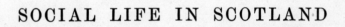
SOCIAL LIFE IN SCOTLAND

T.

SOCIAL LIFE

IN

SCOTLAND

FROM EARLY TO RECENT TIMES

BY THE

REV. CHARLES ROGERS, D.D., LL.D., F.S.A. SCOT.

VOLUME SECOND.

KENNIKAT PRESS
Port Washington, N. Y./London

SOCIAL LIFE IN SCOTLAND

First published in 1884
Reissued in 1971 by Kennikat Press
Library of Congress Catalog Card No: 70-118498
ISBN 0-8046-1246-3

Manufactured by Taylor Publishing Company   Dallas, Texas

CONTENTS.

CHAPTER X.

PAGE

THE PARLIAMENTARY AND JURIDICAL . . 1

CHAPTER XI.

THE ECCLESIASTICAL 69

CHAPTER XII.

CHURCH DISCIPLINE 163

CHAPTER XIII.

PUBLIC SPORTS 256

CHAPTER XIV.

GAMES AND PASTIMES 317

CHAPTER XV.

SOCIAL CLUBS 355

SOCIAL LIFE IN SCOTLAND.

CHAPTER X.

THE PARLIAMENTARY AND JURIDICAL.

DURING that period of the monarchy which preceded the eleventh century the revenues of the State were derived from the rents of demesne lands, export and import customs, fines, and escheats. These revenues were collected on the unsupported authority of the sovereign by officers whom he personally named. Up to the reign of Malcolm Canmore there is no record of any national convention or other legislative assembly. Subsequently legal procedure in Scotland began to assume an English impress. Scottish sovereigns became familiar with Anglican modes. Margaret, Queen of Malcolm Canmore, whose pious and useful life closed in the Castle of Edinburgh on the 16th November 1093, was daughter of Edward, last of the Anglo-Saxon kings. A connection with England was renewed when in the year 1100 Maud, daughter of Malcolm and Margaret, espoused Henry

I., and so became the English queen. At the court of his sister Maud, David I. mainly resided, till in 1124 he succeeded to the Scottish throne. A national convention was held in the reign of his brother and predecessor Alexander I., when in 1107 it was declared that Turgot was chosen bishop of St Andrews "by the king, the clergy, and the people." William the Lion, who commenced his reign in 1165, assembled several conventions, which transacted business as representatives of the clergy, the barons, and *probi homines*. These last were vassals of the crown, who, bound to render suit and service at the king's court, were on this account included in legislative announcements. Practically they took no part in public concerns, leaving these to be conducted by the sovereign, the clergy, the officers of State, and the great barons.

At a National Council held in 1230 there were present one bishop, one prior, two earls, one of these being one of the two Justiciars, the High Steward, and one other baron. The Assembly of Nobles which on the 5th February 1283 acknowledged the Maiden of Norway as heir to the throne, consisted of thirteen earls and twenty-four great knights and barons. And the Convention at Brigham of March 1289, relative to the proposed marriage of the infant queen, included about fifty earls and barons and a like number of ecclesiastics. The first Scottish Parliament

met at Scone in 1292 on the summons of the king,
John Baliol.

Burghs were first recognized in connection with
national affairs, when on the 23d February 1295 the
seals of six burghs were affixed with those of the
nobility and barons to an instrument relative to an
alliance with France.   In the Parliaments of Robert
I. are named along with the clergy and barons, " the
chief persons of communities," till, at a Parliament
held at Cambuskenneth on the 13th July 1326, were
voted to meet war and other costs, " a tenth penny of
all rents " by those described as earls, barons, *burgesses*, and free tenants of the realm.

On the part of the lesser barons—the *probi homines*
of the twelfth, thirteenth, and fourteenth centuries —
attendance at the king's court, and latterly in Parliament, was felt as an intolerable burden.   In order
to their relief it was agreed in a Parliament held
by David II. at Scone in September 1367 that they
might be allowed to complete their harvests, by
leaving public business to the care of a Committee.
Eighteen months later, when a Parliament assembled
at Perth in February 1369, business was delegated in
like manner.   Two Committees were chosen, of which
one was subsequently known as the Lords Auditors,
the other became prototype of two distinct bodies—
afterwards to be prominently associated with national
affairs—the Privy Council and the Lords of the

Articles. Consisting of twenty-seven members, the Committee of the Articles were nominated at an early stage of Parliamentary business, when the House adjourned in order that they might prepare the bills. And when Parliament reassembled, it was simply, without discussion, to grant confirmation. In 1535 the Lords of the Articles were authorized to make Acts with the whole power of Parliament; they exercised this power by imposing a tax. Referring to his absolute authority in Scottish Parliaments, James VI., in a speech which he delivered at White-hall in 1607, spoke thus: "This I must say for Scotland, and I may trewly vaunt it; here I sit and governe it with my pen. I write and it is done, and by a clearke of the Councell I governe Scotland now, which others could not do by the sword. For here must I note unto you the difference of the two Parliaments in these two kingdomes. For there, they must not speak without the Chancellor's leave; and if any man do propound or utter any seditious or uncomely speeches, he is straight interrupted and silenced by the Chancellor's authoritie. . . . If any man in Parliament speake of any other matter than is . . . first allowed by mee, the Chancellor tells him there is no such bill allowed by the king. . . . If [in any law] there be anything that I dislike, they rase it out."

The Committee on the Articles underwent various

changes. Under Charles I. in 1633 it was ruled that the bishops make choice of eight lay peers; and that the peers elect eight bishops, when the sixteen so chosen should add to their number eight commissioners of shires, and eight of burghs. Parliamentary attendance was reduced to two days, the first for choosing the Lords of the Articles, and the second to sanction what their lordships had devised.

At the commencement of the Civil War, the Committee of the Articles was abolished. During his ascendancy, Cromwell, who sought a common Parliamentary representation of the three nations, appointed for Scotland thirty members, of whom twenty were to sit for counties, and ten for burghs. But this mode being generally obnoxious, Scotland was during the Commonwealth represented in the single legislative chamber by officials of the government, or by English officers. The former Parliamentary system with the Committee on Articles was revived at the Restoration. In 1690, when the Scottish Convention agreed to accept the government of the Revolution, they stipulated that the Committee of Articles should cease.

What had mainly tended to the ascendancy of the court, by the ready acquiescence of the Estates in the delegation of their authority, was the poverty of the lesser barons. While burgesses were entitled to elect representatives, a corresponding privilege was

denied to landowners, who were constrained, under
a penalty, to attend personally. That attendance involved the heavy cost of taking part in a
pageant which accompanied each Parliament at its
opening. This was called the Riding of the Parliament. Members of the three Estates assembled at
Holyrood Palace, each attired according to his degree,
and mounted on richly caparisoned horses and preceded by trumpeters, rode to the place of meeting. In
the procession the commissioners of burghs and the
lesser barons rode first, next the great barons and
the clergy. The great officers of State followed up,
preceded by the Lord Lyon, heralds, and pursuivants,
bearing the national insignia. Last rode the Sovereign,
attended by his pages, and followed by the royal
guard. Entering the Parliamentary chamber, the
members were addressed in a discourse by the
court preacher, and after some routine business, were
expected to return to Holyrood. To the lesser
barons the ceremony was a cause of embarrassment.
Their personal and horse trappings were understood,
in most instances, to exhaust the revenues of a year.
James I. sought to relieve the rural landowners of
Parliamentary attendance, by allowing a representation, but his proposal was at the time not carried
out At length by a statute passed in 1567 the
barons were allowed to send commissioners from
their several counties, but were also called upon to

defray the costs of the elected. The allowance as costs was in 1661 fixed at £5 daily from the day of leaving home to that of return; but this sum was greatly inadequate. Those entitled to vote at the election of commissioners of shires were by statute in 1585 declared to be "such as have forty-shilling land in free tenandry held of the king." This qualification was undisturbed for two centuries and a half.

Prior to the reign of Robert II. (1371-1390) the Acts of Parliament were composed in Latin, a language in which hitherto all public business and private correspondence had been conducted. The earliest existing MS. which presents any considerable body of the laws in the vernacular is ascribed to the year 1455; it is preserved in the Advocates Library.

From the earliest times the Scottish Parliament met in one house, but the members were not allowed to occupy the same footing, for the great barons and the clergy sat on benches, the officers of state on the steps of the throne, and the commissioners of shires and burghs upon "furmes." Parliaments assembled at Cambuskenneth, Scone, Perth, and Aberdeen, commonly at Edinburgh, where the king chiefly resided. At Edinburgh the Estates convened so early as the reign of King Robert the Bruce. The Parliament Hall of Edinburgh Castle (now the garrison hospital) was reared in 1434.[1] A spacious chamber, 80 feet in length and 30 in breadth, with an open chestnut roof, richly decorated, it was appropriated to other uses prior to the 3d of February 1489-90, when we find that the Estates assembled in the Tolbooth. The Parliament House of Stirling Castle, a Norman structure, with a hall 120 feet long, was used up to 1571, when in September of that year a Parliament was there held in presence of the infant James VI. The structure was then in considerable disrepair, and when the New Tolbooth at Edinburgh was reared in 1561, it was opened as the Parliament House. Within the New Tolbooth Charles I. held a Parliament in July 1633, subsequent to his coronation. In the same vicinity, adjoining St Giles' Church, a building was in 1640 reared for the accommodation of the Estates. Of this fabric the great chamber, still known as the Parliament House, forms the hall of the College of Justice. Measuring 122 feet in length by 40 in breadth, with an open oak roof, springing from corbels of various designs, it forms an apartment admirably adapted to its present purpose. In the *Laigh* Parliament House were for a time accommodated the records of the kingdom.

Besides enacting laws, the Scottish Parliament imposed taxes for ordinary and extraordinary purposes,

---

[1] Exchequer Rolls, iv. 579.

the latter including the coronation and baptismal ceremonies, the destruction of freebooters, and the suppression of insurrections. Taxes were ordinarily imposed upon the land, but in 1692 Parliament levied a poll-tax with a view to meeting the arrears which had occurred in the remuneration of public officers and of the army during the four years which had elapsed since the Revolution. By the poll-tax statute, every person of both sexes, whether householders or lodgers, were required to pay into the Exchequer 6s. yearly. A cottar who followed a trade was also required to make a payment of 6s. From servants who received more than £6 of wages were levied one-twentieth part, and from tenants one merk per hundred of the landlord's valued rent. Burgesses of royal burghs were assessed according to means and substance. From persons who held rank as gentlemen were exacted £3, and from landowners with £50 and under £200 of valued rent, £4 ; with £200 and under £500, £9 ; and with £500 and under £1000, £12. Those whose valued rents exceeded £1000, and all knights and baronets, were required to contribute £24, while barons were expected to pay £40, viscounts £50, earls £60, marquises £80, and dukes £100. The poll-tax proved unpopular, and was discontinued.

The Scottish Parliament ceased when, on the 1st

May 1707, the political Union with England was
fully consummated. In the Treaty it was provided
that Scotland should in the Parliament of the United
Kingdom be represented by sixteen Peers in the House
of Lords, and in the House of Commons by forty-five
members. By the Reform Act of 1868 the representation in the Lower House was increased to sixty.

With the event of the political Union it was hoped
by English statesmen that the Scottish national
insignia, consisting of the crown, sceptre, and sword,
would be borne to the Tower of London, but the
removal of the symbols was disallowed. In a large
wooden chest they were deposited in the Crown
Room of Edinburgh Castle, of which the door was
made fast.

The original insignia of the Scottish monarchy,
including the crown royal and the coronation stone,
were by Edward I. removed to London in 1296,
when John Baliol was deprived of his sovereignty.
A coronet with which, in the absence of the ancient
crown, Robert the Bruce was crowned at Scone, was
also snatched by English invaders. But a new crown
constructed for the coronation of David II. in 1329
continued to be used at every coronation till 1650,
when it was at Scone placed on the head of Charles II.
Elegantly fashioned, and richly adorned with
jewels, it was in the reign of James V. surmounted
with two concentric circles, displaying at the point

of intersection a mound of gold, enamelled, also a large cross patèe. The circumference of the crown is 27 inches. The sceptre was constructed for James V. in 1536 during his visit to France. To James IV. the sword of state was in 1507 presented by Pope Julius II. ; it is accompanied by a sheath, which is adorned with filigree work, embracing Papal emblems interwoven with acorns and oak leaves.

The regalia were not only used at coronations, but at the opening of every Parliament were borne in procession, and in the place of meeting deposited on a table in front of the throne. When the Lord Chancellor presented a bill for royal sanction, the Sovereign or the King's Commissioner touched it with the sceptre, an act which gave effect to it as a legal statute.

After being used at the coronation of Charles II. in 1650, the national symbols were removed for safety to the Earl Marischal's castle of Dunnottar. The Earl being a prisoner in England, the defence of the castle was entrusted to Captain George Ogilvie of Barras, with a garrison of one hundred men. Faithful to his trust, Ogilvie nobly held out, but as the army of the Commonwealth had triumphed everywhere, permanent resistance was hopeless. What strength might not secure was attained by stratagem. On the counsel of the Dowager Countess Marischal, Mrs Grainger, wife of the minister of Kinneff, a parish

in the vicinity, asked permission of the English
commander to visit in the castle the Governor's
wife, her friend Mrs Ogilvie. The commander having acceded to her request, Mrs Grainger and her
waiting-maid entered the stronghold. After a brief
interval they returned, each bearing a supposed gift
from the governor's wife. For Mrs Grainger held in
her lap what passed as a bundle of lint, while her
attendant carried what was described as the hards of
flax. To those possessing the deeper penetration of
the north it would have appeared obvious that a
beleaguered garrison would not readily surrender
any portion of clothing or the material for producing
it ; but Cromwell's commander and his staff happily
were unsuspecting. The commander, it is alleged,
helped Mrs Grainger to her horse, and if this
tradition is correct, he had some opportunity of
remarking the weight and form of her burden. By
the handmaiden were borne the sceptre and sword of
state. Never before had Scottish females entered on
so daring an enterprise.

The women quitted slowly the precincts of Dunnottar Castle, but hastily traversed the remainder of
their journey to Kinneff Manse, about five miles
distant. There did the venerable Countess Marischal
hail the success of a stratagem which concerned the
honour of the kingdom and the credit of her house.
The minister of the parish hastened to complete what

his wife had begun so skilfully. The sequel is depicted in a narrative which Mr Grainger supplied to
the Dowager Countess : " The 31st March 1652.   I,
Mr James Grainger, minister at Kinneff, grant me to
have in my custody the honours of the kingdom, viz.,
the crown, sceptre, and sword. For the crown and
sceptre I raised ane pavement stone just before the
pulpit in the night tyme, and digged under it ane
hole, and putt them in there and filled up the hole, and
layed down the stane, just as it was before, and
removed the mould that remained that none would
have discovered the stone to have been raised at all.
The sword again at the west end of the church amongst
some common seatts that stand there, I digged doun
in the ground betwixt the two foremost of these seatts,
and laid it doun, within the caice of it, and covered
it up, so that removing the superfluous mould, it
could not be discovered by anybody. And if it shall
please God to call me by death before they be called
for, your Ladyship will find them in that place.—
James Grainger." [1]

Mr Grainger survived the Restoration, and was
privileged to see " the honours " transferred from the
earthen floor of his parish church to their former
place of keeping—the Crown Room of Edinburgh
Castle. There were the regalia, on 26th March 1707,
locked up and secured.

[1] Register of Deeds, 1702.   General Register House.

So long as the regalia rested in the Union strong
box, Scottish nationality was asleep. Scotland at the
Union had two Secretaries, the number ·in 1714 was
reduced to one, and when the Marquis of Tweeddale retired from the office in 1746, it was not filled up. What
Scottish business fell to be transacted was nominally
entrusted to the Lord Advocate, but the bulk of
government patronage was really in the hands of one
or two powerful families, who therewith aggrandized
their friends and rewarded their adherents.   Professedly on account of the two Jacobite insurrections
Scotland was denied the privilege of embodying a
militia. The royal palaces were, without repair, allowed
to crumble into ruins.   To a grazier were leased the
royal gardens at Stirling, while the other precincts of
the palace were appropriated to hog-feeding, or allowed
to become the resort of gamblers and tinkers, and a
haunt of the profane.   Such indeed was the condition
of the precincts of Stirling Castle so lately as 1855,
when it was the privilege of the present writer to
induce the authorities to promote a salutary change.
Till about thirty years ago, Stirling Castle was in its
various structures exposed to those modernizing
changes which have deprived it of its ornaments.
The older palace was early wrecked, and in
1777 the highly ornate palace of James V. was
dismantled of its fittings, including its superb oak
carvings, and ruthlessly converted into a barrack. In

like manner were broken up the Parliament House
and the Chapel Royal, the former being converted
into a barrack, the latter into a store of arms.

At Edinburgh was experienced as keenly as in the
provinces the bitterness of alien rule. Within the
Castle, the historically precious chapel of Queen
Margaret was unroofed, and allowed to fall into decay.
An hospital was formed of the ancient Parliament
House. The royal apartments, in one of which
James VI. was born, were converted into a canteen,
or rooms in which soldiers were indulged with liquor.
Amidst the remonstrances of the citizens and the
protests of the Corporation, a block of barrack rooms
was reared in the Castle, which, sufficiently adapted
for a rural mill-work, was calculated to deface a city
otherwise remarkable for architectural beauty. The
palace of Holyrood was allowed to crumble, ánd its
Abbey Church so to suffer from neglect that its roof,
in December 1768, fell into the interior, crushing in
its fall the gracefully sculptured columns, and wrecking the royal tombs. Then children began to use in
their diversions the skulls and other bones of Scottish princes. The skulls of Lord Darnley and Queen
Magdalene were exposed and borne off. Less than a
century ago, the Lord High Commissioner to the
Church of Scotland was compelled, in lack of accommodation elsewhere, to hold his levees in a tavern ;
and so lately as 1844 did the General Assembly meet

for the first time in an appropriate hall provided by the State. Within the last forty years the Lords Ordinary of the Court of Session listened to pleadings and gave judgment amidst the stir and bustle of the Parliament House.

Nor were the national registers better cared for than the public buildings. The paramount duty of preserving the records, not only for legal and constitutional purposes, but as monuments of history, was suggested by the Lord President Forbes, and about eighteen years subsequent to his decease, the sum of £12,000 for the erection of a Register House was granted by the king from the fund of the Forfeited Estates. But this grant was for nine years resolutely withheld. At length on the 27th June 1774 the Register House was founded, but funds for the completion might not be had till half a century later.

Prior to the depositure of the national records in the Register House, they were kept in hogsheads in the Laigh Parliament House, of which the northern wall was bordered by the damp earth of St Giles' churchyard. The custodiership being loosely discharged, volumes were borrowed and lost. A portion of the Records of the Privy Council were bought as waste paper, and in 1794 eight volumes of the Register of Sasines were, at a public sale, purchased by a bookseller, who honourably restored them. The latter incident led to a movement, which, in the first instance fruitless, aroused a spirit of inquiry. Some influential person, seeking to confirm his title to certain lands, hoped to procure evidence from records not contained in the hogsheads. And a notion possessed him that what was lacking might be found in the Crown Room. Interesting the Barons of Exchequer, they procured a royal warrant authorizing an examination. The instrument being directed to the Great Officers of State, these, on the 22d December 1794, assembled in the Castle. Under the guidance of the Governor, they proceeded to the Crown Room. In the words of their report, it was "secured by a strong outer door of oak wood and two strong locks, the keys of which were not to be found, and the only window barricadoed on the outside by cross-bars of iron, and a wooden frame within." The report continues, "when one set of doors was forcibly entered, another set, consisting of strong iron bars, had to be wrenched open." When at length the interior was reached, there was found in an arched chamber, and resting under six inches of dust, a large oaken chest. Though this was large enough to contain many registers, the Commissioners on examining their warrant concluded that lawfully they might not proceed further. So the search was abandoned, the strong barricades which secured the apartment being stoutly replaced.

The uncertainty which attended the existence of

the national insignia was a source of deep concern to Sir Walter Scott, who waited a suitable opportunity for instituting an inquiry. His personal intimacy with the Prince Regent at length enabled him to effectuate his purpose. By a warrant from the Regent, dated the 28th October 1817, the Great Officers of State, including Sir Walter as a Principal Clerk of Session, were appointed Commissioners to enter the Crown Room, and therein make due search for the regalia. On the 4th February 1818 they executed their mission. As the key of the great chest could not be found, the lock was forced. On the lid being raised were found, under several inches of dust, the long-hid treasures. These were the crown, the sceptre, and the sword of state; also a gold-topped silver rod,-which was the Chancellor's mace. With the exception of the sceptre, which was slightly bent, the insignia were in excellent preservation. They are now exhibited in the Crown Room.

Of the ancient Officers of State the highest in rank was the Chancellor. Constituted by Alexander I., he in the reign of Alexander III. received a salary of £100. The royal fiefs were administered under his authority, and he could grant or recall royal charters. Keeper of the Great Seal, he by its use rendered valid the regal writs. As President of Parliament, he was conversant both with the civil and the canon law; and usually chosen from among the clergy, he brought to that order much of the influence which it possessed prior to the Reformation.

When Walter, son of Alan of Oswestry, was by David I. appointed civil administrator of his house-hold, he was styled *senescale*, that is, senior servant, the seniority implying dignity and rank. The office so created became that of High Steward, which in the person of Walter's representative, Robert II., was merged in the monarchy. As a substitutional officer James I. appointed a Master of the House-hold, who furnished and arranged the castles and palaces, and was chief of the royal henchmen, pages, and yeomen. A Constable was first appointed in the reign of Alexander I. ; he kept the king's sword, led the royal army, and was chief of the barons. From the reign of David I. the office was hereditary in the family of De Morevile, and when that family ceased it was combined with the office of *March-scale*, or Marischal. The Marischal was keeper of the stable and master of the horse ; he enjoyed high rank and exercised a powerful authority. The Marischal's office became hereditary in the family of Keith.

The Chamberlain had (as the name of his office implies) charge of the *camera* or treasure-chamber. He presided in the exchequer court, which derived its name from the chequered cloth which covered the table at which he sat. Under his presidentship assembled the Court of Four Burghs, by which the laws of trade and commerce were framed and administered. To the Chamberlain those who considered themselves aggrieved by the decisions of inferior courts prosecuted an appeal; and the penalties imposed by his decisions became a portion of his revenue. These must latterly have been very considerable, for while in the reign of Alexander III. the Chamberlain's salary was £200, his receipts for feudal casualties, escheats, and other perquisites, amounted in a single year to £5313. To lessen the power of the Chamberlain, which had become formidable, James I. established the office of Treasurer. To the Treasurer the sheriffs and other collectors of the national revenue presented their accounts at intervals. Subsequently a portion of the Treasurer's duties were discharged by the Comptroller, who superintended the royal manors. This officer also exercised those functions which at a modern period were discharged by the Barons of Exchequer. In 1596 James VI. appointed as Great Chamberlain the Duke of Lennox, the office, which had become honorary, being made hereditary in his house.

James I. appointed a Lord Privy Seal. By impressing a small seal or signet, this great officer rendered valid writs and gifts less important than those reserved for the great seal in the keeping of the Chancellor. The Secretary was an officer who constantly with the king, received memorials and complaints, and was by the sovereign instructed how to deal with or dispose of them. By his signature royal decrees were made valid. The Lord Clerk Register was keeper of the public archives and Clerk of Parliaments; he also kept the minutes of the Privy Council and of the higher judicatories. The King's Advocate was the sovereign's legal adviser, and by royal authority prosecuted defaulters in the public courts.

These high officers, deriving their honours from the sovereign, were official members of the Privy Council. They also had seats in Parliament, but when the number of State offices had indefinitely increased, it was in the year 1617 found essential to restrict to eight those permanently invested with legislative authority.

During the reign of David II. a Secret Council was nominated. The king was without issue, and as the succession to the throne was attended with difficulty, it became essential that the question should be considered by the officers of State in secret, also by other councillors of position and experience. The difficulties to be surmounted were these. On the one hand it was known that the king had indicated a willingness to transfer the sovereign authority to the English monarch, while on the other hand Robert the Steward, next in the order of succession, was twice married, and his first wife, Elizabeth Mure, was within the

degrees forbidden by the canon law, while his marriage had lacked the Papal sanction.   By those who
joined in the secret deliberations, it was resolved that
the independence of the kingdom be openly maintained, also that the crown be settled upon the
Steward and his eldest son by Elizabeth Mure. When
that son, who afterwards reigned as Robert III., was
from sickness unable to conduct the Government,
his elder son, the Duke of Rothesay, was appointed
to administer in national concerns along with a
council of eighteen persons.   Councils for advising
the sovereign were thereafter appointed as necessity
arose, till 1489, when a Privy Council for aiding the
royal authority was constituted permanently. Of this
body, the records since the year 1545 have been preserved, and, under careful editorship, are now being
issued in printed volumes by the Lords of the
Treasury.

The Privy Council usually consisted of fifty members, those additional to the officers of State being
specially chosen by the sovereign.   As the executive
of the State, the Privy Council enforced police regulations, and determined important questions relating
to civil and criminal affairs.   In judicial concerns
it was indirectly associated with another court—the
Lords Auditors of Parliament—which, like the Privy
Council, was entitled to review the judgments and
decrees of inferior judges.   Changeable with each

Parliament, the Lords Auditors consisted of six churchmen, six great barons, and five commissioners of burghs, of whom several were ecclesiastics. For judicial duties, neither the members of the Privy Council nor the Lords Auditors were specially qualified; and to remedy the defect, James V. in 1532 established, under Papal sanction, a new tribunal intended to combine the functions of the Lords Auditors and of the Privy Council. Of this tribunal, the judges were styled Lords of Council and Session, and there were, along with a president, seven lay and seven clerical members. By the Pope it was understood that a churchman would uniformly be chosen to preside, and by churchmen was the presidential office held till the Reformation. In 1579 the power of choosing a president was granted to the court itself, but after some changes the right of nomination was reserved for the Crown.

The ordinary lords were at first chosen by the King and Parliament, afterwards by the latter. In the course of testing his prerogative, Charles I., in 1626, displaced the Lord President and six ordinary lords, the remaining eight being allowed to continue on obtaining new gifts of their offices, thereby acknowledging that their former appointments had lapsed on the death of the late king. In the further exercise of arbitrary power, Charles addressed letters to the Lords of Session, commanding them in certain

instances to delay judgment or to hasten it. In a
letter addressed to the Court of Session on the 25th
November 1626 he, in a matter concerning the Earl
of Murray, charged the Court " not to medle." The
abuses which attended such unworthy interference
became unendurable, and the priest-ridden monarch,
in 1641, was necessitated to agree that Scottish judges
should not be appointed without Parliamentary
sanction. This provision was rescinded at the Restoration. [1]

In 1640 the spiritual side of the Court of Session
was abrogated by statute. But the privilege possessed by the sovereign of nominating unsalaried
judges, styled Extraordinary Lords, continued a
source of irritation till the reign of George I., when
these supernumeraries were abolished. At its institution, the Court was endowed with " 10,000 golden
ducats of the chamber," derived from the bishoprics
and monasteries ; but the amount was levied so un-
satisfactorily that in 1549 the salary of an ordinary
lord did not exceed £40. The salaries, augmented
from time to time, were, at the Restoration, equal to
£200 sterling. In Queen Anne's reign, each lord
had a salary of £500. The present salary of a Lord
Ordinary is £3000, that of the Lord President £4800,
and of the Lord Justice Clerk £4500.

[1] See " Register of Royal Letters during the Secretaryship of
the Earl of Stirling," 1884, 2 vols. 4to, *passim*.

By Act 11 George IV., the Lords of Council and Session were reduced to thirteen. Formerly the fifteen judges sat together in one court; but, according to modern arrangements, five judges styled Lords Ordinary decide on all causes in the first instance, the remaining eight judges being arranged in two distinct Courts, called the First and Second Divisions, four sitting in each Court. In the First Division the Lord President presides; the Lord Justice Clerk in the Second. To the First or Second Division causes are brought for review from the Lords Ordinary, or, in legal phrase, from the Outer House. In the Court of Session legal business long proceeded tardily, with the result that while law agents became rich those involved in litigation were by slow stages severed from their estates and homes. When in 1727 the celebrated Duncan Forbes of Culloden became Lord President he devised an Act of Sederunt, which provided that no cause might be protracted in Court beyond the period of four years. Prior to this provision many causes had been continued twenty years, involving members of successive generations in legal uncertainty and lamentable discomfort.

Collaterally with the Court of Session exists the College of Justice, of which the judges are described as senators, and which in its membership includes the whole legal faculty,—advocates, writers, extractors, and clerks.

Prior to the Reformation a Consistorial Court in every diocese was conducted by a judge named the Official, who was appointed by the archdeacon. To the Official's adjudication were reserved matters relating to legitimacy and divorce; also to movable succession, the fulfilment of covenants, and cases of slander. By the Officials were certified the Public Notaries, whose fitness and personal qualities largely availed in times when four-fifths of the nation were unable to write. Ere the Court of Session was established the chief legal business of the kingdom was conducted in the Consistorial Courts of Edinburgh, Glasgow, and St Andrews. Before the Reformation appeals from the Consistorial Courts might only be determined at Rome. These appeals were prohibited in 1560, while on the 8th February 1563 Consistory Courts were superseded by a principal Commissary Court established at Edinburgh. The Commissary Court, which consisted of four commissioners or lay judges, was gradually merged in the Court of Session. In 1836 it was abolished as a separate jurisdiction. By the statute 4 George IV. c. 97 each county is formed into a separate commissariot, the sheriff being commissary.

To the Lyon Court are referred all questions relating to armorial bearings. The sole judge in this court is the Lyon King, whose authority in Scotland is similar to that exercised in England by

Garter King of Arms. Lyon derives his title from his bearing a lion rampant in the emblazonry of his official robe. One of his earlier duties was to convey messages from the sovereign to foreign courts. He now appoints messengers-at-arms and superintends them. On appointment Lyon formerly underwent the ceremony of a coronation. Sir Alexander Erskine, Bart. of Cambo, was on the 27th July 1681 crowned Lyon King at Holyrood Palace by the Duke of York; he was the last who was so distinguished.

The Druids exercised the earlier jurisdiction; they framed laws and executed them. Their courts and legislative assemblies were held on natural or artificial eminences fenced by a ditch and rampart, and which were styled *mod-dun*—that is, enclosed mounds. When the Saxon superseded the Celtic tongue the name *mod-dun* was vulgarized into maiden; hence the maiden castle of Edinburgh, the *maiden* craig of Dumfriesshire, the *maiden* rocks of Carrick and Fife, and the *maiden* stones of Ayton, Garrioch, Tullibody, and Clackmannan—all the localities so named being associated with ancient courts.

But the scenes of early jurisdiction have in not a few instances been distinguished as mote-hills, *mod* being converted into the Anglo-Saxon *mote*, and *dun* represented by its English equivalent. There are mote-hills in the counties of Roxburgh, Dumfries, Wigton, Lanark, Ayr, Stirling, Perth, and Aberdeen.

In memorial of the ancient ditch and rampart, courts of law are still *fenced* by the macer in a form of words. The mote-hill was latterly a place of execution. Thus on the mote-hill of Stirling in May 1424, Murdoch, Duke of Albany, and several members of his family, were publicly beheaded under the charge of treason.

Coeval with the Druidic age, and prior to the Roman invasion, a species of legal government was conducted through the instrumentality of a Toshach and a Maormar. The Toshach was an officer ranking with the Thane of the Saxons. Elected to his office by the chiefs of a province, these submitted to his arbitration, and in the field accepted his leadership. Galgacus was chosen Toshach by the Caledonians in their early struggle with the Romans. The descendant of a Toshach whose power had been prolonged was regarded as a prince, and latterly was crowned. The Scottish King was a Toshach at the first. A Toshach founded clan Mackintosh; the name is in English the son of the Thane.

Exercising a separate and independent jurisdiction, the Maormar ruled over his clan, and became their supreme lawgiver and judge; the subordinates of the Maormar were *Maors,* or lesser judges. By Malcolm Canmore Maormars were designated earls, while Maors latterly ranked as barons of baillieries, or inferior officers by whom the mandates of provincial judges were put into execution.

Retributive justice, dispensed harshly to the poor, was tardy among the opulent. At the dawn of history we find trial by ordeal in full operation. A murderer taken red-hand was convicted summarily. But when the criminal, whether charged with murder or theft, pleaded not guilty, and could not be directly convicted, he was allowed to clear himself by compurgation. This was accomplished when a number of leal men swore that they believed him guiltless. The compurgators varied from one to thirty, but usually twelve persons were impanelled. If compurgation failed, the accused person appealed to the Divine judgment by challenging his accuser. Judicial combats were witnessed by churchmen in the belief that the innocent would triumph. Knights were allowed to do combat by proxy. Accused persons might elect to be tried by ordeal. The administration of the ordeal was a monastic privilege. There was trial by fire, also by water. Trial by fire was successful when the accused passed over a red-hot iron unscathed, and by water when, if thrust into a lake, he swam safely to shore. In the year 1180 it was ruled by statute, that "na baron have leyff to hald court of lyf and lym, as of jugement of bataile or of watir, or of het yrn, bot gif the scheriff or his serjand be thereat, to see gif justice be truly kepit thar as it ow to be."[1]

[1] Innes's "Scotland in the Middle Ages," Edin., 1869, 8vo, pp. 183-7.

Trial by the right of wager in battle existed in the reign of David I., the accused being allowed to elect this mode of proving his innocence in preference to "the purgation of twelve leal men." In 1230, during the reign of Alexander II., it was provided by statute that any one acquitted by an assize should not for the same offence be required to submit to an ordeal.

With compurgation and ordeal subsisted a system of compensation, whereby those guilty of public or private offences made recompense both to the persons injured, and also to the State. In the earlier portion of our written law rates of compensation are enumerated. The king is valued at a thousand cows, the king's son and an earl at one hundred and fifty cows, and a villein or ceorle at sixteen cows. A married woman is estimated one-third under the value of her husband. For the wounding of an earl the compensation was nine cows, of a thane three, and of a serf or ceorle one. Next to the revenues derived from the Crown lands and customs, the escheats levied from delinquents proved from the thirteenth century to the sixteenth a chief national resource.

For the more efficient administration of justice, David I. appointed a supreme magistrate, or chief justice, styled the Justiciar. He sat *in curia regis*, and from time to time held circuit courts or justice-ayres.

By William the Lion a second Justiciar was appointed, with his jurisdiction in the Lothians. In the reign of Alexander III. the chief of the Comyns was appointed Justiciar of Galloway. On his temporary conquest, Edward I. divided the kingdom into four judicial provinces, two justices, an Englishman and a Scotsman, being appointed to each province. On the restoration of the national independence, King Robert the Bruce divided the country into two judicial districts, one to the north, and the other to the south of the Forth. At the chief burgh of each shire the Justiciar held a court three times a year, not only for administering justice, but also in applying it. The fines imposed by the Justiciar were paid into the exchequer, with the exception of a tenth reserved for the use of the Church.

Though occupying the royal judgment seat, the Justiciar was not by any of the kings invested with the entire judicial authority. From the Parliament of 1488, James II. received the following counsel :— " It is avisit and concluded, anent the furthe putting of justice throw all the realme, that our souerane lord sall ride in proper persoune about to all his Aieris ; and that his *Justice* [the Justiciar] sall pas with his hienes, to minister justice, as beis thocht expedient to him and his Counsale for the tyme."

During a judicial circuit in southern counties made in the same year James occupied two months;

he was accompanied by the Chancellor, the Justiciar, the Treasurer, the Clerk Register, and the Justice Clerk. To the last named officer pertained the duty of making from the records extracts of fines. These he placed in the hands of sheriffs, stewards, and bailies for recovery.

In 1491 Parliament ordered that justice-ayres "be held, set and halden twis in the yere, that is to say, anys on the griss [grass], and anys on the corne."

The proceedings of the justice-ayres from November 1493, and ending July 1513, have been preserved. They are contained in two MS. volumes which, on the 5th March 1880, were deposited with the Clerk of Justiciary, after being for 150 years in the custody of the Faculty of Advocates.

In 1526 Parliament enacted that " our Sovrane Lord be personalie present at the halding of Justice Aires, geif it pleses his Grace ; " also " that na Justice Aires be haldin na part, without our Sovrane Lord and his Justice be present." From ordinary justice-ayres, appeals might be prosecuted to the King's Council, or to the Judicial Committee of Parliament, or to Parliament itself. An appeal bore the strange title of " ane falsing of dome."

The office of Justiciar shared the fate of other great appointments of State by passing into a personal office. Early in the sixteenth century it was conferred on the Earl of Argyle. The Earl is named as Justice General in a court which, on the 25th August 1526, was held by his deputy. In the reign of Charles I., Lord Argyle resigned the appointment, but continued to act as Justice General for the sheriffdom of Argyle and Tarbert, and of the Western Isles. After other changes, the sinecure office of Justice General was in 1793 conferred on James, third Duke of Montrose. By a legislative act passed 23d July 1830, the office was, on the ceding of the existing interest, declared to be merged in the Lord Presidentship of the Court of Session.

Early in the twelfth century Scotland was divided into sheriffdoms, which again were subdivided into wards or bailiaries, or constabularies. The sheriff was king's lieutenant within his particular district. The decrees of the courts of regality and barony were executed under his authority, while from district collectors he obtained their drawings of the public cess, and made account of them to the exchequer. The office of sheriff became hereditary, the duties being delegated to some one in the neighbourhood acquainted with legal affairs. The chief landowner of a bailiary was, as a territorial magnate, constituted the hereditary bailie. Each royal castle was governed by a constable, the field of his jurisdiction, styled the constabulary, extending only to the castle and its precincts. The constable of Roxburgh Castle was also sheriff of the county.   When a royal castle, as at Dundee, was associated with a burgh, disputes as to jurisdiction between the constable and the magistrates were not infrequent.

The coroner or crowner was constituted by Edward I.   It was his office to compel attendance at the law courts of those charged with crime by seizing their cattle and corn, or securing them personally in ward. An office so liable to abuse was early superseded ; it only remains as one of the civic titles enjoyed by the Lord Provost of Perth.

By the magistrates of burghs, especially those of Stirling, Perth and Edinburgh, was possessed a jurisdiction in *blood wits*, that is the right of trying and pronouncing judgment on persons charged with murder.   Thus John Cheislie of Dalry, the assassin of the Lord President Lockhart, was, in 1689, summarily tried and condemned by the magistrates of Edinburgh.

The Justice of Peace Court, instituted in 1609, was empowered to check civil broils and punish those who were disorderly.   In 1617 two Justices were appointed for every parish.   Agrarian controversies, or those relating to matters of husbandry, were settled in courts of birlaw.   Of these courts the judges were selected by husbandmen and approved by sheriffs or other local magistrates.   *Birley-men* attended to the rights of outgoing and incoming tenants.

In 1672 was established the High Court of Justiciary, which included five Lords of Session as commissioners or judges, under the presidentship of the Lord Justice Clerk. With headquarters in Edinburgh, the commissioners were authorized to hold circuit courts at Dumfries and Jedburgh, Stirling, Glasgow and Ayr, also at Perth, Aberdeen, and Inverness. From 1708 circuit courts began to be held at the places named twice a year. While in inflicting punishment English judges are ruled only by statute, those presiding in the criminal courts of Scotland are regulated by common law, that is, the practice of their own courts. That practice has widely varied. The early punishments were singularly harsh. For libelling the Lord Justice General, Dowall Campbell was, on the 24th February 1673, sentenced to have his tongue bored, and to stand two hours in the cuck-stool or pillory. For committing an assault, Andrew Drummond was, on the 29th November 1703, sentenced to be set on the cuck-stool, and "there to have his neck and hands put in the same, and his lug nailed thereto the space of an hour." In a circuit court held at Stirling on the 20th May 1709, the Lords of Justiciary sentenced Thomas Smyth and Janet Walker, for the offence of adultery, "to be taken to the mercat cross of Falkirk, and there to stand with a paper on their breasts bearing these words in great lettres, 'Thir are adulterers;'" also to be taken to the parish church of Muiravonside on Sunday, the 29th inst., and to be placed at the church door with the same placard pinned to their breasts. On the 21st November 1726, Isobel Lindsay, whose illegitimate child had died soon after birth under circumstances of suspicion, was by the High Court sentenced to be " by the hands of the common hangman, scourged through the streets of Edinburgh at the five usual places thereof, receiving at each place five stripes upon her naked back, and thereafter to be carried to the Correction-house, there to remain five months." On the 28th December 1726, George Melvil " a notour thief," was " set on the trone, and had his nose pinched." For theft, David Alison was, in October 1727, " pillored," " pinched in the nose," and " sent to the Correction-house." In March 1728, Jean Spence, " a notour thief," was " pillored," " hir lug nailed," and " hir nose pinched."

There being no county or district prisons other than the cells of the tolbooth, criminals were seldom sentenced to imprisonment, and then only for periods rarely exceeding six months. Other punishments were cruel, but imprisonment was farcical. Prisoners in the tolbooths of Edinburgh, Stirling and Perth were till within the last sixty or seventy years allowed to indulge a species of diurnal revelry. The means of conducting their jollities were procured from the good-natured public, to whom the prisoners lowered from a cell-window a small box, with the words inscribed upon it, " Pity the poor prisoners." The box received contributions of tobacco, liquor, and fruit. Banishment from the sovereign's "hail dominions, furth of Scotland," or from one district of Scotland to another was a common sentence. On the 3d July 1711, the Lords of Justiciary banished Euphan Clark from the shires of Forfar and Perth, for ten years. And on the 16th March 1726, Thomas Pyne was banished from the country north of the Tay. The ordinary place of exile during the eighteenth century was " his majesty's plantations in America."

In 1742, several persons who had violated the sepulchres of the dead, were sentenced to "scourging and banishment;" in 1823, an offence of the same character was visited with seven years' transportation. So long as the publication of Popish doctrines was held to be penal, those who exercised the rites of the Romish faith were subjected to trial and punishment. At the Aberdeen circuit court, held on the 3d May 1751, Mr Patrick Gordon, residing in the castle of Braemar, was, on the charge of being " habit and repute a priest, jesuit, or trafficking Papist," found guilty on confession, and was sentenced " to be banished furth of Scotland," " with certification that if ever he return, he, being still a Papist, shall suffer the pain of death."

Ordinary sentences of banishment were accompanied

by the provision that the convicts would be publicly
whipped in the event of their covertly returning.
Thus on the 6th October 1749, the judges of the
Inverness Circuit sentenced Christian Ironside to perpetual banishment from Scotland, declaring that " if
ever she shall return, she should be taken to the head
burgh of the shire in which she is apprehended, and
thereafter, upon the first market-day, whipped through
the town by the hands of the common hangman,
receiving the usual number of stripes upon her naked
back." In November 1790, the magistrates of Stirling applied to the Commissioners of Justiciary for
counsel as to whether they would subject to a public
whipping a woman who had returned from banishment, and was in a state of pregnancy. Scourging
through the market town was a common sentence. So
recently as the early part of the present century,
persons convicted of perjury were by the Lords of
Justiciary sentenced to be scourged.

A first act of theft was, irrespective of the value of
the articles stolen, visited with some leniency ; but
conviction as " a notour," or habit and repute thief,
was ordinarily punished by death. From 1790 to
1830, were in the High Court sentenced to death as
" notour thieves," in 1790, William Gadesby ; in
1791, John Paul and James Stewart ; in 1797, John
Young ; in 1799, Andrew Holmes ; in 1811, Adam
Lyell ; in 1815, William Honyman and John Smith ;

in 1816, John Black ; in 1817, John Long and Thomas Mitchell ; in 1819, Burne Judd and Thomas Clapperton ; and in 1829, Jacob Laird. The majority of these offenders had robbed with violence.

The last criminal who, in Scotland, was hanged for forgery, was Malcolm Gillespie, a native of Dunblane. As an officer of Excise, he had distinguished himself in the revenue service, and having retired on a pension, settled at Skene, Aberdeenshire. But he indulged in financial speculations, and so fell into the offence for which he suffered. On the 28th September 1827, convicted by a majority of the jury, he was executed at Aberdeen on the 16th November following. It may be remarked that the judge who passed sentence upon Gillespie was reputed for his humanity, and that the advocate-depute, who resisted commutation of the sentence, was known to the writer as mild, gentle and beneficent. But the humanities in relation to the administration of the criminal law were sixty years ago most imperfectly understood.

Prior to undergoing the highest penalty of the law, criminals guilty of heinous offences were subjected to torture. In 1689, Cheislie of Dalry, who in a state of lunacy assassinated the Lord President Lockhart, was at his trial examined by torture, and being sentenced to death, was drawn on a hurdle to the market-cross of Edinburgh, where his right hand was struck off. Thereafter he was dragged to the gibbet in the Grassmarket. His body was thereafter hung in chains at the spot now covered by the suburban mansions of Drumsheugh.

Alexander M'Cowan, who at the circuit court held at Perth in May 1750, was convicted of murder and robbery, was sentenced to have his right hand struck off prior to execution. The last criminal hung in chains in Scotland, was one Leal, a messenger in Elgin, who at the Inverness Circuit in 1773, was found guilty of robbing the post, and sentenced to death. According to the Inverness Register of Deaths his body was "hung in chains, at Janet Innes's cairn."

The Justiciary Court now sits each Monday during session, and in spring and autumn proceeds on circuit. In determining causes, the Court is assisted by a jury of fifteen persons, chosen by ballot out of forty-five jurors summoned. The jury may decide by a majority and in addition to the usual deliverances of guilty or not guilty, they are privileged to adduce a verdict of not proven. Formerly when a panel was found not guilty, he was, in the Justiciary Record, described as " clenzit ;" and when guilty, as "fyllit ; " if sentenced to death, the recorder set forth that he was " justifiet." Scottish jurors anciently pledged themselves to maintain honest judgment in these gingling rhymes :

> " We shall leil suith say,
> And na suith conceal, for na thing we may,

So far as we are charged upon this assize,
Be God himsel, and be our pairt of Paradise ;
And as we will answer to God, upon
The dreadful day of Dome."

As public prosecutor, the Lord Advocate was formerly privileged to insist on the conviction of every
prisoner by menacing the jurors with "assizes of
wilful error," that is, with personal penalties. Among
the articles of grievance represented in 1689, the
Advocate's power of menace against juries was included. The right of menace was withdrawn. By an
act passed on the 31st July 1868, the Lord Justice
General, the Lord Justice Clerk, or any single judge
in the Court, was authorized to preside alone at any
criminal trial.

Apart from the legal tribunals directly sanctioned
by the Crown, and in which the judges were justiciars, and sheriffs, and other magistrates, both of
county and burgh, there existed courts of regality and
barony, in which justice was roughly and arbitrarily
dispensed. For a feudal baron was practically invested in the sovereignty of the territory conveyed to
him by his charter, and even when the soil was
alienated, he continued to exercise a jurisdiction over
those who occupied it. And he was bound by no form
of process, or restrained by any law, statutory or
common.

By statute four crimes, murder, rape, robbery, and

fire-raising, were, as "pleas of the Crown," reserved
to the jurisdiction of the King's judges ; nevertheless
the lord of regality asserted the power of dealing with
every description of felony within his feudal domains.
He owned the right *fossa et furca*—that is, of punishing by pit and gallows. Under the right *furca* the
baron could suspend on a gibbet any of his vassals.
The punishment *fossa* was of a twofold kind, since
the baron could immure in a pit or dungeon, or
sentence to death by drowning. In earlier times the
regality prison was a species of pit, partly or wholly
underground. In the episcopal castle of St Andrews,
founded by Bishop Roger in the year 1200, a circular
pit was formed in the rock on which the stronghold
rests ; it is nearly thirty feet in depth, with a diameter
at top of seven feet, and at base of twenty-seven.
Therein offenders against the Church or State were
to be immured, and within it in 1544, under the
charge of heresy, were confined Friar John Roger prior
to his secret assassination, and in 1546 the pious
reformer, George Wishart, previous to his martyrdom.
Regality prisons were latterly constructed under the
arches of the older bridges ; also within the damp
vaults of unoccupied castles. Within lochs and ponds
and in ditches female convicts were soused or drowned.
In the baronial court of Sir Robert Gordon of Gordon-
ston, held at Drainie on the 25th August 1679,
Janet Grant was, on a charge of theft to which she

pleaded guilty, sentenced to be drowned next day
in the Loch of Spynie. From the practice of the
regality courts in extinguishing by water the lives
of female offenders, the government of James VII.
adopted this mode of silencing those women who
ventured to impugn the king's arbitrary rule.
Charged with denying that James was entitled to
rule the Church according to his pleasure, Margaret
M'Lachlan, aged sixty-three, and Margaret Wilson,
a girl of eighteen, were on the 11th May 1685 made
to perish in the waters of Blednoch.

In the earlier times lords of regality could seldom
read or write; hence they appointed bailies to preside
in their feudal courts, and otherwise to act on their
behalf. Latterly a bailie was appointed to preside in
every regality court. The abbot and monks of Cupar
had on their home estate a principal bailie and two
deputies. At the Regality Court of Dunfermline
certain officers connected with the several districts
of the jurisdiction were statedly examined concerning
"bludes"—that is, as to blood-shedding, whether
by slaughter or wounding. On the 6th October 1631
Andrew Alexander "gave up ane blude committed
between William Craik and James Barclay." By
the Regality Courts of the north was exercised a
rigorous authority. Content in their records to
enter the names and offences of accused persons,
and the names of jurors, the result of a trial was

expressed by such words as "clenzit" or "con-
vickt." To those in the latter category are usually
added the words "hangit" or "drounit." In the
Book of the Regality of Grant are presented sentences of unparalleled severity. A lad, Donald Roy
Fraser, charged with plundering "the socke of a
pleughe," was on the 14th June 1692 convicted on
his own confession, when the bailie of court, James
Grant of Galloway, sentenced the prisoner "to be
nailit be the lug with ane irene naile to ane poste, and
to stand ther for the spaice of ane hour without
motione, and be allowed to break the griss nailed
without drawing of the nail." Having on the 22d
May 1696 convicted two ignorant persons, a father
and daughter, of "stealing and resetting of scheip,"
the bailie of Grant ordered the delinquents to execution. But as "supplication" was made for them by
their neighbours, who besides offered to become
security for their future good behaviour, the bailie
recalled the death sentence, and substituted the following : "That Patrick Bayn be taken immediately
from court to the gallow foot upon the moor of
Ballintore, and tyed thereto with hemp cords, and his
body made naked from the belt upward, and then to
be scourged be the executioner with ane scourge by
laying upon his body twenty-four stripes to the
effusion of his blood." The daughter was sentenced
to be "scourged with thirty stripes till her blood rin

doun, and thereafter to be banished from Strathspey."
On the 2d September 1697 Ludovick Grant of that
Ilk and his bailie, sitting on the bench together, gave
sentence that three persons guilty of horse-stealing
should be carried prisoners from the court to the pit
of Castle Grant, there to remain till Tuesday next,
and under guard carried to the gallow-tree of Ballintore, and to be all three hangit betwixt two and four
in the afternoon till they be dead." Another offender,
Thomas Dow, was at the same time sentenced to be
bound to the gallows during the time of the execution,
and thereafter to have his left ear cut off, and to be
scourged and banished the country."

By regality courts were also determined civil
causes, and enacted binding regulations in regard to
home products. Thus, on the 29th January 1669,
the judge of the regality court of Dunfermline considering " the low pryces and waitts [weights] that
is given for beer and malt, ordained brewers and
tapsters to retail and sell the same at sextein pennies
the pynt (instead of twenty) in the several parishes
of the regality, under the penalty of ten merkis scotts,
toties quoties."

Through the claims asserted by the lords of
regality, criminals were not infrequently rescued
from the jurisdiction of the ordinary courts. For
a lord of regality could repledge a criminal in the
king's court by offering security that he would

be tried in his own. Or he might claim the right of sitting with the king's judge, and thereby impede the even course of justice.

Than the regality court, a less important feudal jurisdiction was the court of barony. In the barony court a thief might be punished by a capital sentence, if caught with the fang, "that is, if captured while bearing the article stolen." Yet sentence of death could be pronounced only when the criminal was brought up within three suns after committing his offence. Ordinarily the judge of the barony court was expected to confine his administration to the enforcing of statutes for preserving game, and protecting orchards and rabbit warrens. He might also punish summarily those who wantonly destroyed certain saplings of the forest. Hence the rhyme :—

> " Oak, ash, and elm tree,
>   The laird may hang for a' the three ;
>   But for saugh and bitter weed
>   The laird may flyte, but mak naething be't."

Freeholders and landowners, disqualified from holding regality or baronial courts, might act as soyters at a justice ayre. Under authority of the ayre courts, soyters passed upon inquests, and attended to the due execution of sentences. In south-eastern districts the soyter exercised an authority similar to that of the provincial sheriff.

During the reign of William the Lion freeholders

were charged to attend the courts of justiciars and sheriffs. In 1449 the command was renewed by statute, while in 1540 it was ordained that those freeholders who owed suit and service in the regality and other courts were to be fined for non-attendance. At " the head court of the bailyearie of Cunningham held within the tolbooth of Irvine," on the 6th October 1674, the depute " unlawed and amerciated ilk of the absentis in the soum of fyfteen pund scotts money for their contumacie, conforme to the act of Parliament." And from " the Register of the Stewartry of Menteith " (1639-1733), we learn that the heritors and freeholders were bound to be present at each of the head courts held three times a year. On the names being called, those who failed to answer were each amerced in a penalty of £50. In 1672 a statute provided that all freeholders, magistrates, and dignified persons of the shire should wait upon the Commissioners of Justiciary at their several circuits. The rule being found burdensome, a new regulation was made on the 1st May 1760, whereby the attendance of noblemen, barons, and freeholders, was dispensed with, the sheriff and his deputies excepted.

By public statute heritable jurisdictions, regalities, and constabularies, were, from the 25th March 1748, abrogated and dissolved, while a sum of £150,000 was granted from the exchequer as compensation to the

holders. To ,barons and their bailies were reserved the
right of inflicting penalties against those convicted of
assault, to the extent of twenty shillings, or by
" setting the delinquent in the stocks, for any time
not exceeding the space of one month." In civil
causes baron-bailies were allowed to decern for debts
not exceeding forty shillings, also for the recovery of
" mails and duties " from their own tenantry. The
owners of baronies did not readily acquiesce in being
deprived of their higher authority, and some of
them continued to appoint their officers of justiciary long after such appointments could exist only
in name.

A new judicial system supervened. Of every
county, the Lord Lieutenant was appointed High
Sheriff, while under him, yet of independent authority,
was nominated as Sheriff-Depute, an advocate who
had at least three years' practice in the Court of Session. The sheriff-depute was authorized to hold
occasional courts, but his duties were chiefly to consist
in considering appeals from the judgment of his
substitutes.

For the office of sheriff-substitute was required no
special qualification, persons of local respectability
being willing, like London vestrymen, to undertake a
round of arduous and irksome duties, rewarded solely
by the dignity of office. Our lamented friend, the
late Dr Hugh Barclay, sheriff-substitute of Perthshire,

in one of his entertaining publications, facetiously
refers to a sheriff-substitute, who, "practising as an
apothecary, dispensed justice and medicine alike in
scruples, and was conversant with injections and
ejections alike; he could also purge witnesses."[1]

At length the importance of securing an effective
sheriff-substitute was so generally recognized that in
1787 a small salary was allowed.   This was, about
twenty years later, fixed at £200, the appointment
being still conjoined with some other office.   In
1825 it was ruled that the qualifications of every
sheriff-substitute should, on his appointment, be certified by the President of the Court of Session, also
by the Justice Clerk.   Increased emoluments were
also provided; these have been augmented by subsequent acts.

To the sheriff and his substitute belong extensive
criminal jurisdiction, but the more important causes
are, at the discretion of the Lord Advocate and
his deputies, reserved for the Court of Justiciary.
The sheriff and his substitute may try criminal causes
with or without a jury; they may inflict imprisonment for a year, or impose penalties to the extent of
fifty pounds.

A dempster or doomster was associated with the
court of Parliament; he was *Indicator Parliamenti,*

[1] "The Local Courts of England and Scotland."   By Hugh
Barclay, LL.D.   Edin., 1860, p. 20.

the conclusions of Parliament being expressed by his voice. The office of heritable dempster to Parliament was, by Robert II. in 1349, confirmed to Andrew Dempster of Cariston. By David Dempster in 1476 were claimed before the Lords Auditors " ten pundis amerciament of fee ilk parliament," also a fee of each justice ayre held in Forfarshire,—claims which the Auditors allowed. On the 7th October 1476, judgment was given in a cause by the mouth of Alexander Dempster, in presence of the king sitting in the Parliament-house with the crown on his head, and the sceptre in his hand. From the earlier times a dempster was connected with every court which exercised criminal jurisdiction. When a criminal was convicted and sentence of death recorded, the dempster was called upon to repeat the sentence aloud. On a hand-bell being rung by the presiding judge, the dempster entered the court. After repeating the words of the sentence, he added, " And this I pronounce for doom." If the dempster was not forthcoming or his duty was imperfectly discharged, it was held that a death sentence might not be carried out. At a circuit court held in Glasgow on the 10th May 1723, Margaret Fleck, a married woman, was, on the charge of rough-handling her infant child so as to cause its death, declared guilty of murder and sentenced to death. The sentence is in the Justiciary Record entered thus:

THE PARLIAMENTARY AND JURIDICAL.

" The Lords Commissioners of Justiciary having considered the foregoing verdict of assyse returned against Margaret Fleck, pannel, they in respect thereof by the mouth of Thomas Cochran, Dempster of the Court, decern and adjudge the said Margaret Fleck, pannel, to be taken from the tolbooth of Glasgow upon the 5th day of June next to come, to the common place of execution at the tounhead of Glasgow, and there betwixt the hours of two and four of the clock in the afternoon, to be hanged by the neck upon a gibbet until she be dead, and ordain all her moveable goods and gear to be escheat and inbrought to his majesteis use."

But Thomas Cochran, dempster and executioner of Glasgow, would not make valid a sentence which the evidence (as it appears on the record) did not justify. Undeterred by his refusal, and the universal sympathy of the people audibly expressed, the two circuit judges, Lords Dun and Pencaitland, sanctioned the following minute :

" After wryting and signing the above sentence of death against Margaret Fleck, pannel, the Dempster above named and insert refused to pronounce the sentence to her. And their Lordships having desired the Sheriff Depute to provide another Dempster instantly, or else to do it himself, he craved their lordships might delay the same till the next day, against which time he should have one provided. Which being condescended to by their Lordships, they continued pronouncing of sentence against the said Margaret Fleck till to-morrow at nyne o'clock ; with certification that if the Sheriff Depute did not provide a Dempster against that time, they would oblige him to do it himself, and ordered the above sentence to be delete and scored ; and continued the Court and whole dyets thereof till that time."

Next morning one Robert Yeats, in consideration

of his being appointed dempster of the court, made the doom legal by pronouncing it.

On the 16th March 1773 the Commissioners of Justiciary abolished the office of dempster, and decreed that sentence should be pronounced by the presiding judge, and afterwards read by the Clerk. The abolition arose from an indecent exhibition in the High Court, thus described by Sir Walter Scott. The office of dempster having become unexpectedly vacant, one Hume, who had been sentenced to transportation as an incendiary, consented temporarily to fulfil the office. Brought into court to pronounce sentence of death upon a fellow prisoner, he omitted the duty, but warmly reproved the judges for the severe sentence they had imposed upon himself. Hume was forcibly ejected, and it was forthwith determined to avoid the recurrence of so unseemly a demonstration. Early in the present century Lord Justice Clerk Eskgrove introduced the English custom, whereby the judge in pronouncing sentence of death wears a black cap.

It has been alleged that in regalities connected with ecclesiastical establishments, dempsters were unemployed. This is an error. In seeking to extirpate heresy by burning the devoted confessors, Resby and Craw, Bishop Wardlaw of St Andrews appointed as dempster and executioner to the regality a person named Wan, whose office became hereditary in his family. The hangman's acres, situated at Gair Bridge, near St Andrews, are still in possession of Wan's representatives. Till the year 1773 ordinary sentences passed in court were publicly intimated by the macer.

The dempster of court usually executed the sentence which he pronounced. An executioner was appointed to each principal town.. He was usually styled "the lockman," since in right of office he possessed the privilege of helping himself to a *lock* or handful of farm produce from every sack in the market-place. The hangman's measure was subsequently determined by a timber cap or iron ladle, given by the magistrates to every executioner on his appointment. The executioner of Stirling's collecting cap is preserved in the museum of that burgh.

A century ago, when capital sentences were becoming less frequent, and hence the executioner's office less needful, disposers of grain began to hold that the summary opening of their sacks and the appropriation of their produce was an intolerable infliction. At Dumfries market in 1781 a grain dealer named Johnstone deforced the burgh executioner in his attempt to open his sacks, and in consequence was sentenced to imprisonment. But the magistrates who gave judgment, apprehending that Johnstone's example might induce a general resistance, sought the advice of counsel. By the legal authority consulted,

the executioner's claim and the magisterial action
upon it were approved; but the demand continuing
to induce complaint, it was in 1796 wholly withdrawn, while the executioner's salary, payable by the
burgh, was proportionably increased.[1] Till the close
of the century every burgh lockman had his free house
and stated salary, varying from £8 to £10 sterling,
together with a special fee for every execution.

The lockman of Edinburgh was an officer both of the
Justiciary Court and of the municipality. From the
Exchequer he received a salary of five pounds, while
latterly, in commutation of his market privilege, he
had granted him by the Town Council a weekly allowance of twelve shillings. The execution fee considerably varied. In 1780 James Alexander, lockman of
Edinburgh, was by the city chamberlain paid for
service at an execution 13s. 4d., with a fee of 2s. 6d.
for the use of his rope.[2] Subsequently the lockman
received two guineas at every execution.

The Edinburgh executioner was arrayed in grey
trousers and vest, with a black velvet coat, trimmed
with silver lace. The corporation evinced especial
care that he should be properly habited in executing
his office upon notable offenders. In reference to the
execution of the Regent Morton the Burgh Records

[1] "M'Dowall's History of Dumfries." Edin., 1867, 8vo, pp.
694-5.

[2] "Edinburgh Town Chamberlain's Accounts."

present the following entry: "2 June 1581.—The
prouest, baillies, and counsale vnderstanding that
James, Erle of Mortoun, is to be execut to the deid
afternone for certaine crymes of lese maiesty [high
treason], ordains Androw Stevinṣoun for honour of
the towne to caus mak ane new garment and stand of
claythis of the townis liveray to thair lokman with
expeditioun, and Johne Robertsoun, thesaurer, to
refound to him the expenssis."

The Edinburgh lockman had his dwelling in the
Fishmarket Close, and was expected to occupy a seat
specially allocated to him in the Tolbooth Church.
In his "Traditions of Edinburgh," Dr Robert Chambers
remarks that the lockman, John Dalgleish (frequently
named in the "Heart of Midlothian") was a regular
communicant, but was accommodated at a special
table when all the other communicants had retired.

Those who were appointed to the hangman's office
were seldom noted for their personal virtues. From
the Burgh Records of Glasgow we derive the following: "7 September 1605.—John M'Clelland, beand
apprehendit as suspect of theft and challengit thairfoir, and be the clemencie and grit mercie of the
proveist, baillies, and counsale of this burgh was put
to libertie, and fred out of the tolbuith and prissoun-
hous thairof, vpon conditiouns gin ever he sould be
found within the town agane to be hangit without
ane assys, as the act maid thairvpone of his awin

consent the auchteine day of Januar 1605 yeiris at
mair lenths beiris, and being now laitlie apprehendit
and to vnderly ane assys the day and dait heirof for
sindrie crymis of thift, and be wertew of the said act
justlie to suffer deathe, nevertheless the proveist,
baillies and counsall, desolat of ane executour, to
execute the hie justice [on] malefactouris, hes acceptit
admitit and resaveit the said John to be thair executour in the same justiciarie, and hes dispensit with
the said act and crymes of theft committit be him for
acceptatioune of the said office." The minute proceeds that M'Clelland had agreed that if ever he
quitted the office, or fulfilled his duties unworthily,
he would consent " to be hangit to the deid."
M'Clelland also agreed that he would not execute his
office elsewhere than in the city of Glasgow without
" speciall leif and licence." On these considerations
the provost and magistrates ordained that anyone who
" be word or deid" ventured to molest him would be
amerced in fyve· pundis, to be directly applied to
his personal benefit.

On the 19th October 1576 the bailies of Edinburgh
suspended the lockman from office on account of
" his monyfald offenssis in oppressing of the peple for
common tulze" [broils]. In his place they appointed
" Dustyefute " [probably an old pedlar] to act "during
thair willis." On the 25th August 1617 the Kirksession of Perth resolved to inform the Town Council

of the vicious life of James Stewart, the burgh executioner, likewise concerning his " cruelty and oppression
against poor weak persons." In the reign of Charles
II. Alexander Cockburn, executioner at Edinburgh,
who was convicted of murder, was executed by the
hands of Mackenzie, the hangman of Stirling, whom
it was believed he had wantonly traduced. John
High or Heich accepted office as executioner at
Edinburgh in 1784 in order to escape the sentence
of death pronounced upon him for an act of theft;
he survived till 1817.

Gibbets were reared on eminences styled gallow-
hills; also where two roads met, and on lonely muirs.
A lime tree at the gallows ford, near Crieff, marked
the scene of many executions in freebooting times.
When a highlander passed the sombre erection he
uncovered, and, expressing a blessing upon himself,
added words of execration upon the instrument of
doom.

The Edinburgh gibbet anciently stood at the Burgh
Muir, about a mile north-westward of the city. But
on the 24th August 1586 the Town Council resolved
to rear a gibbet in a more convenient locality. " In
respect," proceeds the Council minute " that the awld
gallowis in the Burrow Mure is failled and decayand,
bayth in the tymmer wark and the wallis, and that
the sam stands vpoun the grund quhilk is now sett in
few, thairfore ordanis the sam to be removit and

tayne downe, and ane new gallows of pillers of stayne
with wallis to be bigget and rayset narrer the towne
in the place devyset thairfore and pottet be my lord
provest, and als consents to contract with ane masoun
for doing thairof for the sowme of twa hundreth
mark, and the masoun to furneis all necessars of
stayne, lyme, and warkmanschip, and the said sowme
to be payet furth of the entres syluer of the said
mwre."

Of two gibbets subsequently erected at Edinburgh, that chiefly in use stood in the Grassmarket.
An execution which took place there in 1774 is thus
described by Major Topham :—

"The houses from the bottom up to the top were lined with
people, every window crowded with spectators to see the unfortu-
nate man pass by. At one o'clock the City Guard went to the
door of the Tolbooth, the common gaol here, to receive and conduct their prisoner to the place of execution, which is always in
the Grass Market, at a very great distance from the prison. All
the remaining length of the High Street was filled with people,
not only from the town itself, but the country around, whom the
novelty of the sight had brought together. On the Guard knock-
ing at the door of the Tolbooth, the unhappy criminal made his
appearance. He was dressed in a white waistcoat and breeches,
usual on these occasions, bound with black ribands, and a night-
cap tied with the same. His white hairs, which were spread over
his face, made his appearance still more pitiable. Two clergymen
walked on each side of him, and were discoursing with him on the
subject of religion. The executioner, who seemed ashamed of the
meanness of his office, followed, muffled up in a great coat, and
the City Guards with their arms ready, marched around him.
The criminal, whose hands were tied behind him, and the rope

about his neck, walked up the remaining part of the street. . . .
When the criminal had descended three parts of the hill which
leads to the Grass Market he beheld the crowd waiting for his
coming, and the instrument of execution at the end of it. He
made a short stop here, naturally shocked at such a sight, and the
people seemed to sympathize with his affliction. When he
reached the end he recalled his resolution ; and after passing some
time in prayer with the clergyman, and once addressing himself to
the people, he was turned off and expired." [1]

Till the commencement of the present century, on
the evening prior to an execution, the magistrates of
Edinburgh indulged a procedure which they described
as " splicing the rope ; " they met at Paxton's tavern
in the Exchange, and made their arrangements over
liquor.   After every execution at Paisley, the burghal
authorities had a municipal dinner.   The execution at
Paisley of Thomas Potts, in 1797, incurred a cost of
£33, 5s. 3½d., of which the sum of £13, 8s. 10d. was
expended on the civic feast, and the further sum
of £1, 14s. 3d. on the entertainment of the executioner and his assistants.

As an instrument of death, the gibbet was reserved
for criminals of the baser sort.   Offenders of rank
sentenced to death were decapitated.   At Edinburgh
was used a " heiding sweird ; " which we learn from
the Burgh Records was always sharpened before use.
In February 1563, the old heading sword being

<hr>

[1] " Letters from Edinburgh in 1774 and 1775," by Edward
Topham, Lond., 1777, 8vo, pp. 59-61.

"failzit," a two-handed sword was acquired in its
stead. The famous decapitating instrument known
as the *Maiden*, was constructed in 1565. A behead-
ing machine so named was, in 1541, introduced at
Halifax in Yorkshire, its appellative being derived
from the Celtic *mòd-dun*, originally signifying the.
place where justice was administered. Preserved
in the Museum of the Society of Antiquaries, the
Edinburgh " Maiden " may be thus described : Into
an oak beam five feet in length, are fixed two
upright posts ten feet in height, and twelve inches
apart. Between these uprights in a deep groove
works a steel blade, laden with a portion of lead
weighing seventy-five pounds. When the executioner
unloosed a rope by which the laden axe was supported in the upper part of the groove, it fell
heavily on the neck of the criminal which rested on a
cross beam, and thereby produced instant decapi-
tation. At least one hundred and twenty persons,
including the regent Morton, were by the Edinburgh
" Maiden " deprived of life. In 1710 its use was
abandoned. The heads of remarkable offenders were
anciently placed over the Nether Bow, or on a pike
at the Tolbooth.[1]

By the hands of the executioner were performed
many odious functions. In 1436, Sir Robert Graham,

[1] Paper on the Maiden, by W. T. M'Culloch, in " Proceedings
of the Society of Antiquaries of Scotland," VII., pp. 535-562.

the chief assassin of James I., was by this officer nailed to a tree, then torn with pincers, and latterly crowned with a red-hot crown. The hangman wielded special instruments of torture. In 1593, the Earl of Orkney's brother was charged with conspiring against his life, and of being assisted in his plotting by Alison Balfour, " a notour witch." Alison, a married woman of untainted fame, declared her innocence, but her supposed perjury was held to aggravate her offence. Her limbs were by the executioner thrust into the caspieclaws, an iron frame, which was gradually heated till it burned into the flesh. As confession could not be obtained, her husband was, in her presence, torn in the rack, or " long irons." Next her son was thrust into the boot, an iron cylinder into which the legs were inserted from the feet to the knee-joints, when by the executioner were delivered fifty-seven malletstrokes on wedges resting between the case and the limbs until flesh and bones were crushed. Next was brought in Alison's little daughter, to whose hands were applied an iron screw, called the pilniewinks, which, thrusting the nails into the flesh, made the blood spurt from the finger points. Sooner than endure this last spectacle, Alison offered to own herself a witch ; she was now burned by the executioner.

By the Scottish Privy Council, on the 23d July 1684, was accepted a new instrument of torture.

The minute testifying its reception proceeds thus :
" Whereas the boots were the ordinary way to ex-
piscate matters relating to the government, and that
there is now a new invention and engine called the
Thumbkins, which will be very effectual to the
purpose and intent foresaid, the Lords of his Majesty's
Privy Council do therefore ordain that when any
person shall by their order be put to the torture, the
said boots and thumbkins both be applied to them, as
it shall be found fit and convenient."   A few weeks
later the cruel myrmidons of a tyrant experimented
their new instrument on the hands of the afterwards
celebrated Principal Carstairs, whom they desired to
confess that he knew of a confederacy for excluding
the Duke of York from succession to the throne.
Carstairs endured the application of the new " engine "
by the executioner for one and a half hour, yet
refused to divulge aught which might embarrass
his associates.   By the government of the Revolution,
the instrument of torture was presented to him in
token of admiration and respect.

A pair of thumbkins of large size, which belonged
to the burgh of Montrose, is preserved in the National
Museum at Edinburgh.   It resembles a miniature pair
of stocks with a strong central screw.   The thumbs
were by the executioner thrust into two apertures,
who screwed down the upper bar till the bones were
crushed.

Confession was also extorted by means of a prickling iron shirt; it was contrived by General Dalzell, and applied by him to imprisoned Covenanters. Fire-tongs were used, when the thumbkins and iron shirt were not at hand. The points of the tongs being made hot, were extended between the shoulders, and applied to each arm till the flesh was burned to the bones. When confession did not follow, the tongs, heated a second time, were applied under the arm-pits.

The application of torture was specially approved by James VII., under whose government it became common. Not improbably its prescription by the Romish Church may have reconciled to the usage a prince who preferred ecclesiastical usages to the sanctions of humanity. By a decree of Pope Innocent IV., in 1282, magistrates were enjoined to subject heretics to torture in order that they might be urged to confess both against themselves and against others who cherished their obnoxious opinions. In 1640, torture was inflicted in England for the last time; and on the 11th April 1689, the Scottish Parliament declared "that the use of torture without evidence and in ordinary crimes is contrary to law."

The method of destroying by fire those charged with heresy or sorcery was clearly derived from the practice of burning criminals adopted by the Druids. By the executioner the victim was bound with ropes to a stake raised upon a heap of coals and timber; he

was then surrounded with faggots, strewn with tar.
Having tightened the rope around the victim's neck,
the executioner applied fire to the heap, which
instantly blazed up. Within less than an hour the
body was consumed.

Scourging was a common punishment. The magistrates of Edinburgh scourged by various modes.
Ordinary offenders were whipped "at the poultry
market," greater offenders "in the correction house,"
and "riotous criminals from street to street." For
scourging each offender the Edinburgh executioner
received in the seventeenth century a fee of one pound
Scots ; the payment was subsequently increased.

The mode of flogging from street to street somewhat varied. On the 10th December 1538 the
magistrates of Haddington sentenced a thief to be
whipped through the town, "bundyn at the erse of
ane cart." In 1697 the Town Council of Hawick
sentenced two women for theft "to be taken out
of the irons at the tolbuith and publicly scurged
thro' the hail toun in the market day, and at the east
end of the toun to be brunt on the chiek with the
letter H, and thereafter to be banished the toun by
touck of the drum." In May 1753 Agnes Blyth was
for hen-stealing sentenced by the Sheriff of Edinburgh
to be whipped through the streets and thereafter
banished from the country.

Deprivation of the ear, or "lugging," was anciently

THE PARLIAMENTARY AND JURIDICAL.

inflicted by the executioner upon runaway serfs, latterly on notorious felons. Branding was common. The branding iron of Dunfermline was a rod two feet long, having a square lump of iron at the end, on which were engraved the letters *Dun-Reg*, that is, Dunfermline Regality. The square end of the instrument being made hot was by the executioner thrust against the offender's forehead. Female offenders were branded on the cheek.

"Setting on the Tron" was a punishment which prevailed at Edinburgh. It implied that the offender was to be placed in the pillory or jagg at the public weighing place. There were also pillories at St Michael's Well and the Fishmarket. Blasphemers were pilloried. Women who in the seventeenth century were at Edinburgh convicted of impurity were sentenced to be ducked in "the quarry hole," a filthy pool near Leith. Commutation of punishment of a remarkable kind occurred in 1701, when five persons who at Perth were convicted of theft, and would have been executed, were allowed to escape death on accepting "perpetual servitude." One of the number, appropriated as a worker in the silver mines at Alva, had fastened upon his neck a metal collar inscribed thus :—"Alexander Steuart, found guilty of death for theft, at Perth, the 5th of December 1701, and gifted by the justiciars as a perpetual servant to Sir John Areskin of Alva."

The collar, now preserved in the National Museum, was dredged from the Forth, in the waters of which the unhappy culprit had doubtless sought relief from his miseries and serfdom.[1]

Burghal order was strictly enforced. In 1650 the magistrates of Linlithgow inflicted penalties on certain burgesses who had acted towards them with disrespect. One burgess was fined for "not giffing reverence," that is, not rendering obeisance to a bailie; another for having "in his great raschness and suddantie destroyed the head of the toun's drum" was deprived of burghal freedom, fined £50 and obliged to "sitt doune upon his knees at the croce at ten houres before noone, and crave the provest baillies and counsall pardone." On the 5th September 1663 the Town Council of Dumfries deprived the wife of a burgess of municipal privileges for venturing to appeal to the Sheriff against a judgment of the burgh court. The municipal decree is in these words :—" Considering the great abuse of their authoritie by Elizabeth Gibson . . . by writing an address to the Sheriff Depute of Nithsdaile for repairing a wrong done by one of our burgesses to her, whereby she has endeavoured to move the Sheriff Depute to encrotch upon the privileges of this burgh, contrairie to the bound prerogative of a burgess's wife; therefore the magistrates and counsel discharge her of any

[1] "Chambers's Domestic Annals," iii. 247.

privilege or libertie she can claim of freedom of trade within this burgh."

The courts of law, numerous as they were, long failed to repel insubordination and check lawlessness. With his Jedwood axe and desperate followers, the Border moss-trooper defied the officers of justice, and at times set the royal authority at nought. When summoned as an offender before the Privy Council, or other court of law, the great barons attended with their armed retainers. Of such retainers the great Earl of Douglas possessed two thousand, a number which rendered him more powerful than the Government. "The backing of parties at the bar," as attendance at the law courts with a body of followers was called, was in 1579 prohibited by statute, but the practice did not then wholly cease.

Prior to the sixteenth century, the lesser barons mainly relied on the support of their powerful neighbours. To these they granted bonds of manred, in which in lieu of shelter and protection they made pledge of service. Manred obligations were prohibited by statute in 1457, but for two centuries later, bonds styled of "manrent" were granted by one baron to another in pledge that revenge would not follow on an act of injury, or that long-continued grudges would peacefully subside.

Personal liberty in the eighteenth century was not quite secure. Between the years 1740 and 1746 a magistrate of Aberdeen, along with the Town Clerk Depute of the city, proceeded without fear of law to kidnap persons in the adjoining districts, and to despatch them to the American plantations. About six hundred men were so seized and borne off. After the battle of Culloden, in 1746, the Duke of Cumberland exercised towards the discomfited insurgents the same harsh measures as had in 1691 been extended towards the Macdonalds of Glencoe. Under form of law, civil tyranny was only less formidable than military violence. The factor's "snash" exercised upon his industrious father, led the poet Burns to compose his odes on the dignity of labour, and on the rights of humanity, which, while intensifying his own fame, have materially tended to repress sycophancy on the one hand and to crush tyranny upon the other.

CHAPTER XI.

THE ECCLESIASTICAL.

WHEN worship in the grove and upon the hill-top had ceased, and the religious rites of the rock-basin had passed away, the earlier inhabitants conducted their religious solemnities upon the shores of estuaries, by the margins of lakes, at wells, and upon river-banks. The apostle of Cumbria, St Ninian, had his cave or cell on the shores of the Solway, near which in 397 he reared the " candida casa," or church of Whithorn. His ministrations among the southern Picts were followed by those of Kentigern or St Mungo, who planted his mission on the Clyde. Palladius, consecrated in 431, laboured among the northern Picts from the isles of Orkney to the Tay. The next great apostle, St Columba, eclipsed by his ministry of untiring zeal the labours of his predecessors.

Columba began his mission in 563 by planting his headquarters at Iona, so called from the words *Innis-nan Druidneach,* the isle of Druids. For there the worshippers of Baal conducted a great school and possessed a principal seat. At the lapse of another

century St Cuthbert began his devoted pastorate on
the south-eastern border.

As the Druids had received their appellative from
worshipping in the groves, so the apostles of the new
faith were named *Ceal dé,* pronounced Kildé, that is,
worshippers of God.   Every Christian missionary
became known as a Culdee.

In the wake of the converts at Iona arose monasteries at Abernethy, Lochleven, and Dunkeld, and in
the tenth century at Brechin.   Lesser Culdee settlements were planted at Glasgow, Dunfermline, Dunblane, Muthill, Scone, Culross, Melrose, Abercorn,
Inchcolm, Aberlady, and Coldingham; likewise in
northern parts at Mortlach and Monymusk.   With
each monastery were connected twelve brethren, who
chose a thirteenth as abbot or chief.

Unconnected with the Roman see, the Culdees
sedulously pursued their unambitious labours.   It
was by a law of Adamnan, abbot of Iona, passed in
697, that women were freed from the services and
severities of war.   By the Culdees were formed
shires or *parishes,* the words originally being
of like import.   Parishes, which the Culdees had
indicated in the ninth, were fully constituted four
centuries later.   To the Culdees also was due that
literary activity through which, prior to the twelfth
century, ecclesiastical MSS. were preserved and
illuminated.   Votaries of graceful art, designers of

elegantly sculptured tombs, and not destitute of science, they cast light upon an age which without them had been uninteresting and obscure.

In 825 the king of the Picts abandoned his capital at Abernethy on the Tay, choosing as his residence the promontory, then named Muckross, overlooking a bay upon the eastern shore. With the king quitted Abernethy, the college of monks, who were there sustained by his bounty, while for their use he reared a small convent, which to his new capital brought the name of Kilrymont, or church at the heather mount.

In the eighth century the Roman Bishop began to class the regular with the secular or Columban clergy, with a view to their being secured under Catholic rule. At a Council, held in Scotland during the progress of this century, the way was opened up, while at another Council held at Scone in 906 Constantine II. and Kellach the bishop pledged themselves to support the Roman Church. Not long subsequently Constantine abandoned his sceptre, after a reign of forty years, and entering the monastery of Kilrymont became its abbot.

One of the earliest features in the degeneracy of the Roman Church was manifested in a system of relic-worship, which legends were fabricated to sustain. When Constantine was abbot of Kilrymont the name of the locality was changed to St Andrews,

the change of name being, as usual, justified by
a legend. About the year 368 it was alleged that
from Patras in Achaia proceeded on a voyage Regu-
lus, a Greek monk, who, possessing certain bones of
St Andrew the apostle, was in vision directed to
carry them to an island in Western Europe. Voyag-
ing two years, he was at length stranded in the
bay opposite the cliff of Muckross, afterwards
Kilrymont. There he landed, and occupying a cell
to which his name was given, desired that the
place of his disembarkation might be called after
the apostle whose bones had preserved him in his
voyage and enabled him in safety to reach the shore.
Sanctioned by the royal abbot the invention was
accepted, and hence St Andrew was accepted as
the patron-saint of Scotland. The original influence
of the monastery of Iona was now on the decline,
the fabric had by the Danes been burned in 797, and
again in 801, while in 805 the structure was dilapidated by pirates, who also slew several of the monks.
Meanwhile St Andrews was recognised as a religious
metropolis. And there, as a becoming shrine for
the bones of St Andrew, was erected a chancelled
church with a tall square tower, the latter a substitute
for the round tower which had sentinelled the Culdee
convent at Abernethy.

During the reign of Malcolm Canmore the sim-
plicity of the Culdee system became absorbed in the

splendour of the Catholic ritual. Secular churchmen still held office, but as they gradually departed
from the scene their places were supplied by the
regular clergy. As a Saxon Princess Queen Margaret
was strongly inclined to the Romish worship, also to
Anglican modes. Personally clad in magnificent
attire, she prescribed imposing vestments for her
clerks and monks, which, under her personal super-
intendence, were prepared by the ladies of her court.
Impressing her illiterate husband with a love of
devotion he kissed her favourite books, and in every
religious concern was persuaded by her counsel.
Attended by the king, she addressed the assembled
clergy, enjoining upon them a stricter observance
of Sunday, with the more frequent celebration of
the Holy Communion. She particularly enjoined
abstinence in Lent; she herself not only fasting
in Lent but during the forty days which preceded
Christmas.[1] Mainly through her instrumentality the
Culdee system was broken up. When nearly a cen-

[1] See "Life of St Margaret, Queen of Scotland," by Turgot,
Bishop of St Andrews, translated from the Latin by Wm. Forbes-
Leith, S.J., Edin., 1884, 4to. By the sanction of Pope Innocent
IV. the queen's remains were on the 18th June 1250 disinterred
and, encased in a silver shrine adorned with precious stones,
were placed under the high altar of the Church of the Holy Trinity
at Dunfermline, which she had founded. Queen Margaret was
canonized by the Pope at the special request of her remote
descendant James VII.

tury later the Columban Church was superseded by
the Roman clergy it was found that many lands
which had belonged to the Church were by ecclesiastics alienated to their children. To prevent a continuance of the evil David I. insisted on that provision
of the canon law which prohibited marriage to the
clergy. Founding ten religious houses David
planted them with churchmen noted for their intelligence. Under their encouragement and that of their
successors fields were enclosed and tilled, orchards
planted, and gardens ornamentally laid out. During
the three centuries which followed, many of the Roman
clergy were distinguished for their virtues. Under
their fostering care learning was maintained, and such
knowledge as the laity possessed was imparted in
schools under their authority. By churchmen were
founded nearly all the Universities. Fostering science
they furnished the earlier architects and produced the
elder scribes and record-writers. In their registers
have been preserved the seeds and roots of history.
They were the first husbandmen, and the original
traders. They exercised an abundant hospitality.
By their influence was serfdom stamped out and
extinguished.

From a remote age had been claimed by the great
landowners the privilege of *gryth* or sanctuary, that
is, the right of protecting a criminal from the avenger,
and of securing him shelter till the day of trial. To

this description of sanctuary belonged the Cross Macduff in Fife. Instrumental in overthrowing Macbeth, Macduff received from Malcolm Canmore a right of gryth, which at a central point was denoted by a cross. During the thirteenth century, the right of sanctuary possessed by the great barons enabled them to grant in return for a nominal rent the privilege of trial in their regality court rather than in the public tribunal.

The Church claimed a right of sanctuary on higher grounds. Places of worship might not be polluted with blood, and he who sought revenge at the altar was held guilty of sacrilege, for which no degree of penitence could atone. By an ecclesiastical decree it was ultimately ruled that every church which was consecrated and had the right of baptism and burial, should possess the privilege of sanctuary, and which it was stipulated should extend to thirty paces around the burial-ground.

In connection with Scottish abbeys, the privilege of sanctuary was made the subject of a letter which, in 1200, was addressed by William the Lion to Pope Innocent III. who returned an answer defining and restricting it. The right of sanctuary was enlarged by David I., regulated by Alexander II., and by James III. and James V., considerably restrained. At Lesmahago in Clydesdale, also at Dull in Athole, the extent of the sanctuary or gryth was denoted

by a sculptured cross. Four stones, each graven
with a cross, remain at the four angles of the gryth
which at Torphichen surrounded the church and
preceptory of the Knights Hospitallers of St John;
it measures a mile on each side. The gryth of
Macbrubha of Applecross extended to six miles on
all sides of the church. Special rights of sanctuary
were granted by Malcolm IV. to the church at
Innerleithen. The sanctuary at Wedale, or Stow,
was confirmed by William the Lion. Within the
sanctuary of Holyrood abbey a fugitive, in 1337,
might claim refuge by tolling a bell. When James V.
laid out the extensive park at Holyrood, which
includes Salisbury Craigs, the whole territory was
embraced within the sanctuary of the abbey.

As protection from arrest within the gryth of the
ancient abbey was, at the Reformation, reserved for
debtors, many insolvent persons up to a recent
period have, pending a settlement of their affairs,
obtained shelter within the sanctuary of Holyrood.
Early in the present century, the debtors sojourning
in Holyrood abbey came to be familiarly known as
" the abbey lairds." On a payment of two guineas,
the Bailie of Holyrood, an officer appointed by the
Duke of Hamilton as hereditary keeper of the abbey,
granted to the debtor seeking sanctuary, letters of
protection.

The clergy maintained a high prerogative. By his

coronation oath the sovereign was bound to extirpate
those whom they might pronounce heretical. The
oath was, at the command of the Pope John XXII.,
accepted by David II. in 1329, and to his royal
successors it was administered up to the period of
the Reformation. Thereafter the Reformers adapted
the oath to changed ecclesiastical conditions, taking
the sovereign bound to uproot all those who professed the Romish faith. William III. rejected the
persecuting clause, and at the Union in 1707 the oath
was abrogated.

Both in legislating and in the administration of
justice the Romish Church exercised a chief authority.
On the judicial bench the clergy sat as judges or
assessors, and few ventured to question decisions, in
support of which might be fulminated the thunders of
excommunication. At a time when the barons seldom
exceeded twenty, there sat in Parliament thirteen
bishops, fourteen abbots, five priors—in all, thirty-two
ecclesiastics. Churchmen held provincial councils, and
though at these the king was allowed a voice his
representatives were two doctors of the civil law, who
were bound to subserve the policy of the Church.
Nominally the sovereign was executor of the Church's
acts; in reality they had their sentences carried out
by the prompt action of a conservator.

From the reign of David I. in the twelfth century
to that of Queen Mary in the sixteenth, each monas-

tery represented a miniature state. The abbot held
a rank, regal of its kind. Clothed in the dalmatic, he
was crowned with a mitre, bore a crosier as his sceptre,
and made valid his acts by a seal or signet. Addressed
as " My Lord," he claimed high authority since his
office was specially held through "divine permission."
In his progresses, he rode upon a mule sumptuously
caparisoned, and attended by a considerable retinue.
When he visited churches, the bells were rung on his
approach. Abbots became sponsors to children of the
blood-royal, and enjoyed the privilege of conferring
knighthood. Children of the great barons served
them as pages, and the distinction was coveted.

Under the abbot ranked the precentor or chanter,
the sub-chanter, the cellarer, the sub-cellarer, and the
treasurer. Next in order were the chamberlain, the
refectioner, the hospitaller, the infirmarer, and the
almoner. The porter was a lay brother, and his office
was usually hereditary. The porter of the monastery of Paisley founded the Renfrewshire family of
Porterfield ; the door-warden of the abbey of Arbroath
established the house of Durward ; and the family of
Usher derived its name from those who as *huissier* or
door-keeper held office in a religious house.

The learning and religious fervour which originally
characterised the dignified clergy gradually became
less marked till about the middle of the fifteenth
century, when Scottish ecclesiastics indulged an un-

blushing licence. Ignorant of theology, they were imperfectly acquainted with the very elements of knowledge. Nearly every religious house became a focus
of corruption, whence issued those noxious influences,
which contaminated the young and debased the old.
Had not the monastic authorities wielded a power
made strong by superstition, they had by an outraged
populace been driven from their haunts several years
before they actually fell. At length the ruling clergy
took alarm. On the 27th November 1549 a "General
Convention" was held at Edinburgh to determine
how heresy might be restrained. Fire and faggot,
it was felt, had reduced confessors to ashes, but had
failed to arrest the progress of inquiry. The Convention therefore determined to remove some causes
of complaint. Without attempting to conceal the
degrading profligacy of their order, the members
called upon their brethren to renounce concubinage,
dismiss from their dwellings lewd persons and blasphemers, and to forbear wrecking the ecclesiastical
endowments in gifts to their illegitimate offspring.
The Convention also made provision for educating
the illiterate monks, for checking itinerant traffickers
in indulgences, and for restraining the grievous abuses
which had crept into consistorial courts. Non-resi-
dence was a prevailing evil. Within the college
attached to Elgin Cathedral were dwellings for
twenty - two canons, but in reality one hundred

churchmen were retained on the bishop's staff, apart from their cures and scenes of pastoral labour. By the Convention residence was insisted upon and pluralities were restrained. To persons ignorant of letters, or otherwise unqualified, clerical orders were denied.

The reforms did not avail, for at a Provincial Council held in January 1551, it was admitted that few persons attended ordinances, and that those who came jested during service, and conducted secular business; others sported in the church porch, also in the churchyard. From the Church had religion been dissociated, nor within a corrupt atmosphere could piety be revived. In the month of August a catechism sanctioned by the Council, and issued in the name of the Archbishop of St Andrews, was printed in the vernacular, and forthwith circulated "among rectors, vicars, and curates," also among secular persons, though not indiscriminately. The production, calm in tone and composed in no ungraceful diction, prudently prescribed a careful observance of the moral duties. Had it appeared a century before, it might have awakened reflection. But the wound which it attempted to heal had festered and become incurable.

The downfall of the Romish Church might not much longer be postponed. In point of morals a national reproach, its existence had become an incubus on free thought and on civil progress. By his scathing wit had Sir David Lyndsay subjected to scorn the arrogance of the higher churchmen, while, less conspicuously, the Earl of Glencairn, James Wedderburn, Town Clerk of Dundee, and some others, had in unpretentious rhymes attacked the doctrines and practices of the parochial clergy. Ultimately the Roman Church succumbed to the terrible invectives which accompanied the ministrations of John Knox. In 1555 this great reformer discoursed in private at Edinburgh to the barons and other leading persons inclined to the Reformation, and succeeded in overcoming the apathy of some and in arousing the energy of others. In 1556 the Edinburgh citizens demolished the sculptured images at St Giles' Church, and at the annual feast of St Giles cast the canonized figure of the saint into the North Loch. Popular tumults for the suppression of Romish error occurred elsewhere. In June 1559 the multitude at St Andrews unroofed and wrecked its magnificent cathedral. In the following year the Reformed doctrines were publicly acknowledged, and Romish worship disallowed.

Of the two archbishops who in 1560 held rule in Scotland, John Hamilton of St Andrews was, under the charge of treason, hanged at Stirling on the 1st April 1570 ; Archbishop James Beaton of Glasgow proceeded to France in July 1560, and ιhough subsequently restored to the temporalities of his see, continued to reside in Paris till his death in 1603. Thereafter the Roman Catholic Church in Scotland was placed under English archpriests. Subsequently the Scottish Mission was ruled first by Prefects-Apostolic and afterwards by Vicars-Apostolic. On the 4th March 1878 the Scottish hierarchy was restored, and a Catholic Archbishop of St Andrews re-appointed under Papal sanction.

The catechism of Catholic doctrine, issued at St Andrews in 1551 in the name of Archbishop Hamilton of St Andrews, was composed by John Wynram, the sub-prior, who afterwards joining the Reformers became superintendent of Fife. On the 29th April 1560 Wynram was appointed, along with Knox and several others, to prepare a work "on the policy and discipline of the Kirk." The result was the production of the "Book of Discipline," which, approved by a portion of the nobility on the 20th of May, was sanctioned by the General Assembly which met at Edinburgh on the 20th of December. At that Assembly were present six ministers, with thirty-six laymen who appeared as commissioners from congregations and parish churches. To the Assembly was submitted a list of forty-three persons for appointment as readers or teachers or parish ministers. Among these were several landowners or lesser barons, one of whom, noted for his zeal, was Hugh

Wallace of Carnell, representative of that illustrious
hero who 260 years before had successfully asserted
the civil liberties of his country. A " Confession of
Faith " as a further basis of doctrine was ratified by
the Estates on the 17th July 1560, while on the 27th
January 1561 the " Book of Discipline " was in the
Tolbooth of Edinburgh subscribed by the reforming
nobles. Churchmen yielded to the inevitable. The
higher clergy accepted the change in silence, and
some in the humbler orders rejoiced in being eman-
cipated from a system which had fettered and crushed
them.

The Scottish Reformed Church, founded by Knox
on the Genevan model, was not wholly republican.
The episcopal order was dispensed with, but in its
stead were appointed as overseers of the parochial
clergy a body of superintendents. These were
assigned to the districts of Edinburgh, Glasgow,
Aberdeen, St Andrews, Brechin, Dumfries, Jedburgh,
and Kirkwall, and the counties of Ross and Argyle.
Each superintendent was required for eight months
in the year to itinerate in the work of planting
churches, or to preach three days weekly to existing congregations. The superintendent of Angus,
John Erskine of Dun, was an accomplished layman.
Each superintendent received a money salary of 400
merks, with a stipend in victual of 144 bolls meal,
96 bolls barley, and 48 bolls of oats.

To supply with religious teachers those parishes which lacked stated pastors was devised an office similar to one which bore the same name in the unreformed church. George Wishart was a Catholic *reader*, and it was because of having in the exercise of this office preached the reformed doctrines that he was condemned. Under the reformed system a reader conducted divine service in vacant parishes, and in other parishes read publicly to the people the English Scriptures. Church service at the Reformation usually commenced at nine, but the reader entered his desk often so early as seven o'clock. Afternoon service closed at four, when the reader returned to his desk and read till six. In the morning his lessons were selected from the Old Testament, in the afternoon from the New. Several parish priests became readers. While in towns the office of reader was combined with the custodiership of the parish registers, in rural parishes the several offices of reader, schoolmaster, session-clerk, and leader of the psalmody were held by the same person. By the General Assembly of 1581 readers were declared to be no longer essential, but they continued to be employed till 1645, when the order was suppressed.

At the Reformation the reader's salary averaged forty merks ; but when after a trial of two years a reader was found qualified to exhort, he was remunerated with a stipend of one hundred merks. On the 12th

March 1643 the Kirksession of Newbattle, under the ministry of Mr Robert Leighton, afterwards Archbishop of Glasgow, agreed that the reader and schoolmaster, William Hamilton, should receive a salary of "tua hunder merks."

In 1567 the Church embraced 289 ministers and 715 readers; in 1750 there were 833 parochial charges. Between the endowments provided for the reformed pastors and those enjoyed by the higher clergy under the former system, the contrast is striking. The revenues of the bishopric of St Andrews in 1275 were equal to £37,000 of modern money, the stated value at the Reformation being £45,000. Eleven other bishoprics were also liberally endowed, and several abbeys and monasteries were famous for their opulence. In 1561 the rents of benefices were divided into three parts, two being retained by the Romish clergy, while the remaining third was dedicated to the support of the Reformed Church and to public uses. In reality, only a third of a third was allocated to the new teachers. The sum actually allowed was £2400 Scots, which, had all the parishes been supplied with pastors, would have provided to each incumbent a stipend not exceeding fifty merks. As minister of Edinburgh John Knox had a stipend of 400 merks, nominally £20 sterling. For the ministers of Glasgow, St Andrews, Perth, Aberdeen, Stirling, and Dundee were provided stipends varying from £12 to £15. But other parish ministers rarely possessed incomes exceeding 100 merks, that is, about £5 sterling. Certain pastors supplemented their endowments by keeping taverns. Nor were the revenues of the clergy two centuries later very materially improved. To the General Assembly of 1750 a committee of their number presented a report, showing that while the average annual value of glebes was £4, 2s., no fewer than 704 out of 833 parish ministers had stipends under £100, there being 272 under £50. One parish minister had a stipend so low as £24.

The scholarship evinced by the parochial clergy in preparing sketches, historical and descriptive, of their respective parishes, and which were embraced in the "Statistical Account of Scotland," published in 1791-9, induced the enterprising editor, Sir John Sinclair, to interest himself in securing for the order a more satisfactory provision. With some influential coadjutors he pressed the subject on the attention of the legislature, with the result that in 1810 an Act was passed providing a grant of £10,000, so as to augment the smaller livings to a minimum of £150. An effort now in progress to provide for every parish minister a stipend of £200 has met with wide support. Under that amount in annual value are at present no fewer than 225 livings.

From the time of Queen Margaret in the eleventh

century the Scottish clergy had, according to their degree, worn showy and imposing vestments. Such a mode of clothing was obnoxious to the Reformers, who sedulously eschewed it. They clothed themselves in hodden grey, wore coloured neckerchiefs, and preached in gowns of blue serge. By the General Assembly of 1575 ministers' wives were prohibited from using "all kind of light and variant hues in clothing, as red, blue, yellow, and such like;" also "silk hats and hats of divers and bright colours;" also from "wearing rings, bracelets, buttons of silver, gold, and other metal."

Subsequent to his accession to the English throne James VI. sought to induce the Scottish clergy to adopt attire similar to that worn by their English brethren, and to this end obtained Parliamentary sanction. A statute was passed which provided that ministers should attend the church courts in their gowns, but the ordinance was disregarded.

Though an important step in reformation was apparently secured, when on the 19th March 1543 Parliament enacted that it should "be lawful for all men to read the Old and New Testaments in the mother tongue," the provision was practically inoperative. For while few persons could read, the majority were ignorant of the first principles of religion. Nor were copies of the Scriptures to be procured save at a cost which rendered the acquisition

impracticable. Hence at the Reformation the Protestant clergy permitted a mode of instruction which
in these times might be regarded as unseemly. On
Sunday evenings the people were invited to witness
dramatic renderings of scriptural scenes ; the practice
continued till 1575, when it was abandoned.

Through the intervention of the Church it was in
1579 enacted by Parliament that "all gentlemen
householders and others worth 300 merks of yearly
rent, and all substantial yeomen or burgesses being
householders and esteemed worth £500 in lands or
goods, shall have a Bible and a Psalm-book in the
vulgar language in their houses for the better instruction of themselves and their families in the knowledge
of God, under a penalty of ten pounds." Consequent
on this provision the Town Council of Edinburgh made
public proclamation that "Bybillis were to be sawld
in the merchant booth of Andrew Williamson, on the
north side of the meill mercat." And it was by the
city corporation subsequently ordained that householders should present themselves before the magistrates with Bibles in their hands, and that "for
eschewing of fraud" such books that were presented
should have the owner's name written upon it by the
Town-Clerk.

Subsequent to the middle of the seventeenth century, the public reading of the Scriptures was generally dispensed with, while the services, including

both prayers and sermons, became oppressively tedious. In 1662 the Diocesan Synod of Dunblane, under the presidentship of Bishop Leighton, resolved to discontinue the custom of "very short texts and very long sermons." The Synod also resolved to provide for "daily public prayer in churches, morning and evening, with reading of the Scriptures." During the recollection of the present writer, the reading of the Scriptures was by a portion of the rural clergy omitted in their public services.

As at the Reformation the Romish clergy were deficient in religious knowledge, it became a chief object of the Protestant ministry to familiarize with Divine truth those who engaged in the pastoral duties. Accordingly members of each Presbytery, then styled "the Exerceis," met weekly, with the view of aiding and stimulating each other in the modes of exhorting or lecturing, or conducting the other duties of a faithful pastorate. At each meeting one of the brethren was appointed to *exercise*, that is, interpret, another to *add*, that is, exhort, while all were expected to take part in confirming or censuring what the two officiating brethren had in their services expressed. In 1638 the Presbytery of St Andrews at their weekly meetings were proceeding through St John's Gospel with an exercise and addition upon every verse. When the exercise was concluded, the brethren who had conducted it were removed, while the others delivered their "censures." When any prominent faults were remarked these were noted, and the offender affectionately admonished.

To the aid of the clergy in their parochial work, also for the general instruction of the laity, was issued shortly after the Reformation a translation of Calvin's Catechism. This was superseded by Mr John Craig's Catechism for "the commoune people and children," which appeared in 1581 in the Scottish vernacular. As a further exposition of Calvinistic theology appeared at Edinburgh in 1591 a translation of the Heidelberg Catechism; this continued in general use till under sanction of the General Assembly were issued in 1649 the Larger and Shorter Catechisms framed by the Westminster Assembly.

By the Scottish Reformers forms of worship were approved and utilized. The Book of Common Prayer, known as the second Prayer Book of Edward VI., was framed in 1552 under the direction of the six chaplains of Edward VI., one of whom was John Knox.[1] With perfect confidence in the thoroughly Protestant character of a work so prepared, the Lords of the Congregation in 1557 resolved that the book should be used "in the several kirks"—both the lessons and prayers. The Prayer Book of Geneva was substituted in 1559. This, subsequently modified by

[1] See "Genealogical Memoirs of John Knox," 1879, 8vo, pp. 83-86.

Knox and others, became known as "The Book of Common Order," or Knox's Liturgy. With reference to this book the General Assembly in 1564 ordained " that every minister, exhorter, and reader shall . . . use the Order contained therein in Prayers, Marriage, and ministration of the sacraments."

But the Book of Common Order being chiefly a compendium of Scriptural doctrine was, in the devotional department, long regarded as not wholly supplying what was needed. By successive General Assemblies had committees been appointed to effect an extension, while in reality no change was produced. At length the subject of a new Liturgy was by Charles I. proposed in 1629 to the Scottish Bishops. By the king was the subject renewed when in 1633 he was crowned at Holyrood. To gratify the royal wish a committee was appointed, and had their report been submitted to a General Assembly, it is not improbable that there had been a satisfactory adjustment. Unhappily the king consulted Archbishop Laud, whose natural impetuosity and extreme ecclesiastical opinions wholly disqualified him for dealing with the strong susceptibilities of a people ever jealous of anglican interference. By Laud it was determined with the royal sanction that, along with a new Liturgy, the constitution of the Scottish Church should be entirely changed. As a preparatory step he, on the 23d May 1636, issued his " Canons and

Constitutions Ecclesiastical," a work adroitly intended
to uproot the stems of Presbyterian government.
Having indicated the royal purpose as to a new
ceremonial, Laud, in the following year, promulgated
his Service Book. Intensely ceremonial as was the
character of its teaching, this book might have
escaped hostility if it had stood alone. But as a
sequel to the " Canons " it was doomed.

The introduction of the Service Book in St Giles'
Church on Sunday, the 23d July 1637, was attended
with memorable consequences. As the Dean of
Edinburgh had from the book read only a few sentences, a woman who sat near listening to the strange
words, momentarily persuaded herself that mass was
being offered. Hastily standing up, she threw towards
the Dean's pulpit or reading-desk the small folding
stool on which she had been seated, and lustily
called out, " Will ye say mass at my vera lug."
Confusion followed, and the bishops and clergy
retired.[1]

[1] Who threw the stool is a question not decisively settled. The
prevailing belief is that the thrower was Jenny Geddes, an herb-
woman, but Wodrow, in his " Analecta," maintains that the tradition of his time gave the credit to Mrs Mean, wife of John Mean,
a pious merchant, who, as a vigorous upholder of Presbytery,
had been exposed to persecution. (See " Chambers's Domestic
Annals," vol. i. 545; ii. 103.) In the National Museum at Edinburgh is preserved a folding camp-stool, with the date 1565 cut
in the frame, which the donor, James Watson, writer in Duns,

Next day the Privy Council met, and framed a vehement manifesto. But no overt repression of public sentiment might be safely ventured upon. The country was aroused, and committees or "Tables" met daily in the capital. On the 1st March 1638 the National Covenant was solemnly renewed in the Greyfriars' Church, many of the adherents subscribing their names significantly with their blood. Laud, with the king, meditated revenge, but the power of the throne might not cope with the nation in arms. On the 22d September 1638 the Service Book was recalled.

Ecclesiastical formalism and arbitrary government invoked in their resistance a warm co-operation on the part of the earnest and patriotic sections of two nations which had heretofore viewed each other with jealousy and aversion. When the Assembly of Divines, at which the Scottish Church was represented, was sitting at Westminster, the celebrated Samuel Rutherford, in a letter to a correspondent, dated 25th May 1644, remarked that he and his Scottish colleagues had that day offered to the Assembly "a part of a Directory for Worship, to shoulder out the service-book." In 1645 the Directory agreed upon by the Westminster Divines was

described as that which in St Giles' Church had knocked out the Service Book.

sanctioned by the General Assembly, and confirmed by Parliament.

Upon the struggle followed a decisive result. Hitherto morning and evening exercises had been conducted daily by the minister or reader in the churches of the principal towns, while on these occasions prayers were read from the Book of Common Order. But the introduction of the Service Book had created a prejudice against all Liturgical Forms. Where the daily services were continued, the Book of Common Order was unopened, save by those who loved ritual and cherished it. At the Restoration its use was revived in connection with episcopal forms. But when Presbytery was re-established at the Revolution, the daily service in the Tron Church of Edinburgh, and in other congregations, became known as " the preaching." At Edinburgh " daily preaching" or devotional exercises continued till about the middle of the eighteenth century, when, owing to a paucity in the attendance, they were discontinued.

A solitary attempt made in the eighteenth century to introduce into the Scottish Church the Book of Common Prayer has hitherto escaped notice. Among the episcopal clergy who retained their livings subsequent to the Revolution was Mr James Gordon, minister of Banchory-Devenick. By his Bishop he had, for asserting extreme opinions and indulging intemperate language, been temporarily deprived ; he

remained among the Presbyterians, probably in the
hope of reviving the English ritual. The Kirksession
Register of Banchory-Devenick, under the 27th July
1712, has this entry : "Given out of the public
money for the incident charges of sixty-two service
books which were distribut amongst the parochiners
in order to setting up the English Liturgy in this
church, £3, 5s. 6d." From subsequent entries during
the same year it appears that two hundred copies of
the English Book of Common Prayer were distributed
among "such of the parochiners as were capable to
make use of them."

In 1857 Dr Robert Lee, one of the deans of the
Chapel Royal, began to introduce in the services of
Old Greyfriars' Church, of which he was minister, a
liturgical form of worship. He read prayers from an
"Order of Public Worship," which he had prepared
and printed, and of which copies were distributed in
the pews. At the instance of some recalcitrant
brethren his procedure was impugned in the local
Presbytery, and on an appeal the use of printed
forms of prayer in public worship was by the General
Assembly of May 1859 emphatically disallowed.
Yet the Assembly of 1858 had issued as aids to
devotion a collection of "Prayers for Social and
Family Worship," and as this work, admirably
adapted for its purpose, has met with growing acceptance, it may reasonably be hoped that by a future

General Assembly will be provided some Liturgies or Forms of Prayer suited for congregational use.

Vocal music was earnestly promoted by the reformers. The Roman Church sung chants in Latin, a language unintelligible to the laity. To induce singing in the vernacular the reformers established, under sanction of Parliament, " sang-schools " for " the instruction of youth in the art of music." These magistrates were required " to erect and set up " in the several towns. Instructors were lacking. In the Chapel-Royal a staff of musicians was maintained up to the period of the Revolution, but these were often sinecurists, and all were imperfectly recompensed. Fourteen in number their united salaries in 1623 did not exceed £67 sterling.

During the covenanting struggles, Psalm singing was by those in hiding indulged sparingly. At the commencement of the eighteenth century an interest in sacred music considerably revived, and in 1713 the General Assembly recommended to Presbyteries " to use their endeavours to have such schoolmasters chosen as are capable of teaching the common tunes;" further that schoolmasters not only pray with their scholars but also sing part of a psalm with them, at least once a day. Yet congregational singing was, during the progress of the eighteenth century, performed roughly. The music ordinarily lacked melody. Precentors or leaders of the Psalmody long continued to be much underpaid. Within the last forty years the precentor of Dunino, in Fife, was content to earn a fee of 10½d. by travelling each Sunday a distance of eight miles.

At a period when Psalm-books were few, and the majority of every congregation were unable to read, the precentor repeated each line before singing it. In May 1746 this practice was disapproved by the General Assembly, which enacted that "the praises of God be sung without the intermission of reading each line." Schoolmasters were at the same time enjoined "to instruct the youth in singing common tunes." In some parishes of Ayrshire, where the earlier Presbyterian modes obtained a firm root, the practice of "reading the line" was continued till the present century.

Subsequent to the Reformation was used in devotional singing "John Knox's Psalter," in which the metrical Psalms are set to music in the harmony of four parts. There was substituted in 1564 the version of Sternhold and Hopkins, slightly modified. This was, however, disapproved by James VI., who believed that he could prepare a version considerably more euphonious. His purpose of preparing a new metrical version was announced in his "Poetical Exercises" in 1601, also in many subsequent letters. But James's ambition to have his words combined in public devotion with those of the poet-king of Israel

was not justified by any qualification of learning or
of genius. After his death in 1625 thirty-one metrical
renderings from his pen were found among his papers,
but none of these was suited to congregational use.

What James left unaccomplished a poet-statesman
actively took up. On the 28th December 1627 Sir
William Alexander obtained a royal letter from
Charles I., authorising him to issue as "The Psalmes
of David, translated by King James," a metrical
translation he had prepared, with the exclusive privilege of issuing it for the period of twenty-one years.
Further, as the alleged production of his "late most
deere and royall father of blessed memorie," Charles
commended the Psalm-book to the English bishops,
to be sanctioned by them for use in the Churches of
England and Ireland; also to Archbishop Spotswood
of St Andrews, that he might sanction it in Scotland.
The fiction as to the authorship, patent as it was,
received no serious contradiction. The English
bishops simply ignored the royal request, while the
General Assembly, also the Scottish Convention of
Burghs, protested strongly. From a new edition Sir
William eliminated certain phrases which, as borrowed
from the heathen poets, the General Assembly had
condemned; but the opposition continued. Nor was
more successful a further issue in 1636, accompanied
with musical notation, and which in form and character of type was intended as an accompaniment to

the Service Book. It did not escape remark that what Laud had disapproved in connection with the English Church he was not unwilling to obtrude upon the Scottish Establishment.

In 1647 the General Assembly commissioned several brethren to examine the paraphrase of the Psalms transmitted by the Westminster Assembly, and to collate the same, with the versions of Sir William Mure of Rowallan, and Mr Zachary Boyd at Glasgow, two contemporary poets; also with Sternhold's translation then in use. After advising with Presbyteries, the Assembly's Committee sanctioned the version of Francis Rous, already approved by the Westminster Assembly; the last thirty Psalms being revised by the earnest and zealous John Nevay, minister of Loudoun. Rous's version, adopted by the Church in 1649, was in the following year published with music. Early in the present century the General Assembly approved an overture suggesting a new translation of the Psalms, and with a view to the object appointed a Committee. By this Committee were consulted several eminent persons. In reply to a letter requesting his aid, Sir Walter Scott respectfully declined, and expressed a belief that "the beauties of Hebrew poetry are not very capable of being transferred into the language and poetical dress of any other nation, except in the shape of prose translation." From Thomas Campbell, Thomas Moore,

and Dean Milman were also received letters of declina-
ture. In 1822 the project was abandoned. By a
Psalmody Committee, appointed by the General
Assembly of 1862, was issued in 1868 the "Tune
Book " now in congregational use.

The earliest Scottish hymnal in connection with
the reformed Scottish Church is the " Compendious
Buik of Godlie Psalmes and Spirituall Sangis," issued
in 1578 by the brothers John and Robert Wedderburn. Partly founded on the hymns of the Protestant
Church of Germany, the Wedderburn collection largely
consists of parodies or adaptations of secular ballads,
of which the tunes were popular. Several of the compositions are direct satires on the Romish Church.
Though not sanctioned by the General Assembly or
used by congregations, the Wedderburn hymns were
long acceptable to the common people.

In 1706 the General Assembly recommended to the
several Presbyteries to endeavour " to promote the
use of the scriptural songs in private families ; " also
to facilitate the Assembly's work in preparing these
songs for general acceptance. They further recommended Presbyteries " to buy up the printed copies
of the songs and compare them with the originals and
make further amendments thereon." By the General
Assembly of 1708, the subject was referred to their
Commission, with powers to collate " the printed
version, with Presbyterial suggestions, and thereafter

" to conclude and establish, publish and emit," a version for public use. What was the result of that movement does not appear; but in 1742 an overture was presented to the Assembly " about turning passages of the Scripture into metre," on which it was agreed to refer the subject to the Commission. Three years later [1] a tractate entitled " Translations and Paraphrases of several Passages of Sacred Scripture," was by the General Assembly submitted to Presbyteries. In 1751 the collection was by the Assembly recommended to private families, and thirty years later, sixty-seven Paraphrases and five Hymns were issued for the use of congregations.

Against the introduction into the Psalmody of metrical compositions by modern writers, some of the elder clergy emphatically protested. The proposal was innovating; it savoured of a Prelatic leaning, and the elegant verse of uninspired men might induce a deviation from the truth itself. So reasoned the isolated or the feeble. But opposition to the reception of the Church Paraphrases was not confined to the clergy. When the Paraphrases were first sung in the parish church of Corstorphine, a considerable

[1] The collection of Paraphrases issued in 1745 contained nineteen compositions by Dr Isaac Watts; three by Dr Robert Blair, author of " The Grave; " three by the Rev. William Robertson of Greyfriars, father of the historian; and one by the Rev. Thomas Randall, minister of Stirling.

portion of the parishioners renounced their connection with the Established Church, and formed in
the district a new congregation in connection with
the Associate Synod.

In the parish church of Mauchline, Ayrshire,
Paraphrases were first sung in 1805, or about a
quarter of a century after being generally in use.[1] For
the purpose of increasing the number of Paraphrases,
the General Assembly of 1827 appointed a Committee
to make a proper selection; but action was indefinitely postponed. Hymn-books, specially sanctioned
by their chief courts, are now in use by nearly every
communion of Scottish worshippers.

To Scottish reformers instrumental music in connection with public worship was especially obnoxious.
The reason is obvious. It was in the Romish Church
used in the cathedrals and principal churches.
Though much inferior to those now in use, the
church organs in pre-Reformation times were constructed carefully and at considerable cost. For " a
pair of organs" to the Chapel Royal of Stirling in
1537, also for a set of organs to the King's Chapel
at Holyrood in 1542, William Calderwood received
£66 Scots.[2] Church organists were liberally recompensed. At the Reformation every place of worship
which contained an organ was assailed by the popu-

[1] Mauchline Parish Register.
[2] Treasurer's Accounts.

lace. The organs were broken up, and the materials sold for behoof of the poor. The organs of the chapels royal were for a time preserved, but the Earl of Mar, as Captain of Stirling Castle, had the organ of its chapel-royal pulled down, under the apprehension that its music might induce the young king to prefer the Romish worship. His procedure was on the 28th August 1571 approved by Parliament.[1] Within the chapel-royal at Stirling a new organ was built not long afterwards, but it was in Divine service rarely used.

The strong prejudice against the use in public worship of instrumental music was intensified when in 1617 James VI. gave orders to repair the organ in the chapel-royal at Holyrood, and at the same time affix to the seats of the choristers carved figures of the apostles. Thus with the revival of instrumental music became associated in the popular mind the worship of images and the restoration of the mass. So keen was the excitement that the bishops gave counsel that the reconstruction both of the organ and of the stalls should be delayed.

More resolute than his royal father, Charles I. in 1631 issued an edict commanding the erection of an organ in every cathedral and principal church. The edict was disobeyed, while the General Assembly of 1638 subsequently ruled that any further attempt to

[1] Acta Parl. Scot., III. 62.

thrust on the Church instruments of music should be
strongly resisted.

For fifty years the question as to instrumental
music had quietly slumbered,. when in 1687 James
VII., in the course of adapting the Abbey Church of
Holyrood for the practice of Catholic worship, introduced in the edifice a large and magnificent organ.
After his abdication it was by a mob of Edinburgh
apprentices torn to pieces and burned.

The erection at Holyrood of a costly organ osten-
sibly in connection with the Roman Church served to
confirm the popular belief that instrumental music
was a device and appliance of the Papacy. So universal was the persuasion that even the clergy of the
episcopal communion performed their sacred offices
without the music of the organ. When one hundred
and twenty years had elapsed since the last of the
Stewart kings had associated instrumental music with
Romish ceremonies, Dr William Ritchie, minister of
St Andrew's Presbyterian Church, Glasgow, ventured
with the approval of his congregation to use an organ
in the ordinary services. The instrument was played
in St Andrew's church on Sunday, the 23d August
1807, when a sensation followed which may not ade-
quately be described. The Presbytery was assembled,
and at their bar appeared the Lord Provost leading a
deputation of influential citizens, who had come to
protest against the alleged innovation. In their

protest the Presbytery joined, passing a deliverance " that the use of organs in the public worship of God is contrary to the law of the land, and to the law and constitution of our Established Church." Thus was the newly erected organ put to silence; but its framework remained in St Andrew's Church till it actually fell to pieces.

At length the baldness of Presbyterian worship began to be generally admitted, and persons in every district were found to interest themselves in the improvement of the Psalmody. In 1829 the congregation of the Relief Church at Roxburgh Place, Edinburgh, with the approval of their minister, Mr John Johnston, had an organ built in their place of worship. There was a loud clamour, and by the Relief Presbytery Mr Johnston was called upon to desist or submit to deprivation. With his people he in self-defence severed his connection with the Synod. The next effort was made in December 1845, when a congregation of Independents at Edinburgh, under the ministry of Dr Lindsay Alexander, began to use an organ in their place of worship. From the constitution of the Independent Church the ruling of a congregation is supreme in its devotional concerns. In reality no opposition was attempted.

For a decided change in public sentiment there was a slow preparation. At length, in the spring of 1863, Dr Robert Lee, who had already been

reproached as an innovator, while worthily attempting to amend the Church's services in the devotional
department, ventured a step further by introducing
a harmonium into his place of worship. Even at the
brief lapse of twenty years the intrepidity of the
course taken may not readily be estimated, for while
nearly all the elder clergy continued to associate instrumental music with Popery, or a Romanizing ritual,
there floated about a rumour that the minister of Old
Greyfriars church was a Jesuit in disguise, while the
prediction was hazarded that he would yet become
openly unfaithful in like fashion as two centuries before
had proved that apostate to Presbytery, James Sharp
of St Andrews. Confident in his cause, Dr Lee defended his procedure in an historical narrative, which
might not be questioned as to its facts, or refuted in
its conclusions. And exercising powers of debate
of a rare order, he overcame in discussion all
who grappled with his arguments. If instrumental
music was longer to be withheld as an accompaniment in worship to the melody of the voice, the
course was only to be justified by considerations of
expediency. Therefore the General Assembly of 1864
wisely determined that "such innovations should
be put down only when they interfered with the
peace of the Church and the harmony of congregations." By this resolution, Dr Lee felt that his
cause was won. At the cost of £450, readily contri-

buted by his church members, an organ was erected for the use of his congregation. For the first time it was used on the morning of Sunday, the 22d April 1865, and the chords then vibrated awakened a wide response. In the Free Church the introduction of instrumental music has considerably lingered, mainly owing to an opposition, keen and uncompromising, under the leadership of the late Dr James Begg; yet a resolution of the General Assembly of 1883, similar to that passed in the Assembly of the Established Church in 1864, will induce an improvement in congregational melody similar to that which is now to be remarked wherever musical instruments are used in Divine worship. In the Free Church opposition to the use of the organ in sacred worship has all but ceased.

In resisting the prostrations of Romish worshippers, Scottish Reformers fell into an opposite extreme. At their instance the people were not only permitted, but encouraged to enter places of worship wearing their hats, and throughout the service from its commencement to its close to eschew kneeling or other attitude of reverence. For many years subsequent to the Reformation, Scottish Presbyterians sat in church covered except at prayer, when hats or bonnets were drawn aside or taken off. During the entire service, the congregation remained seated. The extreme length to which the clergy expatiated in prayer might excuse the arrangement, but did not entirely justify it. When the pious Leighton became Bishop of Dunblane, he endeavoured to effect a change. Under his direction, the Diocesan Synod, on the 11th October 1664, "recommended ministers to exhort their auditores that in tyme of Divine service they behave themselves in a most decent and humble manner, but especiallie that in tyme of prayer they be exhorted either to kneel or stand."[1]

Early in the eighteenth century the practice of standing at prayer became common; it was universally continued till within the last ten or fifteen years, when Scottish worshippers began to kneel or reverently to bend forward upon the pew-desks. In rural congregations, standing at prayer is continued, while in some places of worship in which has been adopted the modern system, a few persons conspicuously persist in adhering to the not ancient usage of their ancestors. In some country parishes, and occasionally in city churches, do persons of the humbler order enter their pews and become seated before uncovering. Within the last seventy years one or more parish ministers of Edinburgh walked from the vestry to the pulpit wearing their hats.

Devotional reverences were prohibited only in connection with congregational worship. From the

[1] "Register of the Diocesan Synod of Dunblane," 1662-88, Edin., 1877, 8vo, p. 17.

period of the Reformation onward till the seventeenth century the Moderator of the General Assembly constituted the court by praying upon his knees. And in performing household worship, the act of kneeling was deemed an indispensable accompaniment.

To persons of rank or substance, or in positions of authority, an expression of reverence, even from the pulpit, was not deemed inappropriate. For a century subsequent to the Reformation, the clergy bowed from the pulpit towards the pews of the principal landowners, who, if present, were expected to acknowledge the compliment. To the English Puritans this practice was obnoxious; hence a resolution by the General Assembly of 1645, in these words : " That ministers bowing in the pulpit, though a lawful custom in this Kirk, be hereafter laid aside, for the satisfaction of the desires of the reverend divines in the Synod of England, and for uniformity with that Kirk."

In the islands and uplands the period for commencing divine service was regulated less by any strict adhesion to a fixed hour, than by the consideration whether the more notable parishioners had assembled or were approaching. In a note to the " Heart of Midlothian," it is related by Sir Walter Scott that in a parish in the Isle of Bute, on occasion of the church bell falling out of order, the parish beadle ascended the steeple, and, while imitating the bell-sounds with his voice, interjected at intervals for guidance as to

commencing the service, an intimation that the two
principal landowners were at hand.   Thus—

"Bellùm, Bellellum,
Bernera and Knockdow's coming!"

To his parish church every considerable landowner
added an aisle, which served to accommodate at worship his family and domestics. But *the laird* was not
expected to continue a listener during the entire service, so with his seat was connected a retiring room,
where he might lounge or read.   Each aisle opened
into the church by a gallery, and was approached
by an external stair-case, while the under portion
of the structure constituted the family burial-place.
Those landowners who did not construct special aisles
erected four-sided pews in the area of the church; in
these they worshipped in life, while underneath them
in the soil their remains were deposited.   Also in the
area of the church, pews were reared by Kirksessions,
and leased to sitters for rents, which were applied in
administering to the poor.   Ordinary hearers bore
with them to church small stools on which they sat
at worship.   Church stools and rude forms were in
the church passages occupied by the poor till the
commencement of the present century.   When new
churches were built, the whole area was seated and
apportioned among the heritors according to their
valued rental.

By the Romish Church, the solemnities of religious worship were blended with secular enjoyment. Thus, in the reign of William the Lion, the observance of Sunday was ordained to commence on Saturday at noon, and to continue till the morning of Monday, while the interval was to be employed in sports and pastimes as well as in the practice of devotion. When religion and recreation were associated, it was evident that under the ascendency of the one the other would succumb. Towards the period of the Reformation, Sunday was chiefly to be remarked for marketing and merry-making, while in the evening at six o'clock ordinary secular pursuits might be lawfully resumed.

By the Reformers the secularizing of the Sabbath was especially condemned, and they laboured diligently to overcome it. On the 19th July 1562, the General Assembly by a resolution entreated Queen Mary to check "all vices not punishable by the laws of the realm," among which was "the breach of the Sabbath." But as the petition was unheeded, the General Assembly of August 1575 ruled that "the kirk has power to cognosce and decern upon" (among other offences) "violation of the Sabbath, not prejudging the punishment of the civil magistrate." Sabbath observance, with regular attendance on ordinances, was now strictly enforced, the neglect being made punishable by high censures. At length, on the entreaty of the Assembly, the neglect of church attendance was made penal by statute. In the year 1600, Parliament enacted that those who absented themselves from worship should be amerced in penalties according to a scale. Thus an absenting earl was mulct in one thousand pounds; a lord in one thousand merks; a baron in three hundred merks, and a yeoman in forty pounds. Burgesses were ordained to pay such fines as might be imposed by their several corporations. The statutory law which prescribed, under high penalties, regular attendance on ordinances, was afterwards grossly perverted. It had been framed at the instance of the Presbyterian clergy against profane persons; but when episcopacy was thrust upon the Church, it was used as an engine to crush those who were conscientiously opposed to ritualistic forms and a new ecclesiastical government. The perverted application took origin with an edict of James VI., which, on the 10th June 1624, enjoined all loyal subjects "to hear the word preached, and to participate of the sacraments . . . . in their own paroche." The decree was renewed by Charles I., and the penalties so rigidly enforced that in 1630 the more earnest section of the clergy surrendered their livings, and cast themselves on the bounty of their flocks. Within their several parishes they assembled their adherents for Sunday service in the fields, or on the hill-sides, preaching from tents. These

tents were not cloth-covered enclosures, suspended on
poles as those now in use, but consisted of a movable
pulpit, with a projecting top, in which the preacher
was in his ministrations protected from rain and
wind, also from the sun's rays. Worshippers stood
or leant upon the sward, or were seated on boulders,
or on small mounds.

These out-of-door assemblages were styled *conventicles,* as a term of reproach. But the stigma,
like that of *Christian* applied in derision to the early
converts to the faith of the gospel, proved a memorial
of religious earnestness. There were occasional
triumphs. The public repudiation of the Service
Book in 1637, followed by the subscribing of the
National Covenant in February 1638, and the resolu-
tions of the celebrated General Assembly which met
at Glasgow in November of the same year, proved at
the time the bulwarks of liberty. These bulwarks
were strongly fortified when in 1643 the "Solemn
League and Covenant," as a declaration of faith and
bond of common defence, was accepted by many
earnest persons both in England and Scotland.

With the event of the Restoration oppressive
measures were renewed, for Charles II., who had
himself subscribed the Covenant and experienced
hospitality and help from the Presbyterians, proceeded on his recall to oppress and persecute them.
Restoring episcopacy, he sent as unprovided wanderers

from their homes the lawful successors of those who
had established the Church at the Reformation; he
renewed the royal proclamations against conventicles,
and charging those who frequented them with sedition,
made them liable to fine or imprisonment. A Court
of High Commission was established at the instance
of the primate, Mr James Sharp, who, prior to accepting the archbishopric of St Andrews, was a rigorous
Presbyterian. In order effectually to crush those
with whom he had formerly co-operated, the primate
constituted the new court according to his own
model. Of the forty-four commissioners five could act
in concert with a bishop. Governed by no rules and
unrestrained by any special forms, the members were
commissioned "to do and execute what they shall
find necessary for his majesty's service," and from
their judgments there was no appeal. No indictments
were framed; no witnesses were examined; nor were
defences tolerated. The Act of Fines being renewed
on the king's authority, penalties were exacted from
all whom the Treasurer or the King's Advocate might
name. Among the persecuted were all who preached
without a bishop's license, and all who attended
religious services elsewhere than in the parish church.
The High Commission Court lasted two years; it
might have subsisted longer had the bishops been
less violent.

One of the High Commissioners, James Hamilton,

Bishop of Galloway, had, as minister of Cambusnethan, been a rigid Covenanter. He now persecuted keenly his Presbyterian brethren. On the 26th October 1664 his Diocesan Synod issued the following minute: " By divers ministers present it was represented that many of their parishioners did wilfully absent themselves from the preaching of the word and other divine ordinances, and did refuse to bring their children to the church to be baptized by them, but either kept them unbaptized or took them to outed ministers of their own principles to be baptized privately by them. Therefore the Synod resolved that such persons, after admonition and warning, be cited before the court of High Commission." As to " the common people," the Synod considered that the " honourable judicatorie of High Commission " should not be troubled with them, and further that as " lenity hath rather encouraged them to go on in contempt, his Majesty's Secret Councell" be requested " to send a party of souldiers to quarter upon such obstinate persons in every parish untill they pay twentie shillings Scots for every ten days' absence from the church."

By the Privy Council the desire of Bishop Hamilton and his clergy was promptly satisfied. Into Galloway was despatched Sir James Turner, another renegade from Presbyterian doctrine, and who had exercised his military skill, derived from his experiences in the Thirty Years' War, by crushing the

Covenanters of the west. Turner fulfilled his commission with terrible severity. By his coarse and brutal soldiers he scoured the south-western counties, assailing and mocking the peasantry at their devotions, and plundering them of their substance. Nor would he withdraw his troops or allay his exactions till each of his victims had subscribed a bond in these words: "I have been most civilie, discreetly, and gently delt with in the matter of my fines for my bygane faults." Further, each victim was bound to promise, under a penalty, that he would not be absent from the parish church "two Lord's days together, nor attend conventicles or contribute for the supply of any conventicle preachers."

For relief from Turner and his troops, appeals were urged on every side. By certain parishioners of Girthon it was represented to the Diocesan Synod that even while "they walked according to the law," they had been fined "for alleged disobedience." At length the people, to the number of three thousand, arose in arms, and succeeded in making captive their oppressor.

The cruelties which Turner enacted in Galloway were, in Ayrshire and other counties, notably carried out by John Graham of Claverhouse. This man, popularly remembered as "the bluidy Clavers," was naturally chivalrous and the reverse of implacable. But in the service of a despot he became cruel, being

resolved at all hazards to crush those who resisted an
authority, which he associated with the divine. In
1685 he at his own door shot dead John Brown, the
pious crofter of Priesthill, who persisted in attending
conventicles. A month later he, in attempting by his
dragoons to disperse a body of Presbyterians celebrating the communion, met an unexpected resistance,
and was discomfited at Drumclog. But three weeks
afterwards he gratified his revenge by slaughtering
in their flight those Covenanters who were seeking to
escape from the disaster at Bothwell Bridge. On the
8th May 1685, James VII. had decreed that all who
attended "field-conventicles shall be punished with
death and confiscation." This was Graham's warrant,
and it satisfied him.

With the restoration of Presbytery in 1690, under
the government of the Revolution, it would have
been pleasant to record that the "outed" ministers
reinstated in their livings had, through persecution,
become forbearing. A different picture is to be presented. They refused to tolerate any other sect. On
the 29th November 1705 the Presbytery of Lanark
called upon a magistrate at Douglas "to repress the
conventicles of Quakers" held in that place. Towards
their deprived episcopal brethren, at whose hands
they had in many instances suffered wrong, they
cherished a deep resentment. Through their instrumentality was passed in 1695 a Parliamentary enact-

ment, whereby church ordinances such as baptism and marriage performed by the Episcopal clergy were declared to be irregular. Mr James Greenshields, a native of Scotland, ordained, after his deprivation, by Bishop Ramsay of Ross, opened in 1709 a place of worship at Edinburgh. Charged by the Presbytery of Edinburgh as officiating within their bounds without warrant, he pleaded that he was not amenable to their authority. His plea was rejected, and he was ordered to desist from preaching under the pain of imprisonment. As he persisted he was, at the Presbytery's instance, seized by the magistrates, and thrown into prison. By the Court of Session he was refused redress; but on appeal the House of Lords reversed the judgment. Mr Greenshields was now liberated after enduring personal restraint for seven months. Against the remonstrances of the General Assembly was passed in 1712 the Act of Toleration. Herein it was provided that it was " free and lawful for all those of the Episcopal communion in Scotland to meet and assemble for the exercise of divine worship to be performed after their own manner by pastors ordained by a Protestant bishop . . . and to use in their congregations the Liturgy of the Church of England . . . without any let, hindrance or disturbance whatsoever." But the Act of Toleration maintained an important reserve. All the tolerated clergy behoved to take the oaths of allegiance and abjuration ; also in conducting divine service, to pray for the Queen and the Princess Sophia. By this provision was left open to Presbyterian ministers a wide avenue of attack, for it was abundantly certain that no Episcopal clergyman would venture to renounce his allegiance to the House of Stewart. Of Mr Henry Chrystie, deprived of the living of Kinross in 1689 for refusing to pray for William and Mary, and actually praying for King James, and who was now a non-jurant bishop, it was reported that he exercised his ministry "within his house at Kinross," an offence for which, by the Circuit Court held at Stirling on the 23d May 1709, he was ordered to remove from the parish. On the same occasion were the deprived ministers of Stirling, St Ninians, and Baldernock ordained to desist from exercising their ministry, until they had sworn allegiance to Queen Anne, while the Sheriff Depute of Stirlingshire was menaced with deprivation if he further omitted to shut up the meeting-houses of the non-jurant clergy.[1]

After a time the animosity of Presbyterian ministers towards their deprived and suffering brethren considerably subsided, but the race they had started was keenly followed up. The Jacobite rising of 1715 was held by members of the English government to have been materially abetted by the non-jurant clergy.

[1] Justiciary Record ; "Fasti Eccl. Scot.," II. 597.

Accordingly, Mr Secretary Stanhope, in May 1716, conveyed to the Lords of Justiciary a royal mandate, whereby they were enjoined " to shut up meeting-houses where neither His Majesty nor the royal family were prayed for." To this command the Lords made answer that " while ready to give all dutiful complyance with His Majesty's commands," their forms did not " allow such summar procedure till after tryel."[1] But repressive measures followed promptly. On the 28th June 1716, twenty non-jurant clergymen were by the Justiciary Court prohibited, under a heavy penalty, from exercising their functions, and by the same judicatory, in June 1717, were other twenty non-jurors in like manner put to silence.

On the suppression of the rebellion of 1745-6, the Episcopal clergy were subjected to a new attack. In his devastating progress after the battle of Culloden, the Duke of Cumberland burned their chapels, while by a statute passed in 1746 it was provided that after the 1st September " every person exercising the function of a pastor or minister in any Episcopal meeting-house in Scotland, without registering his letters of orders, and taking all the oaths required by law, and praying for His Majesty King George and the royal family by name, shall for the first offence suffer six months' imprisonment, and for the second

[1] Justiciary Record.

be transported to some one of His Majesty's plantations for life." It was further provided that every
house in which four persons, besides the usual occu-
pants, assembled for worship, was to be held a meeting-
house,[1] and that no orders should be registered but
such as were given by bishops of the Established
Churches of England or Ireland. By the same Act
laymen were enjoined, under heavy penalties and
disabilities, to act as informants, and to cease from
attending the unqualified.

When in 1690 Presbyterian ministers were reinstated in their parochial cures, tent-preaching was
no longer a necessity. While it prevailed, a practice
arose which even the altered ecclesiastical condition
did not wholly supersede. For when the communion was dispensed on the hill-side by popular
preachers, persons gathered on the occasion from vast
distances. And these gatherings were continued long
after the Revolution. To suit the requirements of
those who met, preaching tents were erected in the
churchyard, or in the vicinity of the church. Not infrequently the sacred ordinance was administered in the
fields. When the pious Thomas Boston was minister

---

[1] In the memoir of the Rev. John Skinner, episcopal minister
at Longside, the well-known poet, it is recorded that to avoid
this statutory restriction at a time when its violation would have
been perilous, the reverend gentleman assembled his congregation
outside his cottage, while he conducted service at a window or the
open door.

of Ettrick from 1707 to 1732, it is recorded that on one occasion 777 persons communicated, of whom all save 103 who formed the parochial roll, had assembled from the neighbouring parishes.[1]   On the occasion of the revival at Cambuslang in 1742, about 30,000 persons joined in celebrating the communion.[2]   And in the summer of 1788, 1400 persons communicated in the churchyard of Mauchline, though the communion roll of the parish embraced only 400 names.[3] In 1787 Dr John Burgess, minister of Kirkmichael, in Dumfriesshire, informed the Presbytery that he had "for many years dispensed the Sacrament of the Supper in the open fields."[4]   And at the celebration of his ministerial jubilee in 1883, Dr James Chrystal, minister of Auchinleck (a district associated with covenanting struggles), remarked that at the commencement of his ministry, tent services at the season of Communion were common.   He added that the ministers of neighbouring parishes closed their churches in order to assist in the work of preaching to the great audiences which usually assembled.

Long before its final abandonment, sacramental tent-preaching had proved positively mischievous. In the rural districts each occasion was anticipated

[1] Ettrick Parish Register.
[2] "Fasti Eccl. Scot.," II. 273.
[3] Mauchline Parish Register.
[4] Presbytery Records of Lochmaben.

by the young as a time of special merry-making, and was, as it came round, associated with scenes not only utterly irreverent, but altogether degrading.   On this subject we are indebted to Professor Walker's MS. Referring to "Manse Life at Dundonald in 1780," the Professor proceeds:—"Our grand *Saturnalia* was the Sacrament, or annual administration of the Holy Communion.   It was an occasion of high excitement to every person in the parish, above all to the villagers, who had then the rare importance of receiving visitors and exercising hospitality.   Even the village itself by the concourse of strangers, the bustle of old and young in holiday attire, the display of three or four hucksters' stalls with ginger-bread and sugar-plums, round which we stood and gazed with delight and desire, and the happy flutter of the girls when they were treated by their sweethearts, rose for the time to something like the dignity of a town.   The children, who had often envied those of Irvine its fairs, now felt that their hour of consequence was come, and each believed himself an object of that envy which he had felt.   But far beyond all in the enjoyment of these delicious emotions were the children of the manse, which was as much the focus of excitement to the village as that was to the parish; our visitors being superior both in numbers and in rank.   We had the clergy, the prime movers of the whole, the landed gentry, and several persons from a distance of extraordinary religious pretensions, which they thought entitled them to fill the intervals of devotion with participation in good cheer and social relaxation. Our pleasures therefore were as various as they were great. We had much better than usual, including pastry and other festal luxuries; we had the exclusive privilege of riding the horses of our visitors to water, and of receiving from some of them a halfpenny to be expended at the hucksters' 'stands,' and at these as well as at play round ' the tents ' in the churchyard, which being a novelty, was of course an attraction, we had the flattering perception that our condescension in still continuing to mingle with the little villagers was fully recognized by them. There was but one drawback to our bliss. We sometimes received hints of the serious and sacred nature of the occasion ; and we had to sit quiet under sermons of unusual length. Subject, however, as our gaiety was to these interruptions, and checked as it was at times by a doubt whether it was right to be so very happy, the secular prevailed, I fear, upon the whole over the spiritual emotions of our hearts, during those festive days."

Professor Walker adds : " From the tent, a portable wooden pulpit, sheltered from the weather, and set up in the churchyard, preacher after preacher, mostly incumbents of contiguous churches, addressed a miscellaneous audience, seated on the memorial slabs, or reclining on the graveyard. In that noblest of temples roofed by the blue vault of heaven, and enclosed by the hills and forests in their summer glory, orators of real power found their opportunity to stir to their highest pitch the religious emotions of the people's hearts. The eagerness therefore with which crowds flocked from other parishes to these periodic festivals of devotion is not to be attributed solely to such *feelings* as readers of Burns's 'Holy Fair' (wherein such a scene is described with matchless humour, but with little reverence), might suppose to have been chiefly operative in causing the customary assemblage of so vast a concourse."

Some years before the publication of Burns's effective satire, sacramental gatherings were condemned by the Church courts, and discountenanced by individual ministers. Referring to an Act which, on the subject, had been put forth by the local Presbytery, the session-clerk of Buittle, Kirkcudbrightshire, has in his register the following entry : " January 14, 1750. The Lord's Supper was celebrate in our kirk for the first time in that manner, viz., most part by our selves and with only one assistant minister." On the working of the new system, the Buittle session-clerk continued to make an annual report. On Sunday, the 22d March 1752, he writes : " Our Communion Day, in which there was much satisfaction." These entries follow : " Sunday, 14th July 1754. We had the

Communion with remarkable evidences of our Lord's gracious favour in and about the whole work." "25th July 1762. All the work was most wonderfully countenanced, and was in several respects more satisfying than in former years. We had the like good report of the sacraments administered this summer in most neighbouring congregations." "Sunday, the 2d July 1775. Our Communion Day, a merciful day both of spiritual and temporal favours; and in particular a plentiful warm welcome rain, after a long much-felt threatening drought."

Among the practices of the Romish Church which Scottish Reformers specially condemned, was the frequent observance of fasts and festivals. At Iona the monks fasted each Wednesday and Friday, except at the period intervening between Easter and Whitsunday; but this abstinence was intended for those only who served in religion. By instituting festival days the Romish Church led the common people to consume nearly half the year worse than idly. In correcting a great abuse, the Reformers were not personally blameless. In 1578 the General Assembly appointed a fast to continue for eight days. But abstinence from labour was chiefly associated with the season of Communion. When this sacred ordinance was in 1560 celebrated by John Knox, in St Giles Church, the services were continued daily from Monday till Saturday. And these services implied fasting of a most exhaustive sort, since they usually commenced with daybreak, and were continued till the evening. In the parish register of the Canongate, we are informed that on the 5th May 1566, "the Communion was administered anis at four houris in the morning, the uthair at nyne."

At the Reformation, and long subsequently, the Communion was observed as a week-day service, and in this manner dissociated from that superstitious reverence with which in Romish times the ordinance had been accompanied. Instead of the six days' services which existed at the Reformation, the sacramental days were afterwards reduced to four. In 1643 the Communion services at St Andrews were held on Tuesday, Thursday, Friday, and Saturday.[1] When Sunday was afterwards appropriated as the day of Communion, the previous Saturday was reserved for a preparatory service. The sacramental Fast-day was introduced by the Protesters. For the Thanksgiving Monday is claimed a special origin. In 1630, when the people were deeply agitated by the arbitrary measures of the court, the celebration of the communion in the church of Shotts was attended by a remarkable demonstration. In conducting service, the parish minister, Mr John Home, had been so especially fervent that at the close, the people lingered about refusing to go home. Next morning they assembled

[1] St Andrews' Kirksession Register.

in the church, when Mr Home again preached and succeeded in lulling the prevailing emotion. A thanksgiving service was instituted thereafter.

So long as tent-preaching prevailed a sacramental occasion was attended by the ministrations of ten or twelve ministers. Four usually officiated on the Fast-day, two in church and two out of doors. On Saturday two ministers preached, and the services of Sunday and Monday were supplied by four or six.

In rural parishes the Communion week-day services continue as in former times. But in towns and populous places there is an increasing desire to dispense with extra services. By some Kirksessions the Fast-day has been abolished. On Fast-days the bulk of the population make holiday, and even those who regularly attend the Sunday services demur to surrender a fitting opportunity of renewing old friendships and of re-awakening gentle memories.

In Romish times few persons communicated. The cup was denied to the laity, and the bread used in the ordinance was described so as to inspire awe and fear. The Reformers desired to present in the ordinance the character of a social though sacred feast. They used the elements freely. When Knox in 1560 administered the ordinance in St Giles' church, there were used by the partakers eight and a half gallons of claret. In 1573 and 1574 the congregation of St Giles consumed in the celebration "ane puncheone" of wine, that is, eighty-four gallons.[1] This would imply a large communion-roll, and it was understood that every adult, not under censure, was bound to present himself "at the Lord's Table," not only to make public profession of his Christian hope, but to signify a renunciation of Popery. According to the parish register so many as 1200 persons communicated in August 1566 in the Abbey Church of Holyrood. In royal burghs the elements were supplied to the Kirksession out of the burgh funds, while in rural parishes a special allowance was made by the heritors to the minister under the name of "communion-element money." In reality the cost of the bread and wine used at the communion table was a very small item of the expense incurred by the incumbent. He had to provide entertainment at his house not only for his elders and clerical assistants, but likewise for those parishioners whose homes were distant, also for notable strangers. When early in the eighteenth century crowds at the communion season flocked to the ministrations of Mr Boston at Ettrick, a farmer in the parish, to relieve the minister of an insupportable burden, offered to make the needful provision. On one occasion he cooked three lambs and baked a vast store of oaten and wheaten bread, besides providing thirty beds in the way of lodgment. In certain districts the communion elements were some-

[1] Edinburgh Guildry Records.

what costly. The sacramental bread in western
counties consisted of a friable cake baked with fine
flour and butter, and seasoned with carraways and
orange-peel. Shortbread is used in a considerable
district of Galloway.

In pre-Reformation times those admitted to the
eucharist received tokens in counters of lead. With
these the Reformers dispensed, substituting " cairts"
or cards. After a time were adopted metallic tokens
square or oval, having inscribed the name of the
parish on one side, and on the other a scriptural
text, or the figure of a chalice.

In the eucharist the Romish priest administered the
sacramental wafers to the recipients kneeling, an
attitude obviously implying homage or worship.
In communicating, Scottish Reformers chose a sitting attitude; the partakers sitting together at the
same table. To the rubric inserted in the Prayer
Book of Edward VI. prescribing that communicants
should receive the Lord's Supper in a kneeling posture, John Knox, as one of the king's chaplains,
offered a keen opposition, and as a compromise his
colleagues inserted the declaration that " the sacramental bread and wine remain still in their very
natural substances, and may not be adored."

Though abundantly aware that the act of kneeling
at the Communion table was by his Scottish subjects associated with Popery, James VI., with an

infatuation which impelled him and his descendants
to dynastic ruin, determined that this method of
receiving the sacramental elements should be adopted
and prevail.   As a preliminary measure, he, on the
4th March 1614, issued a manifesto expressing his
royal will that the Communion in all parish churches
should be observed on the following Easter.   The
injunction was unheeded.   James's purpose remained
unshaken.   Experiencing from the Presbyterians a
loyal reception during his state visit in 1617, he
invited the leading members of the Church, also the
nobility and judges, to celebrate the Communion,
kneeling, within the Chapel Royal of Holyrood.
Some obeyed, but Bishop Cowper, as Dean of
the Chapel, communicated sitting; he yielded subsequently.

James would not be overborne.   Already, in 1612,
his Parliament had decreed that the calling of a
General Assembly was his sole prerogative.   No free
Assembly had met for fifteen years, yet the sem-
blance of ecclesiastical approval became essential to
his purpose.   So at his bidding a body of ministers
met at Perth in August 1618, and styling themselves
a General Assembly, passed "five articles" of procedure.   Four of these were innocuous, but along
with them was the injunction that the Lord's Supper
should be accepted kneeling.   The "Articles of Perth"
were in 1621 ratified by Parliament.

While making strong trial of his prerogative, Charles I. enjoined that on Easter Sunday, 1627, the Communion should—the partakers kneeling—be celebrated at Edinburgh. The celebration ensued, but, save by seven persons, kneeling was omitted. Charles was fierce, and vowed a terrible revenge. The Edinburgh ministers, willing to propitiate the royal favour, diffidently approached the throne, begging that in order to allay popular discontent, the kneeling ordinance might be relaxed. Obstinacy is a chief characteristic of the oppressor. Charles sentenced the clergy for their temerity to appear before the Archbishop of St Andrews to be reproved by him according to his pleasure. No further censure ensued, but another result obtained widely. People dreaded to celebrate an ordinance which, observed in the customary manner, implied persecution. In many parishes the Communion was suspended till the administrative change, which, in 1637, followed the public rejection of the Service Book. By the General Assembly of 1638, the convocation at Perth which had sanctioned "the articles" was declared illegal, and its acts null and inoperative. In the matter of kneeling those brethren who favoured anglican modes were relieved and satisfied. On the 21st October 1638, the collegiate ministers of St Andrews, Alexander Gladstanes, son of the archbishop, and George Wishart, afterwards Bishop of Edinburgh,

administered the Communion " in the old session
form." [1]

During the Commonwealth the communion was
irregularly observed.   In 1653 an ex-Provost of St
Andrews complained to the Kirksession of the parish
that the Lord's Supper had not been celebrated for
three years, whereupon the lay members " seriously
recommended to the ministers to consider how this
might be remedied."   Yet three years further elapsed
ere the ordinance was resumed.[2]   Writing in 1655,
Nicol the diarist remarks that the Communion was
then administered at Edinburgh after an interval of
five years.   During the troubled times which followed,
the observance was partial and intermittent.   In 1701
a more frequent celebration was enjoined by the
General Assembly, and by that judicatory in 1711 it
was suggested that Presbyteries should arrange so
that the ordinance might be dispensed in their
parishes "through the several months of the year."
In the highlands and islands a reluctance to partake
of the Lord's Supper is bound up with the popular
superstitions.   At a recent date it was found by a
Committee of the General Assembly that, in some
insular parishes, the Communion was dispensed at
intervals of from five to fourteen years.

One of the few usages of the Romish Church
retained by Scottish Reformers was the mode of

[1] St Andrews' Kirksession Records.   [2] Ibid.

summoning congregations to worship by tinkling a bell. But bell-chimes, as savouring of Popery, were rejected. According to Martine of Clermont, "the many, fair, great, and excellent bells" of St Andrews' cathedral were, at the Reformation, placed "aboard of a ship to be transported and sold." And the great "Mary bell" of St Giles' Cathedral, Edinburgh, was, in June 1560, taken down and melted for conversion into cannon. The small parish bells were preserved.

When there was no steeple or belfry, parishioners were summoned to worship by a hand-bell. In 1622 the congregation of St Cuthbert's, Edinburgh, were convened in this manner; the beadle going about the parish each Sunday morning, sounding a hand-bell.[1] In seeking to anglicize the Church by a high ritual, Charles I. gave orders that bells of power and weight should be furnished to the great churches. On the 8th December 1629, he informed the Earl of Mar, Lord High Treasurer, that he had appointed Sir Henry Bruce, Master of Artillery, "to deliver unto Maister James Hanna [minister of the church at Holyrood] two broken cannons in the castle of Edinburgh, for providing a peall of bells for the church of Halierood-house." [2] During the eighteenth century

[1] "History of the Church and Parish of St Cuthberts," Edin., 1829, 12mo, p. 49.

[2] The Earl of Stirling's "Register of Royal Letters," I. p. 401.

and subsequently, the exclusive privilege of summoning the lieges to worship was asserted and guarded by the Established Church.

The early history of Scottish bell-ringing is not uninstructive. The bell, a symbol in Israelitish worship, was in their religious rites used by other eastern nations. In Egypt the feast of Osiris was opened by the ringing of bells. The earliest British bells are of iron, the symbol being unknown in the age of bronze.

In forming the primitive hand-bell, the ancient craftsman shaped a thin plate of hammered iron into a form which resembled the Greek cross; thereafter bending the sides together in box-like fashion, he connected them by rivets. The clapper was added by a contrivance which, securing it in its place also served the purpose of a handle.

By Christian missionaries bells were used in summoning the brethren to meals, and the converts to devotion. About the seventh century the iron bell was dipped in molten bronze, and so coated with that metal. A century later, monks cast bronze bells for their several monasteries. These bore handles of an oval form, adorned with lacertine forms. Five centuries later the primitive iron bell was, as a sacred treasure, encased in a silver shrine richly decorated. Those families who by accident or by donative became possessed of an enshrined iron bell were held

to be the favoured of fortune. The ancient bell of
St Fillan, now preserved in the National Museum,
rested till near the close of the eighteenth century
in a churchyard at the loch, or holy pool of Strath-
fillan, and it was held that so long as it there
remained, sick persons bathing in the loch would
experience cure. Lunatics were believed to be
restored to reason when, after being bathed in the
loch, they were for a night detained in the churchyard, with St Fillan's bell bound upon their
heads.[1]

Reared apart from, but in the immediate vicinity
of the monastery, the early belfry or bell-tower was
ascended in the interior by movable ladders. From
the top hand-bells were rung by the monks to summon
the acolytes to prayer ; also to arouse the neighbours
to a common defence against hostile inroads. In
Ireland there are seventy-six of these bell-towers ; two
which remain in Scotland were connected with the
Culdee monasteries of Abernethy and Brechin. All
these towers were reared about the ninth century.
Each was pierced by a narrow door, approached by
a ladder, about two yards from the ground, the lower
portion becoming a safe store-house in circumstances
of danger. Church bells of bell-metal, such as that

[1] "Notice of the Ancient Bell of St Fillan." By the Right Rev.
A. P. Forbes, Bishop of Brechin. In the "Proceedings of Society
of Antiquaries of Scotland," vol. viii., pp. 265-76.

now in use, were in the twelfth century first placed
in the towers of churches.

The earlier churches were caves by the sea-board.
Next in order was the oratory of wattles, supported
by stakes and buttresses of undressed timber. So
constructed was the original monastery at Iona, which
embraced a chapel, a refectory, and a kitchen. In
wattled huts the monks lived in the vicinity, and the
entire establishment was enclosed by a ditch and
rampart. St Oran's Chapel at Iona, reared by the
followers of St Columba, was probably the earliest of
our stone-built churches. The early stone churches
were reared without mortar. Even in the eleventh
century, the principal places of worship were of
imperfect construction. The Chapel Royal of Stirling,
erected in 1120, was covered with thatch.[1] As the
revenues of parish churches were, prior to the Reformation, generally in the hands of monks, funds for
repairing the fabrics were seldom forthcoming. By
the Privy Council in 1563, it was ordained that " all
parish kirks within this realm, which are decayed
and fallen down, be repaired and upbigged," and
further that " they be sufficiently mended in windows, thack, and other necessaries." It was also
enacted that henceforth repairs should be executed
by the parishioners and the parson, two-thirds of the
cost being defrayed by the former, and one-third by

[1] " History of the Chapel Royal," p. ccxlvii.

the latter.   The enactment as to the contribution by
" parsons " had reference to a privilege possessed by
ecclesiastics of taking timber from the neighbouring
forests, and of claiming tithes of the natural produce.   At the date of the statute these rights were
continued.

As the Privy Council orders of 1563 provided only
for repairs, the Court of Session held in 1627 that a
new church could not be erected, save by an Act of
Parliament.   And it was found by the Court in
1628 that "where there is a kirk and a quire [choir],
the parson or his tacksman ought to uphold the quire,
and the parish the kirk ; but where there is no quire,
that the parson ought to uphold the third part of
the kirk."   Till in 1690 it was settled that the repair
and re-erection of churches devolved upon the heritors, nearly every rural place of worship remained
in neglect and disrepair.   On the 21st January
1676, the Presbytery of Lanark remarked, in inspect-
ing the church of Symington, that there were no
glass in the windows, no pulpit, and no reader's seat,
or precentor's desk.   On the 28th October 1660, the
Kirksession of Inverurie ordained that "ilk pleugh in
the parishe bring a load of heather for reparation of
the kirk, againe Wednesday at night next, the last
of this month."   The parishioners of Ettrick were,
on the 25th October 1697, enjoined by the Kirksession to "bring in heather, thack, and divots, lime

and deals, and what necessaries are fit for the repair of the kirk and manse."

The majority of parish churches were long and narrow, and, possessing small windows only in the front wall, were imperfectly lightened. When applying in 1787 for a new church, Dr John Burgess, minister of Kirkmichael, reported to the Presbytery of Lochmaben that the area of the church was "from end to end only an ell wide." The humorous Dr John Muir of Glasgow, who in his early pastorate had ministered at Lecropt, Perthshire, was wont jocularly to remark that he had preached several years in a *trance*, alluding to the extreme narrowness of his rural church. At the celebration of his jubilee in 1883, Dr Chrystal of Auchinleck stated, as an incident in connection with his early ministry, that in consequence of the limited space in the old church, he had been ordained upon a low platform erected in the churchyard.

The practice of interring within the walls of churches, common before the Reformation, was not thereafter abandoned. Mr William Birnie, who in 1597 was admitted minister of Lanark, and afterwards became Dean of the Chapel Royal, issued a publication entitled "The Blame of Kirk Burial, tending to persuade to Cemeterial Civilitie," in which he strongly deprecated intramural interment. The General Assembly also inhibited it. Yet the practice was insisted upon, landowners and others burying their dead under their pews. On the 2d March 1626, James Lindsay of Belstane, being censured by the Presbytery of Lanark " for burying his child within the kirk of Carluke," pledged himself " to build ane yle for his awn buryall." [1]

When at the Reformation cathedrals and monasteries were partially dilapidated, a portion of the precincts was converted into a burial place for the poor. Within the ruins were accumulated rubbish of every sort. Till lately a manure heap occupied the fine western doorway of Paisley Abbey. Thirty years ago the ruin of Lindores Abbey was used as a farm store. Within the cloisters of the abbeys of Elgin and Arbroath wild birds build their nests. The cathedrals of St Mungo and St Giles were happily not unroofed, yet the window-mullions were wrenched out, the columns defaced, and the cornices shattered. The tombs of venerable churchmen were also thrown down, and ancient stone coffins broken open, rifled, and exposed upon the surface. The stalls of prebendaries and choristers were torn down and burned. With the progress of time iconoclastic violence gained strength. During the seventeenth century memorial stones or paintings placed in churches were, as " images," ruthlessly wrecked. In 1640, the Kirksession of Aberdeen enjoined that a portrait of Reid of Pitfoddels be removed

[1] See vol. i., chapter v., pp. 165-6.

from the vestry as " smelling of Popery." The Synod of Perth in 1649 condemned to destruction a sculptured cross standing in the churchyard of Dunblane. And about the same time, the Presbytery of Irvine, at a special meeting at Kilmarnock, commanded the Lord Boyd to remove from the parish church a sculptured effigy which he had reared in memory of his predecessor. In November 1649 Lady Callander was, by the Kirksession of Dalgety, ordered to " take down some images of stained glass," these being described as " idolatrous and superstitious."

Parish manses were originally built and kept in repair by the incumbents, while the estimated value of the structures was, by their successors, made payable to their heirs. But in 1649 it was ruled that a dwelling for every parish minister should be provided by the heritors ; the cost not being under 500 merks, or more than a thousand. Manses were ordinarily constructed at the lowest statutory cost. Those reared in the seventeenth century were composed of clay and turf, held together by bands of timber. The manse of Inverary is in 1723 thus described : [1]

" In the principal house there are these rooms : a hall, a laigh chamber floored within the said hall, a cellar within the said chamber, and another cellar in the east end of the house. A chamber upstairs in the west end of the house, and a closet, with a hanging chamber therein ; a chamber upstairs in the east end of

[1] Records of Presbytery of Garioch.

the house above the cellar ; and a wardrobe above the hall, and a
little room betwixt the wardrobe and the last chamber."

From Professor Walker's MS. " Life of a Manse
Household in 1780," we obtain the following :—

" The manses built in the end of the seventeenth or beginning of
the eighteenth century were very much alike.   They were long and
narrow.   From the smallness of the windows they were badly
lighted, and their four upper apartments were so inartificially
arranged as to leave no space for passages ; they had therefore to
serve as passages to each other.   Dundonald manse was one of the
oldest and one of the worst.   It was roofed with thatch, which
covering had by age been discoloured to blackness, while the
mortar with which the walls were rough cast had acquired a hue
of dingy brown.   Of the same appearance was the byre or cow-
house, the stable, and the outhouses collectively.   These formed
two blocks projecting at right angles from each extremity of the
house, and being connected with a low wall, in which was a
double-leaved gate, too crazy ever to be shut, enclosed a small
front court, if one could dignify it with such a name.   To keep
this free from intrusive vegetable growths no exertion was ever
made, no one having ever felt this to be desirable.   Docks and
nettles flourished without molestation in every corner, exhibiting
peculiar exuberance along an open sewer, called the *glaur-hole*,
which received, but nowhere carried off, the liquid refuse of the
kitchen."

" Such," proceeds Professor Walker, " was the exterior of my
father's manse at Dundonald.   On entering the house a transverse
passage, with a clay floor, full of irregularities, led to the kitchen,
similarly floored, in one end, and to a low-roofed bedroom in the
other, the cellar and dairy occupying the intermediate space.
Above stairs was a dining room in the centre, at one end a tolerable
bedroom, and two small ones at the other.   As the family multi-
plied, portions of the confined space between the rafters and the
tie-beams were enclosed to form two diminutive apartments.   The
interior furnishing of the several rooms was of the simplest

character, consisting either of deal boards, or of dark furze hung on the unplastered walls. When the cloth had rotted off in one apartment, a heroic innovation was made by papering it. But the paper being applied to a wall of unhewn stone, it, in its unplastered roughness, showed a surface as surgy as the sea in a storm. I wish I could add that the discomforts of such a dwelling were relieved by the nicety with which it was kept. But, alas! brooms and brushes were rarely used, and some corners never felt their presence."

With physical surroundings so utterly inadequate, the Scottish minister of the seventeenth century derived his social status solely from the dignity of his office. And as his attenuated revenues precluded the possibility of his making any provision for a family, he might not expect to secure a helpmate who, by education and training, could share his pursuits, and appreciate his conversation. At length, consequent on an Act of the General Assembly of the 23d May 1743 was legalized by Parliamentary statute a Fund for behoof of the widows and children of the parochial clergy, also of the University professors. At or shortly after admission it was provided that every minister or professor should select one of four annual rates to be compensated by a proportionate provision to widows or children. The original rates were £2, 12s. 6d. ; £3, 18s. 9d. ; £5, 5s. ; and £6, 11s. 3d. ; while the relative annuities to widows were £10, £15, £20, and £25. Consequent on some changes the annuities have latterly been increased to £26, £34, £42, and £50, secured by annual rates of

£3, 3s., £4, 14s. 6d.; £6, 6s.; and £7, 17s. 6d. When a contributor dies, being a widower, his child or children are entitled, irrespective of age, and if more than one, equally among them, to a provision of £100, £150, £200, or £250. If a contributor dies, leaving a widow, who survives him for so short a time as not to become entitled to an annuity, a provision to the children is payable, if one or more of them is under sixteen years of age, but not otherwise, and the amount is the same as if the contributor had been a widower at the time of his death. The permanent trustees of the Fund are the ministers of the Presbytery and professors of the University of Edinburgh; there are also elected members. The Fund was devised by Dr Alexander Webster, one of the ministers of Edinburgh, who was assisted in his calculations by the Rev. Dr Robert Wallace and Professor Colin Maclaurin.

During the first four centuries of the Christian Church, opulent and pious persons who founded and endowed churches were content that these should bear their names, while they were assigned seats in the choir as more honourable than in the nave. They were also allowed burial within the walls—a privilege which was extended to their descendants. When in the fifth century the Church was beginning to depart from its original purity, founders were allowed to nominate pastors to the churches they had endowed,

and in the following century what had been by
bishops conceded as a privilege, was asserted as a
right. By a section of the Scottish Reformers, lay-
nomination to benefices was associated with Romish
error, and it is accordingly set forth in the First Book
of Discipline, issued in 1560, that "it appertaineth to
the people and to every several congregation to elect
their minister." But the First Book of Discipline
was not ratified by Parliament, and it soon became
evident that if the privilege of nominating to church
livings was not reserved to lay patrons, the small
portion of money reserved from the rents of the
Church lands for support of the reformed clergy would
be totally withheld. Accordingly, in an address to
Queen Mary in 1565, the Reformers intimated that
they had no desire that patrons should be deprived of
their ancient privileges, while in 1567, when the
Reformed Church was legally established, the rights
of the "laic patronages" were reserved to the "just
and ancient patrones." Between the 25th December
1567, when the "Register of Crown Presentations"
begins, and the 5th December 1571, are recorded 220
presentations, of which 107 are to benefices having
cure of souls. In 1594 forty royal presentations are
recorded. Yet so long as the Presbyterian system
enjoyed an immunity from monarchical interference,
the action of lay patrons and the trial of presentees
by Presbyteries, also provided by statute, worked con-

siderably in unison. This course essentially differed when, in their efforts to place the Church under prelatic rule, James and Charles appointed to benefices those only who became pledged to support their wishes.

In 1649 patrons were deprived, but their privileges were recovered at the Restoration. And on the 10th July 1663, Parliament ruled that under pain of being denounced rebels, all ministers who had entered on their livings during the past fourteen years should seek presentations from patrons, and collation from the bishops. Declining obedience, the more earnest portion of the clergy, to the number of 350, abandoned or were deprived of their charges. After the Revolution, the right of appointing to vacant cures was conferred on the heritors and elders. But this arrangement was brief, for shortly after the Toleration Act had in 1712 been placed on the statute-book, an Act restoring church patronage in Scotland was hastily passed through the House of Commons, and notwithstanding the remonstrances of the General Assembly, was confirmed by the House of Peers. In approaching the Upper House by memorial, the delegates of the General Assembly addressed " the Most Honourable the Peers of Great Britain," thereby ignoring the Bishops; their memorial was rejected till the usual preamble of "the Lords Spiritual and Temporal " was substituted.

In some degree the Church had invited reprisals by suggesting the unwarrantable oppression of the non-jurant clergy, while it was felt that by owing their offices to the favour of the Crown or of the aristocracy, individual ministers were less likely to induce popular discontent. But the consequences were grievously injurious. The exercise full and unrestrained of lay patronage during the eighteenth century, while it failed in checking intolerance, induced that ministerial languor and doctrinal defection which obtained a wide prevalence. In their discourses, omitting any emphatic exposition of cardinal truth, the majority of the clergy covertly preached the doctrines of Socinus. The wide circulation of a work by a Puritan soldier of the Commonwealth, entitled "The Marrow of Modern Divinity," in which the doctrine of free grace was emphatically set forth, excited on the part of the secularizing clergy a desire for its repression. By the General Assembly of 1720 its doctrines were condemned, the people being invited to reject its teaching. Under the leadership of Mr Thomas Boston of Ettrick, the Assembly's deliverance was impugned, and though he and eleven adherents were censured by a subsequent Assembly, the agitation availed in promoting evangelical light in an age which had otherwise been in darkness.

While the embers of the Marrow Controversy were still warm, the General Assembly of 1730 determined that reasons of dissent "against the determinations of Church judicatures" should be unrecorded, implying a desire to stifle all complaints in regard to the settlement of ministers. The resolution was denounced by Mr Ebenezer Erskine of Stirling in a discourse which, in 1732, he preached before the Synod of Perth and Stirling. Sentenced to rebuke, the judgment was confirmed by the General Assembly. Erskine with three adhering brethren having refused to retract, was by the Commission of Assembly in 1733 suspended from the ministry. The four seceding brethren founded, on the 5th December, the Associate Presbytery, while, in a published "Testimony," they set forth that in adopting this course, they regarded the question of the popular election of ministers as subordinate to the public assertion of evangelical truth. By the General Assembly of 1734 the brethren were invited to return to their parishes, but they declined, and were in 1737 joined by four other ministers who seceded from the Establishment.

In endeavouring to shake off secular trammels the Associate Church unhappily proceeded in a course, which more than bordered upon fanaticism. They prohibited their members from entering a parish church under high censures. In July 1741, inviting to Scotland Mr George Whitefield to prosecute an evangelistic tour, they entreated him to accept the

Solemn League and Covenant; but as he refused to abandon the Church of England, of which he was a minister, they openly renounced his fellowship. Appointing a fast to be observed on the 4th August 1742 they, at a meeting held on the 15th of the preceding July, declared that a chief reason for so doing was " because the Lord hath, in His righteous displeasure, left this Church and land to give such an open discovery of their apostacy from Him, in the fond reception that Mr George Whitefield hath met with."[1] In the same "Testimony" they characterize the religious revival at Cambuslang "as awful work upon the bodies and spirits of men, induced by the energy of Satan." Distressed by the recent invention of fanners for winnowing corn, they described the appliance as interfering as a wind-producer with the Divine prerogative. In a manifesto, issued in 1743, the brethren denounced the Christmas holidays by quaintly complaining that " countenance was given to the observation of holy days, by the vacation of our most considerable courts of justice in the latter end of December." They also declared that "the penal statutes against witches" had been repealed, " contrary to the express law of God ; by which a holy God may be provoked, to permit Satan to tempt and seduce others to the same wicked and dangerous snares."

[1] Gillies's " Memoirs of George Whitefield," Lond., 1770, 8vo, pp. 72-7, 118.

Such sentiments, while inducing ridicule on the part of some, excited in others a vehement indignation. In 1781 an Aberdeenshire landowner stipulated in his leases that his tenants would forfeit their holdings, if they took into their service or harboured "seceders," whom he classed with "thieves and vagabonds."

In order to exclude Jacobites and Roman Catholics [1] from burghal administration, a statute was passed in 1745, whereby an oath was imposed on those who sought to become burgesses. By this oath burgesses became bound to profess and uphold "the true religion presently professed within the realm," meaning the Protestant faith. But to a section of the Associates it occurred that the acceptance of the oath gave sanction to the Established Church. Hence arose a bitter controversy which, after two years, resulted in a separation. By the section condemning the oath was constituted the General Associate, by the others the Associate Synod; they were otherwise known as Burghers and Antiburghers. A second separation ensued, when subsequently was agitated

[1] Dr Somerville has recorded disapprovingly that the measures for liberating Roman Catholics from the severe restrictions and penalties instituted by Government in 1779 met with a warm support, not only from individual members of the Church of Scotland, but from the leaders of that party, which had been distinguished for antipapistical zeal. "My Own Life and Times," by Thomas Somerville, D.D., pp. 190-7.

the question as to whether that part of the "Testimony" of 1736 should be maintained or rescinded,
wherein the toleration of Episcopal worship in Scotland was denounced as sinful. To the new separatists
was assigned on the one side the name of the Constitutional Associate Presbytery, and on the other
that of the Original Burghers' Presbytery. Popularly
they were known as the *New* and the *Old Light
Burghers.* After being alienated and opposed to
an extent that members of the one denomination
would by their presence give no sanction to the
ordinances of the other, the two bodies at length
came amicably together. In 1820 they were re-
united under the designation of the United Secession
Church.

A forced settlement at Inverkeithing in 1752 gave
origin to the Relief Church—the name signifying
relief from the burden of patronage. Consequent on
asserting in the General Assembly a former refusal to
assist in inducting at Inverkeithing an obnoxious
presentee, Thomas Gillespie, minister of Carnock, was
deposed summarily. In 1758 he was joined by Thomas
Boston, minister of Jedburgh ; and in 1761 by a congregation at Colinsburgh ; thereafter by several other
"societies" or congregations. Cherishing liberal sentiments, the members maintained the principle of free
communion—that is, of joining at the Lord's Supper
with members of other churches. By the union in

1847 of the Relief with the Secession Church, was constituted the United Presbyterian Church.

These several secessions and changes, inconsiderable at the outset, extended under the exercise of a high-handed patronage. For by a forced settlement public sentiment was outraged almost every second or third year. These settlements were usually effected under a military escort, which by their bayonets and fire-locks guarded Presbyteries in obtruding into the sacred office pastors obnoxious to the flocks. Writing about sixty years ago, Lord Cockburn relates in his "Memorials" how that he knew of a cabinet minister who refused to promote a clergyman from a second to a first charge, on account of what he deemed "the presumption of the parishioners" in venturing to request that this might be done. And when, in 1841, a congregation in Fife applied to a noble earl, patron of the parish, to appoint as colleague and successor to the aged incumbent the ministerial assistant by whose services they were edified, they were informed by his lordship's chamberlain that he could not advise his constituent to accede to "any popular representation." Under such circumstances, congregations from time to time seceded from the Establishment, so that when the Relief and United Secession came together in 1847, as the United Presbyterian Synod, these jointly possessed no fewer than 497 churches.

For many years "the call" or address by the parishioners to the presentee, inviting him to accept the sacred office, had become a mere formality, since there existed no right to call any other, and induction on the patron's gift was a necessary sequence. At length after other efforts to obtain relief had failed, the General Assembly of 1834, on the motion of Lord Moncreiff, agreed by a majority of 184 to 139 to pass the celebrated "Veto" law. This law or resolution provided that " the solemn dissent of a majority of male heads of families, members of the vacant congregation, and in full communion with the church, shall be deemed sufficient ground for the rejection of a presentee." Not long afterwards the presentee to the vacant parish of Auchterarder, Perth-shire, received to his call only two signatures, while nearly all who under the Veto law were entitled to object, signified their dissent. But at the instance of the patron and his presentee, the Court of Session held that the Veto law was illegal, and therefore ordered the local Presbytery to proceed with the induction. On an appeal this judgment was, in August 1842, affirmed by the House of Lords. Thereupon on the 17th November a convocation of ministers who adhered to the policy of the Church was held at Edinburgh. No fewer than 465 ministers were present, and the deliberations continued for an entire week. The result was not made known till the

18th May 1843, when the next General Assembly was held in St Andrew's Church. After constituting the court, Dr David Welsh, the retiring Moderator, declared by a solemn protest that ecclesiastical action was restrained by the recent adverse decision, and laid on the table a " Claim of Right," approved by the former Assembly. Bowing to the Lord High Commissioner, he now retired from the building, followed by those of the brethren present who had in the preceding November resolved to secede from the Establishment. Proceeding to a large hall at Canonmills, the brethren there constituted the first General Assembly of the Free Church, and elected Dr Thomas Chalmers as Moderator. Of 1203 ministers, including those of *quoad sacra* churches, 474 surrendered their livings, a sacrifice to principle without any parallel in modern history.

Liberally supported by friends and adherents, the Free Church yet encountered much inconvenience owing to the refusal by certain landowners of sites for their places of worship. But this system of repression was soon discontinued.

In connection with the Establishment, the Earl of Aberdeen passed through the legislature " a declaratory Act," intended to give greater scope to objecting parishioners; but after a full trial the statute was found promotive of the difficulties which it sought to overcome. One result was inevitable, that if the

Established Church was longer to be maintained, lay patronage must cease. On the 7th August 1874 the royal assent was given to a measure repealing the Act of 1712, and vesting the right of electing and appointing ministers to vacant churches in the several congregations.

Amidst these divisions and conflicts the Scottish people have adhered strongly to the doctrines and principles which prevailed at the Reformation. The bulk of the nation being Presbyterian, the Church of Scotland may be defined as consisting of three sections of clergy, severally denoted by those who receive stipend under the authority of the State; those who are supported by a general sustentation fund, and those who derive support from congregational contributions. Of the two latter sections are many who, upholding the voluntary principle, are opposed to religious endowments. On the other hand, members of the Established and no inconsiderable portion of the members of the Free Church, strongly maintain that the endowment of a settled ministry in connection with a faith approved by four-fifths of the population is a State duty and national obligation. On such points difference of sentiment may only interfere with common concord, when the advocates of one mode of thinking seek to thrust their views obtrusively upon the other. Happily in the midst of existing differences there prevails a general harmony, and a growing desire for mutual co-operation.

The ascendency of the Presbyterians in 1638 was not unattended by feelings bitter and resentful towards those who had opposed them. The Solemn League and Covenant, ratified in 1643 by the Parliaments of both kingdoms, provided that Presbytery be maintained in England, Ireland, and Scotland, and that Popery and Prelacy be extirpated. Though this provision was of brief continuance the idea of Presbyterian uniformity was stoutly maintained by the Covenanters, more especially by that section of which Richard Cameron was the leader. In 1690 the Cameronians objected to the Revolution settlement on the ground that it did not embrace the polity of the Covenant. By the Convention a compromise was effected, when nearly a thousand men connected with the sect formed themselves into a regiment " to recover and establish the work of Reformation, . . . in opposition to Popery, Prelacy, and arbitrary power." But the establishment of the Cameronian Regiment did not wholly supplant the sect of which they were a portion. " Hill men," as they were popularly called, were to be found everywhere in the south-western counties. With views considerably modified, they formed themselves into the Reformed Presbyterian Church, a body which in 1860 numbered 45 congregations ; there are now not more than seven.

A body of persons, somewhat resembling the earlier Hill-men, continue to exist in Sutherland and Caithness, and other northern counties. By the minister of Golspie described as "illiterate, fanatical, and disorderly,"[1] they form a parochial oligarchy, asserting authority over minister and people. Sitting together in a pew close by the pulpit, they each on entering assume a dark cowl, which they wear during service. By motions of the head and low ejaculations they approve or censure the preacher's words. When they specially commend, they with their heels or staves knock gently upon the floor. In the times of tent-preaching, they made choice of ministers who were at the Communion season to conduct the out-of-door services, of which they took the control and regulation.

The Caithness "men" engaged in what was termed *Friday fellowship*—that is, they met each Friday to hear each other discourse on moral and religious themes. Generally self-educated, their discourses were rhapsodical and fragmentary. Austere and censorious, they dealt harshly with the failings of others, but were more than lenient towards their own. By some "men" was claimed the gift of prophecy. Early in the century, John Grant, a member of the brotherhood, renounced his office in the eldership on account of secular advertisements being attached to the parish

[1] "New Stat. Account," xv., 36.

church ; he ultimately retired from ordinances, and
discoursed to his domestics.[1] When attending the
General Assembly of the Free Church, which in
August 1845 was held at Inverness, Dr Alexander
Beith of Stirling found that " the men " were indif-
ferent to the business of the church in its financial
interests, but largely pervaded by the idea of "the
big sacrament," and of "holy services." [2]

When the office of " Reader " had ceased, and the
Scriptures were no longer read in church at morning
and evening services, the General Assembly prescribed that Scripture-reading and prayer should be
conducted in every household. In 1641 the Assembly
instructed ministers and elders " to take care that the
worship of God be performed in families ; " and in
1647 a directory for family worship was prescribed.
In May 1651 the Synod of Perth and Stirling
instructed the Presbytery of Auchterarder to " take
order " that every householder should " practice
family exercise by ane qualified man, or else do it
himself." Deliverances of similar purport continued
to be issued by the ecclesiastical courts. To some
dwellings was attached a small closet or oratory, in
which members of the household could retire for

[1] " Ministers and Men in the Far North," by the Rev. Alexander Auld, Ulrig, Wick, 1868, 12mo.
[2] " A Highland Tour," by Alexander Beith, D.D., Edinburgh,
1874, 12mo, pp. 241, 242.

devotion, and by some families were preserved written covenants of spiritual dedication, which were renewed yearly after the Communion.

During the eighteenth century every Scottish yeoman closed the day's activities by a service of devotion. At eight or half-past eight, assembled in the kitchen the members of the family, along with the hinds and maid-servants. Before the gudeman was placed on a table near the hearth the family Bible, a large edition of the sacred volume. A psalm was sung, all joining in the melody. Next was read a portion of Scripture, and thereafter all knelt down reverently as the gudeman expressed an earnest and comprehensive prayer. In the words of Robert Burns:

> " The cheerfu' supper done, wi' serious face
> They round the ingle form a circle wide ;
> The sire turns o'er with patriarchal grace,
> The big ha'-Bible ance his father's pride :
> His bonnet rev'rently is laid aside,
> His lyart haffets wearing thin and bare ;
> Those strains that once did sweet in Zion glide,
> He wales a portion with judicious care ;
> And " Let us worship God," he says with solemn air.
>
> .   .   .   .   .
>
> Then kneeling down to heaven's Eternal King,
> The saint, the father, and the husband prays.
> Hope ' springs exulting on triumphant wing,'
> That thus they all shall meet in future days,
> There, ever bask in uncreated rays."

Family worship continues, but among those engaged

in husbandry, and in peasants' cottages, it is less
common than at a former period.

During Romish times, Sunday was regarded less
as a day of worship than as the weekly holiday. Few
attended worship, but many engaged in marketing in
the churchyard, and in sports on the village-green.
Proceeding to an opposite extreme, the Reformers
observed the sacred day with a rigid austerity.
Attendance on morning and evening lessons, also
on protracted mid-day services, was strongly insisted
upon, and the neglect made punishable with high
censures. To children were on Sunday prohibited
every domestic pastime.

As a supposed help towards the introduction of an
Anglican ceremonial, James VI. sought to repress the
prevailing morosity. In 1618 he issued a manifesto
authorizing Sunday games, among which as "lawful to be observed" he specified archery, football, and
Morris-dances. The error which it was intended
to surmount, the royal mandate increased and
strengthened, while as it was also extended to the
Puritans of England, "the Book of Sports," as the
king's proclamation was called, was by order of the
Long Parliament in 1643 publicly burned at Cheap-
side. Sunday was associated with especial gloom
during the days of the Covenant. Even in the
eighteenth century, when doctrinal defection prevailed widely, those who had otherwise forsaken the

old paths clung to a cheerless Sunday. On Sunday
morning each window-blind remained undrawn ; and
save in proceeding to church, few walked forth beyond
the bounds of the adjacent paddock. Persons found
upon Sunday discoursing in the highway were classed
with the profane, and styled " Sabbath-breakers." In
those times any proposal to open parks or ornamental
enclosures on the day of rest would have awakened
alarm as a presage of apostacy.

Yet religious education lagged. By persons of
mature years were read such works as Flavel's
" Spiritual Husbandry," Guthrie's " Great Interest,"
Halyburton's " Great Concern," Boston's " Fourfold
State," and Rutherford's " Letters ; " but the only
provision for the religious training of the young was
embraced in the " Shorter Catechism " of the Westminster Assembly. This compendium, suited only
for the experienced adult, was urged upon the memory
of the young ; it was taught in the schoolroom, used
in the nursery and at the hearth, and by ministers
made the subject of instruction at " diets of catechis-
ing." Prior to 1782, Sunday Schools were unknown,
and the earlier teachers were denounced as practising
innovations, and interfering with the functions of the
clergy. In 1799 Sunday Schools were condemned by
the General Assembly, and against those who conducted them the procurator of the Church was
enjoined to proceed punitively under the authorit

of an old Act of Parliament devised against "malignants." During the same period the anathemas of all the Churches were directed against missions; also against laymen who ventured to exhort or preach.[1] During the last sixty years no section of the Scottish Church has failed in missionary zeal.

One of the most hopeful features of our own times is a steadily increasing Christian liberality. Prosecutions for heresy are rare, and earnest interpreters of Scripture are practically unrestrained by the fetters of confessions or creeds. In all the Churches, considerate persons labour to discover the points on which they are agreed rather than those about which they differ. While ministers of different denominations freely exchange pulpits, and assist each other on all fitting occasions, the bulk of the people do not hesitate to approve.

Episcopacy which, associated with arbitrary government, was formerly distasteful, no longer wears a repellent garb, and those who affectionately cherish the memories of Archbishop Leighton, Parson Skinner, and Dean Ramsay, may not unfavourably regard a branch of the Christian Church in which they severally laboured. From the extinct fires of ecclesiastical strife have at length germinated the seeds of a growing concord and increasing amity.

[1] "Memoirs of Robert Haldane and James A. Haldane," Lond., 1852, 8vo, pp. 256, 257.

CHAPTER XII.

CHURCH DISCIPLINE.

In pre-Reformation times the Scottish Church exercised a system of penance, which, while fortifying ecclesiastical authority, was believed to conduce to social order. When social offences were not dealt with directly by the Church, the sentences were, nevertheless, executed under clerical supervision. On this subject the Burgh Records of Aberdeen supply some curious particulars. In 1523 John Pitt, tailor, who had refused to join the Candlemas procession, and conducted himself rudely towards a magistrate and certain burgesses, was sentenced by the Town Council to appear on the following Sunday in St Nicholas Church, "bareheaded and barefooted," and there to publicly acknowledge his offence. In performing his act of penance, he was to wear on his breast a pair of shears, and, in the time of high mass, to carry a wax-candle as an offering to Saint Nicholas and thereafter, on his knees, humbly to beseech the officiating priest to remit his fault. About the same

period Bessie Dempster, convicted before the Town
Council, by a jury, for aspersing David Reid, was
sentenced to undergo various indignities, in which
were included that next Sunday she should go before
the procession in her shift, and entering the church
with a wax-candle in her hand, should offer it " to
the holy blood light," and then, on her knees, beseech
the magistrates and the good men of the town to
request Reid to forgive her.   At Aberdeen, in times
immediately preceding the Reformation, such sentences were common.

While abnegating the doctrine, and renouncing the
ritual of the Romish Church, Scottish Reformers
adhered to the Catholic discipline, omitting only
those forms of penance which bordered on superstition.   And that discipline might be effectually maintained, it was ruled by the first General Assembly, in
December 1560, that elders should be chosen in every
parish to constitute, along with the minister, a local
consistory, or parochial court.   At ordination elders
did not surrender their position as laymen, nevertheless they were privileged to elect one of their
number as a ruling elder to exercise in Presbyteries
and Synods an equal authority with the minister.
To the General Assembly, elders are delegated as
members by Presbyteries, Town Councils, and the
Universities.

In St Cuthbert's parish, Edinburgh, the lay members

of the Kirksession were for a time chosen annually. Those chosen as elders were reputed for their knowledge and Christian experience ; but not infrequently landowners and magistrates of burghs, not being " suspected of Papistrie," were added to the eldership. The Kirksession of Glasgow ruled, in 1599, " that whoever be chosen proveist or baillies after this, sall be enrollit as elderis of the kirke." Kirksessions in royal burghs usually secured at their meetings the attendance of a bailie, who was expected to see their sentences upon delinquents duly carried out. On the 3d October 1564, the Kirksession of the Canongate had before them a parishioner named William Smybert, of whom it was demanded why " he suferit his barin to ly unbaptised ? " Smybert made answer, " I haif my barin baptiset, and that in the qvene's Grace's chapell." Being further posed, " quha wes witnes vnto the child," he replied, " I will schaw no moir at this tyme." This declinature being held an act of contumacy, Smybert was remitted to "James Wilkie, baillie assistar with the kirke," to be by him " haldin in vard," till he would answer discreetly.[1] About the same time the Kirksession of the Canongate, in the presence and with the sanction of John Oswald and James Wilkie, bailies, " commandit Beatrix Moris for disobedience " to be " brankit three houris," and ordained that if ever she be found associating

[1] "Buik of the Kirk of the Canagait."

" with ane under scandel that she be schurgit and brunt in the scholderis."

In 1544 the Town Council of Aberdeen in sentencing Mage Durtly to ask pardon of a neighbour, whom she had offended, by falling before her on her knees in St Nicholas Church, and with a wax candle in her hand, decreed that if she so offended a second time "her crag be put in the jougs." Under magisterial sanction the jagg, as an instrument of discipline, was transferred to the Reformed Church. Attached to the walls of churches, near the principal entrance, it was applied chiefly to obstinate persons, who sought to ignore or escape from ecclesiastical authority. Thus on the 24th April 1608, the Kirksession of Kinghorn received a report from the magistrates " that they had put Jhone Broun in the tolbuithe till he suld ather enter to the gougs or els pay his penaltie."   .

Obstinate offenders were " jagged" on a succession of Sundays, and there were instances in which the punishment was administered each Sunday during a period of six months. That the ministers and other officebearers of a Protestant Church should exercise upon social offenders secular punishment surprised those English soldiers who, in 1650, formed Cromwell's army of occupation. By these the jaggs were pulled down, and the other instruments of parochial discipline burned or broken up.

Subsequent to the Restoration, Kirksessions were in

obtaining secular approval to the jagging of delinquents more careful than hitherto. Thus in April 1668, the Kirksession of Port of Menteith, " after long debate, did judge it most fitt for the bringing of persons to the juges, to make choice of ane of thir two ways, either to desyr the respective heritor to present those in his lands, or to cause a messenger-at-armes with Jon Battison, to bring thereto, or to require the concurrence of a justice of the peace." In June 1697 the Kirksession of Lesmahagow, desirous of severely punishing a shepherd who had shorn his sheep on the parish Fast, passed the following minute : " The Session considering that there are several scandals of this nature breaking forth, recommends to the bailie of the bailerie of Lesmahago, to fix a pair of jougs at the kirk door, that he may cause punish corporally those who are not able to pay fines, and that according to law." To the churches of Merton in Berwickshire, and of Duddingston near Edinburgh, are still attached the ancient jaggs ; the jagg of Galashiels parish is preserved at Abbotsford.

According to the Church of Rome, heresy as an alleged renunciation of the Christian faith merited death by burning. Believing that Popery was a system of damnable error, Scottish Reformers held Romish priests to be worthy of punishment. Sir John Carvet, a priest who, at Easter 1565, had publicly celebrated mass at Edinburgh, was there conducted to the Tolbooth, and being attached by the executioner to the market cross, was subjected to the rough handling of the crowd. Two years previously, at the instance of the Reformers, Archbishop Hamilton of St Andrews had, with forty-seven others, been, for celebrating mass, sentenced to imprisonment; they were liberated by Queen Mary. On the 31st September 1564, the Kirksession of the Canongate, which claimed jurisdiction over Holyrood Palace, placed at their bar a Romish priest, charged with contravening "the order of the Kirk." The narrative of the case is thus detailed in the minutes:

" 31 of September 1564. The quhilk day comperit Sir Johne Scot and biand accusit of certaine crymes committit be him, desyris the copy of the bill and promist to ansuer thairto that day viii. dayes, the quhilk is grantit to him.—The 7 day of October 1564. The quhilk day compeiris Sir Johne Scot, biand requirit to mak ansuer vnto the bill gewin wnto him, ansuerit with stubbornnes, 'I have no thing to do with yow, for ye haue no power over me,' and than produces ane wnsellit Letter subscryuit as he allegit be the Quens Grace Majestie makand mentioun becaus he wes of the Quens Gracis religioun, he wes perservit, and charging thairfor the prowest and baillies of Edinburgh with the Cannogait that thai nor nane of thame wnder all heyest pane and charge, molest nor cumer the said Sir Johne, bot that speciabillie he mycht teche ane schoil quhair he plesit, and becaus that of the wncertitie of the subscriptioun thai command the said Sir John to present the said Letter selit. The quhilk the said Sir John promisis to do."

On the 18th November the process against Scot being resumed, he was " orderit to be delaittit," and

" the Justice Clerk and the Laird of Fordell were ordainit in the name of the eternal God to remove him out of thair husses as ane plane repugner to God and his word." [1]

While retaining the privilege of inflicting upon delinquents corporal punishment, Scottish Reformers also claimed a power which, wielded by sovereign pontiffs, had brought to their knees emperors and kings. By the ancient law of Scotland a person excommunicated by the Church was deprived of his feudal rights ; he could hold no land, and might be seized and imprisoned by the nearest magistrate. Cut off from holy offices, he was separated from the intercourse of relatives and neighbours, while his servants were released from their obedience. Further, it became a trespass to offer him even common courtesy, and to supply him with food or yield him shelter, whether in charity or for coin, was held a deadly sin.

By the first General Assembly held in 1563, John Knox was empowered to frame a form of excommunication ; it was subsequently approved. By its operation, obdurate and contumacious persons were " cut off and secluded " from the society of the faithful and debarred from Christian ordinances, while the civil consequences involved in the sentence remained unrepealed. Every sentence of excommunication

[1] " Buik of the Kirk of the Canagait."

included the words, "And this his sin, by virtue of our authority, we bind and pronounce it to be bound in heaven and in earth."

On the 23d February 1564, the Kirksession of the Canongate resolved anent "persons excommunicated for disobedience and remayning forty dayes wnder the said excommunication," that "letters were to be procurit of the Lordis for warding of thair personis in the castellis of Edinbrucht or Dunbartone, and thair to reman ay and vntil thai satisfie the kirke.   In 1627 the Kirksession of Stow "gave up as ane vagabond" one James Pringle, who had declined the citation of the court; and "it was intimat from the pulpitt that none within the parish should receive him or give him harbour." To the Kirksession of Saltoun, in October 1640, the parish bailie made report that, pursuant to their decree, he had taken poinds from refractory and contumacious persons, viz. : "from Jeane Reid, ane yron pot; from Agnes Litster, ane yron pot; from Marioun Home, ane pan; from Jean Covered, ane pan; from Margaret Fluker, ane coat; and from Helen Allen, ane coat." When in 1647 the Synod of Dumfries and Galloway excommunicated Lord Herries, a Roman Catholic, two tradesmen who had business with his lordship applied, before waiting upon him, for the sanction of the parochial Kirksession.   On the 15th July 1652, Mr James Robertson, minister of Cranstoun, was "publicly rebuikit" by the Presbytery of Dalkeith, inasmuch that on occasion of the marriage of the Earl of Lothian's daughter he had asked a blessing at Newbattle Castle before supper, when one Swinton, an excommunicated person, was present. Among those who joined in the censure was Mr Robert Leighton, afterwards archbishop.

At the Reformation and long subsequently, excommunication was used as an engine wherewith to enforce acceptance of Protestant doctrines. On the 12th July 1580, Captain Anstruther who, in dread of excommunication, had appeared before the General Assembly, made confession that " he had been present at masses in France, though he adhered to the religion professed in this realme ; " he consented to make "public repentance." By the Presbytery of Perth, Gabriel Mercer, in 1595, was enjoined in his seat in church publicly to declare his repentance for having given three days' entertainment to " Elphinstone of Innernytie, an excommunicated papist." And in 1610, Alexander Crichton of Perth was, by the same Presbytery, convicted on confession of eating and drinking, and walking about with Robert Crichton, also described as " an excommunicate papist."

In 1612 the Synod of Fife, which comprehended in its jurisdiction the counties of Fife, Perth, and Forfar, enjoined the members to report the names of "non-communicantis." Among those "delated" were

George, Marquis of Huntly, and Francis, Earl of Errol. The former owned large possessions, was married to the king's cousin, and was greatly esteemed at court. Refusing to conform to Presbytery, he was in his resolution supported by his wife, whose father, Esmè, Duke of Lennox, had, after much vacillation, embraced Episcopacy. By remaining firm in his attachment to the Church of Rome, Lord Errol had suffered imprisonment and considerable loss of fortune. With respect to both noblemen, the Synod resolved that " forasmeikle as all dealing that the Kirk vndertakis against papistrie and the professouris thairof is vneffectual, as lang as no ordour is taken with the principallis," therefor that " the Marquis and his lady as gryt perverteris of vtheris . . . be removed from the countrey, and the Earl of Errol committed to ane more fitt ward than heretofoir." The two noblemen were at the same time excommunicated, while the King and the Archbishop of St Andrews were requested to carry into effect the sentence of banishment and warding.[1]

Continued residence in Scotland as an ecclesiastical outlaw, Lord Huntly found to be impracticable. Accordingly he was, through the influence of his father - in - law, relieved from excommunication at Lambeth by the Archbishop of Canterbury, and in

---

[1] " Letter from Sir Dudley Carleton to Sir Thomas Chamberlain, 24th August 1616." Public Record Office.

presence of several bishops and others, partook of the Communion in the English form. Lord Errol, who came to experience that, as an excommunicated person, he was subjected to many discomforts, publicly renounced Popery in 1617 ; he was thereupon absolved.

For Andrew, eighth Lord Gray, suspected of Popery, but who had expressed his willingness to receive instruction, the Synod of Fife, in 1612, appointed four of their number " to wait on him each Tuesday and Wednesday, for three months, without intermission." During his probation his lordship became bound to " attend the kirk for heiring of the Word ; " further that " he would neither hear masse not sett into his place, priest, jesuit, or excommunicate papist." To avoid further surveillance which had become irksome, Lord Gray, in April 1613, communicated " in the paroche kirk of St Androis." But in 1649, or thirty-six years afterwards, he was discovered to be " a rank Papist," and as such was excommunicated by the Commission of Assembly. By order of the Synod of Fife, in September 1612, George Gordon of Gight (a progenitor of the celebrated Lord Byron), was for " wilfull and obstinate continowans in papistrie, excommunicated in all the kirkes." On the 25th October 1626, Hew Stewart, an excommunicated person, applied to the Presbytery of Paisley to be allowed " to frequent the kirk and hear sermons."

The Presbytery consented on the condition that " he
came in after the first prayer and went out before the
last."

The rigorous prosecution by Presbyteries of notable
persons for refusing to conform to Presbyterian
doctrines formed in the seventeenth century a new
feature of the higher discipline. From 1626 to 1629
the Presbytery of Paisley were chiefly occupied in
pursuing the Earl and Countess of Abercorn, who
were charged with "Papistrie." After many efforts to
evade his inquisitors, Lord Abercorn left the country,
and so escaped sentence. The Countess, who was a
conspicuous Romanist, sought refuge in Edinburgh ;
but she was there, at the request of the Church,
arrested by the Privy Council, and subjected to
restraint, first in the Tolbooth, afterwards in Canongate prison. After an imprisonment of three years,
she, in March 1631, obtained liberation. Suffering
from *squalor carceris*, she was allowed to return to
her house at Paisley, where she not long afterwards
expired.

On the 22d April 1647 the Synod of Dumfries
excommunicated, for non-conforming to Presbyterian
discipline, John, Lord Herries, Lady Herries, the
Countess of Nithsdale, and thirty others. Sentence
was published from the several pulpits. During the
same year, John Wallace of Ferguslee married Margaret Hamilton, a relation of the Earl of Abercorn.

As she was suspected of cherishing Romish doctrine, her husband, under the menace of "process," that is, the preliminary step in excommunication, was by the Presbytery of Paisley, in May 1647, enjoined "to bring her unto Paisley at next meeting of the court, either by land or water." Bedridden and labouring under a serious ailment, Mrs Hamilton, that she might avoid the menaced censure, consented to be carried to the abbey church "upon a wand bed," or frame-work of wattles. In this manner she was borne a distance of four miles.

The most remarkable prosecution for nonconformity was that insisted upon for forty years by the Presbytery of Lanark, against the Earl of Angus, latterly Marquis of Douglas. On the 20th September 1627, the Presbytery of Lanark resolved that in respect "the breither hes direct commissioners at diverse tymes to William, Erle of Anguse, in all lenitie exhorting and admonisching his lordscipe to frequent the kirk on the Lordes day and heir the word of God preached, quhilk his lo. has not obeyed, whairby his lo. gifes vehement suspitioun of his falling away from the treuthe and the confessioun of faithe subscrivit be his lo.; ordaines thairfoir Johne Wilson, beddell of the presbyterie, to go and summand my lo. to compeir personalie before the moderator and breither of the presbytrie of Lanerk, to gif satisfactioun for his offence."

Communicating with the Crown authorities, Lord
Angus secured the royal protection.   By Charles I.
the Archbishops of St Andrews and Glasgow were
enjoined so to negotiate with the Presbytery of
Lanark that the menaced proceedings might be
stopped.   Such a result actually happened, and not
improbably the earl's recusancy might have escaped
further notice, but for his marriage in 1633 to "ane
notour Papist," Lady Mary Gordon, daughter of Lord
Huntly.   There had been communications with his
lordship, who was now Marquis of Douglas, prior to
the 4th of January 1644, when two members of the
Presbytery, who had waited upon him, made report
that they had received his assurance that he had
worshipped in the parish church, and that "he and
his ladie and children would become constant and
ordinaire hearers of the worde."   The Presbytery now
sent commissioners to the Marchioness, who on the
7th March reported that she was willing to attend
church, "as soon as her health sall permitt," and that
the Marquis was "useing means of informatioun that
he may be prepared for subscriveing of the Covenant."
The Presbytery now requested "both of my Lord and
Lady that familie exercise be sett up in their house."
On the 9th May the Marquis, presenting himself at
the Presbytery table, offered at once "to subscrive
the covenant;" but the brethren determined that
the act should be accompanied with greater publicity.

Accordingly they ruled that the minister of Douglas should receive his lordship's oath and subscription on the following Saturday, being the preaching day, before the celebration of the Lord's Supper, and that "in sight of the haill congregatione, having first posed him upon the principal points of poperie, that severallie and publicklie he may disclaime them." When the Presbytery next met on the 13th June, " the brethren appointed to be witnesses to the receiving of my Lord Marquesse of Douglas to the covenant," testified that "all things is orderlie and solemnlie done."

But the Marquis's personal submission did not satisfy the brethren, who at their meeting on the 18th July, in consideration that "my Ladie Marquesse of Douglas doethe still continue obstinate," appointed the minister of Crawford "to give her the first publick admonitione upon Sunday next." On the 5th September, the Presbytery resolved to "delay processe of my Ladie Marquesse Douglas for a tyme, in regaird shee came with her children and rest of the familie obedientlie to church." On the 26th December, the Presbytery, who had been dealing with the Marquis in regard to "familie exercise," refused a request made by him that the duty might not be urged upon him, till he had an opportunity of consulting with the Marchioness when her health, after childbirth, was sufficiently restored.

On the 16th January 1645 the Presbytery enjoined
one of their number " to assure my Lord and his
Ladie, if they give not full contentment in all, they
will enter in processe against them both." This
menace induced the Marquis, on the 13th March, to
make promise that he would " appoint exercise in
his familie." The Marchioness " not being fully
satisfied of her doubts, could not abjure poperie in
swearing the Covenant," but pledged herself to be " an
ordinar hearer of the word." After two weeks the
Presbytery were informed by the minister of Douglas,
that the Marquis had appointed " familie exercise and
was ane ordinar hearer thereof himself, with his
whole familie, except my Ladie." Thereupon the
Presbytery commanded the Marchioness to join " in
familie exercise," and further to become with her
daughters " ordinar hearers of the word forenoone
and afternoone ;" and " that shee should be readie
to communicate on the first occasion." On the 17th
April it was reported that " my Ladie Marquesse consented to be an ordinar hearer of the word," and
was willing on points of doctrine " to receive information ;" but the Presbytery were not satisfied, and
appointed the Moderator to confer with the Marquis.
The Moderator's report, presented on the 1st May,
was favourable to the Marquis personally, since his
lordship had attended his ministrations at Crawford
" the whole day," and had given " ear to the ser-

mons." As to the Marchioness, the court enjoined
that, in order to her "information," she should "hear
sermone upon the Lord's day, forenoone and afternoone;" "also upon the week day," and further "by
constant keeping of the exercises of the familie" and
conferring with ministers. Should these means fail
in convincing her, the Presbytery resolved "to proceed against her ladyship with the process of excommunication."

At all points the Marchioness yielded save one;
she would not abjure Catholicism by accepting the
Covenant. Thereupon the Presbytery examined the
family chaplain as to how the children conducted
themselves. Learning from his testimony that "they
did not always keepe the church," it was ruled that
"they should at no occasion be absent from the
kirke."

To the Presbytery, on the 12th June 1645, it was
reported by their commissioners that both the Marquis and Marchioness had failed to attend services
on the days of preparation and thanksgiving, and on
the Communion Sunday had remained in church
only till the first table was served. On this report,
the brethren determined that the Marquis's children,
capable of receiving instruction, should be "presentlie
sequestered." As the Marquis refused to surrender
his children, the brethren asked counsel of the
Assembly, and on the 13th November the Presby-

tery's commissioners reported the Assembly's judgment, that the Marquis deserved to be "summarlie
excommunicated."

On the 20th November 1645, the Marchioness
compeared before the Presbytery, and being "gravely
examined anent her malignancie and obstinate con-
tinewance in the profession of poperie, and peremp-
torily required without delay to sequestrat her
children, she disclaims any malignant carriage in the
tyme of tryall, professes that in her judgment shee
has renounced the worst points of poperie, and promises to give satisfaction anent her children." The
Presbytery remitted consideration of the case till a
future meeting, but on the 1st day of January 1646
resumed their activities. Of this date their minute
proceeds, that inasmuch as "thair manifold expres-
sions of lenitie and long-suffering towards the Lady
Marquesse of Douglas has produced no other effects
than obstinacie and disobedience," the moderator be
authorised to give the second "publick admoni-
tioune."

The Marchioness again presented herself before the
court to entreat that "the processe against her might
be intermitted for a space." The Presbytery resolved
to delay only till their next meeting.

On the 12th February the Presbytery reassembled,
and found the Marchioness, "be a paper presented
and subscrived with her hand," willing to submit

herself. They appointed two of their number "to conferre with her for trying her sinceritie and ingenuitie be all possible meanes, and to require her children be presentlie removed from Carmichael to Glasgow."

The Marquis of Douglas was absent; he had in the previous summer joined the standard of the Marquis of Montrose with a body of troops. Taken prisoner at Philiphaugh after Montrose's defeat, he was placed at the disposal of "the committee of estates." To that body the Presbytery, on the 5th March, made " humble remonstrance against his liberation, considering of the dangerous consequents that may follow in their bounds if the Marquis sall be returned to his station again." And on the 17th April the Presbytery determined that "whosoever hes been souldiers for James Grahame sall pay a merk, for each dayes attendance, to the poore."

By the Committee of Parliament the Marquis of Douglas was set at liberty. On the 1st October he appeared before the Presbytery of Lanark, when he " was scharplie and gravely challenged for his defectioun in joyneing with the publick enemie, and for prophaning the Lord's table." His parish minister was also censured for admitting him to the communion.

On the 26th November the presbytery's delegates reported that the Marquis had consented to " send back his children to Glasgow, if the pestilence cease within twenty dayes, or otherwayes to Edinburgh." And on the 7th January 1647 the Marquis appeared in the Presbytery room, and in presence of the brethren " humblie confessed upon his knees the breech of covenant by his malignant carriage in the tyme of our late tryall." He also promised " to remove his children to Edinburgh against Candlemasse."

The Marquis must again have hesitated, for on the 4th March commissioners reported to the Presbytery that his lordship " had not satisfied thaim with his confession and carriage before the congregation." They were therefore instructed to " labour to make him sensible of his superficial dealing, and whatsoever may be the secrets of his heart, to require a confessioun." On the 18th March the Presbytery received " a confession," the Marquis affirming that he felt " convinced in conscience " that he had erred " in joyneing with James Grahame and his complices;" he also promised " to adhere to the covenant in all points, whatsoever difficulties sall occure." Holding the confession as " not altogether satisfactorie," the Presbytery required the Marquis to sequestrate his children before their next meeting, under pain of a revival of " the processe." At a meeting held on the 22nd April the Marquis appeared, and excused himself for not " sequestrating " his children on the plea that he was " in want of a paedagog to goe abroad with them." He undertook " within twenty dayes " to provide " such a tutor as sall be recommended for such a charg be the testimonialls of the Presbyteries of Glasgow, Edinburgh, or St Andrews,—university towns, — whom in that case the Presbyterie shall accept." On the 17th July the Marquis appeared to the Presbytery's citation, and made offer to board his sons with the minister of Douglas ; he also named a tutor as their instructor. To this arrangement the Presbytery consented, upon the condition "that he get ane honest man to be chaplain in his familie for establishing familie exercise there."

The Presbytery reassembled on the 1st July, when it was mooted that the Marquis " was prepared to send his youngest sone over to be bred in France." The intelligence created much indignation, and three of the brethren were appointed to proceed to Edinburgh to entreat the interference of the Privy Council. The deputies performed their mission, and the Marquis was, on the 15th July, requested to obey an Act of Council by allowing trial to be made of the young man he proposed to send to France with his son.

After an interval the Presbytery of Lanark resumed their dealings with the Marquis and his household. At a meeting held on the 13th January 1648 the Marquis undertook to send his son Lord William to school at Glasgow. At the same time the brethren resolved that the Marchioness should, up to the 19th of March, receive such counsel as she might desire from her parish minister, with a view to her renouncing "her former erroneous and hereticall pointes," but on the express understanding that should she any longer refuse to abjure her errors, sentence of excommunication would be pronounced upon her. The Presbytery did not again meet till the 23rd March, when they were addressed by "the Ladie Marquesse of Douglas," who in a letter entreated that in consideration of "divers things" she intended to do, they would not further proceed with their menace. The Presbytery resolved to delay passing sentence till the meeting of Synod.

The Marchioness had a long respite, but on the 11th October it was resolved that she should be informed that if she did not render satisfaction, excommunication would certainly ensue. At the same time the Presbytery resolved to report to the Commission of the General Assembly "the heavie oppressions of my Lord Marquesse of Dowglas vpon his tenants." On the 26th October the Marquis, who had been cited, appeared before the Presbytery. He was charged with keeping his son in France, and not providing him with a tutor; with omitting to provide his daughter with a Protestant friend; also with neglecting to engage a chaplain to conduct worship in his household, and the oppression of his tenants. In answer the Marquis agreed to "give obedience," except in the matter of recalling his son, which he said was not in his power. He also "in name of his lady" covenanted that she would "subscribe the Confession of Faith and the Covenant." Surprised that the Marchioness had at length acquiesced in the matter of subscription, the brethren resolved that her signature should not be accepted, till a committee might confer with her. A committee appointed for this purpose was called upon to make report to the Synod.

To the Synod the committee reported that they had found the Marchioness so ignorant "that they durst not receive her subscription." The Synod accordingly ordered the Presbytery frequently to confer with her, "and cause her subscribe every article, as shee came to the knowledge thereof." The Presbytery prescribed to the Marchioness certain portions in the Confession which she should "be labouring to winne to the knowledge of." Two weeks later they resumed consideration of their charges against the Marquis, and notwithstanding of his submission appointed commissioners to meet at Douglas on the 19th inst., there personally to take cognizance of his proceedings. To the Presbytery, which reassembled on the 11th January 1649, their commissioners reported that the Marquis had agreed to attend all the Sunday and week-day services in his parish church, and to provide a tutor for his son, and a chaplain in his household ;

also to retain in his employment such servants only as "shall produce testimonials." With respect to "the oppression of the poor people," his lordship agreed "after much debate" to name six honest men "in the paroche of Dowglasse," at whose advice he would satisfy all just complaints. His lordship begged that he might be allowed to bring his son from Glasgow, and place him at the school of Lanark, pledging himself that the youth would not be taken home without the Presbytery's sanction.

Assembling on the 1st February, the Presbytery remarked that, "in the manifold particulars represented to him," the Marquis's pledges remained unfulfilled, and accordingly determined that, with a view to excommunication, "the second public admonition be given to him." When the Presbytery again met, on the 22d February, a document subscribed by his Lordship was read, in which he "upon his honour" pledged himself effectually to carry out his promises before their next meeting. At the following meeting, on the 8th March, the Marquis informed the Court that he had relieved his people of oppression, and he therefore begged that the process against him might "be discharged." The Presbytery determined that in order to test his Lordship's sincerity, and "on divers other grounds," the process should be maintained.

The minister of Douglas reported on the 19th

April that "my Lady Marquesse" of Douglas· was willing to "confer with him," and "would gladly heare any others whom the Presbyterie would send." He further reported on the 31st May that, having given the Marchioness "some articles to subscribe, she said that it is not needful to subscribe one article after another, but all the articles together." On this point the Presbytery decreed otherwise. A pause ensued, but the Presbytery had not surrendered. On the 13th September they resolved that the Marchioness be invited to subscribe certain of the articles, and that both she and the Marquis be enjoined to attend "public worship upon the Sabbath afternoone." To the subscribing of the articles *seriatim*, the Marchioness continued her objections, and a report by her parish minister to this effect being presented on the 27th September, the brethren held that the Marchioness had "no appearance of the least desire or delight to be reformed ;" and therefore "did ordain that dreadfull sentence of excommunication" to be "on the next Sabbath come fifteen dayes" pronounced upon her by the Moderator. But the Marchioness having in presence of the congregation at Douglas made promise of obedience, the Moderator was content to publish from the pulpit that, while he had. come prepared to publish excommunication, the sentence would be delayed. Of this course the Presbytery approved, while they proceeded to name

a tutor to Lord William Douglas, whom they required
the Marquis to appoint.   To the nomination the
Marquis reluctantly assented, but in evidence of his
Protestant zeal sent to the Presbytery eleven women,
who had by a "confessing witch" been charged with
sorcery.   Though willing that the women whom he
had accused should be subjected to trial and punishment, the Presbytery would not be diverted from
their process against the Marquis and his wife.   On
the 10th January 1650 the brethren determined that
if the Marchioness did not give full satisfaction before
the first day of February, "they must proceede to
the sentence of excommunication."

Again action was delayed.   But on Saturday, the
9th March, two of the brethren waited on the Marchioness, and informed her that if, on the following
day, being Sunday, she failed "to abjure all points
of Poperie" the "dreadful sentence of excommunication against her" would certainly be published.   The
Marchioness yielded, and so after sermon on the
day following "lift up her hand to God" and
testified her acceptance of the Confession of Faith
and of the Solemn League and Covenant.   While
receiving, on the 21st March, an account of these
proceedings, the Presbytery were unexpectedly informed that the Marquis and Marchioness "had sent
one of their daughters to France to a Popish lady to
be bred with her in Poperie."   Holding this as a

breach of faith, the Presbytery gave instructions that both the Marquis's son and daughter should be recalled from abroad. When the Marquis was informed of the Presbytery's request by a committee of their number, he remarked that he could not properly obtemper their demand.

For a time Cromwell's invasion and the "ascendency of sectarians" occupied the Presbytery's attention. But the Marquis and his family were not forgotten. At length on the 15th May 1656, the Presbytery received a report from their commissioners that the Marquis and Marchioness "had ingadged themselves, quhen they have health," to attend ordinances. The Presbytery further insisted that they should set up family worship. It now became obvious that to avoid inconvenient censures the two noble persons had been dissimulating, for on the 4th September the Presbytery found that the Marquis, "his ladie and familie," continued to be "an ill example;" that "he and his ladie cometh scarce to the kirk once in a year," and that "there is no worship of God in their familie." And considering that his lordship "doeth pretend his age and infirmitie to be the cause why he frequenteth not the publick ordinance," the Presbytery insisted that he and the Marchioness should employ a domestic chaplain, under pain of excommunication. Further particulars are lacking, but the suit was probably continued. The Marquis died in 1660, and the restoration of Episcopacy, which occurred in the same year, directed the course of discipline respecting conformity into a different channel.

By Presbyteries and Kirksessions were subjected to discipline those who took part in " the engagement " which, with a view to the relief of Charles I. in 1648, was entered into by the Scottish Parliament with the English cavaliers, and which was attended by an army of about ten thousand men being sent to England, under the command of the Duke of Hamilton. " The engagement," which was really an unworthy attempt to abet despotism, speedily collapsed under the arms of Cromwell; but the attempt was much condemned by the Presbyterian Church. All who took part in it—many through misapprehension, —were, in their respective parishes, called up and censured. For joining in the engagement, the repentance of Sir Robert Grierson is, in the parish register of Mouswald, set forth thus :—

" October 7, 1649. The whilk day, Sir Robert Greirson, the Laird of Lag, efter his publik humiliation made upon his knees in the body of the kirk, and his humble acknowledging his sinne in being accessarie to the late unlawfull engadgement by voting for it in Parliament, and subscryving the act for pronouncing of it, and efter his solemn oath for personal and domestic reparation and preferring the interest of God and religioune before the interest of any mortall man, and other particulars contained in the League and Covenant, he was admitted publicklie to the renewing and subscryving of the same conform to the ordinance of the Presbeterie." [1]

The Duke of Hamilton, who was mainly concerned in the "engagement," was executed at London on the 9th March 1649. His younger brother William, who succeeded him, was in 1650 arraigned, with his duchess, by the Presbytery of Lanark on the charge of having renounced the Protestant faith. To avoid molestation the Duke and Duchess subscribed the Covenant.

During the years 1662 and 1663, the Presbytery of Brechin pursued John Fullarton of Kynnaber, a landowner of the neighbourhood, who with his wife and household had joined the Society of Friends. After a fruitless attempt to induce recantation, " Lady Kynnaber" was on the 9th September 1663 sentenced to excommunication. The servants and the teachers of her children were also excommunicated, the sentence being published from "the several pulpits of the Presbytery." In pronouncing the sentence, individual ministers "did inhibit their parochiners to haunt or keep company with them." At length the laird of Kynnaber, being

[1] With whatever sincerity Sir Robert Grierson expressed his repentance for connecting himself with " the engagement," his procedure in this respect did not make a salutary impression upon his kindred, for his grandson and successor of the same name was a conspicuous persecutor of the Presbyterians, and one of those whose memory is, in the south-western counties, recalled with especial aversion.

upon his death-bed, "subscribed in wreitt a recantation of his former errours," whereupon on the 24th
May 1677 the Presbytery "did relax him from the
dreadful sentence of excommunication under which
he was lying." At the same time the ministers of
Montrose, Craig, and Maryton were appointed to confirm Kynnaber in recanting "his former errours."

In 1666, a man of rare scholarship and superior
gifts, Walter Scott of Raeburn, and his wife Isobel
Makdougal, progenitors of Sir Walter Scott, were
subjected to bitter persecution for embracing the
doctrines of Quakerism. By the Privy Council their
children, consisting of two sons and a daughter, were
"sequestered"—that is separated from them, lest they
should imbibe the parental opinions. At a much
more recent period, Quakers were regarded as danger-
ously unsound. In 1806 the Session-clerk of Newhills,
Aberdeenshire, makes entry that "Alexander, son to
Alexander Melvin in Kingwells, having renounced
the errors of Quakerism, was baptized." Those who
cherished Romish doctrine were denied the privileges
of ordinary citizenship. The Kirksession of Buittle,
Kirkcudbrightshire, on the 9th June 1771, allowed
John Stit, a Protestant, and Katherine Caven, a Papist,
to be proclaimed in order to marriage, on the woman
"subscribing an obligation to forsake the Popish and
embrace the Protestant religion."

While exercising upon others a rigid discipline,

Kirksessions demanded from their own members a careful circumspection. By a course of " privy censures " they secured the purity of their several courts. In December 1565, the Kirksession of the Canongate assembled along with the Superintendent of the kirk [1] and " the haill communicantis, for. tryell of the lif and doctryne of the minister, elderis, and diocanis, reconsilitioun of brodyr, and vthair affairs." On this occasion the Superintendent asked " gif ony persone or personneis, papist or protestantis, had anything to lay to the said Johne [Mr John Brand, minister] in lyf or doctryne that thair thai wald declair as they will answeir before God."

For a time subsequent to the Reformation, the elders selected the ministers' texts, also the portions of Scripture to be publicly expounded ; they also regulated the hours at which divine service should commence and close.

The Kirksession of the united parishes of Anstruther, Kilrenny, and Pittenweem ruled, on the 18th August 1590, that " the preaching sall begin every Sunday at nyne hours, or thereby, that it may end by eleven; that the afternoon's doctrine may begin about ane

[1] Long after the office of Superintendent had ceased, Presbyteries made periodical visitations to parish churches, when the heritors and elders were in the minister's absence " posed " as to his " life and doctrines," while, in his turn, the minister was questioned as to the behaviour of the heritors and elders. Respecting the conduct of the reader, both minister and elders gave report.

afternoon, that it may be ended before three, and the rest of the time may be spent in examination of the heads of the Catechism."

On the 30th May 1598, the Kirksession of St Andrews ruled "that Mr George Gladstanes, minister, proceid in preaching of the second book of Samuell and the buik of the Kingis following upon the Sabboth day." On the 14th October 1621, the Kirksession of Elgin ordered that "when Mr David Philip preaches he turn the glass, and that the whole be finished within an hour."

In certain parishes the subjects of the ministers' pre-lections were registered weekly. Thus on Sunday, the 22nd July 1726, the Session Clerk of Crathie reports that the minister lectured in English on the second chapter of James, and preached in English from Isaiah lxiii. 6, while he also discoursed "in Irish" on the eleventh verse of the 13th chapter of the Romans.

To the Kirksession of the Canongate, John Myll, on the 10th July 1565, made complaint against "John Kirkbo, ane of the diaconis, allegand him to be the causer and fortifier that John Seton tuk his hous oure his head." On the 8th December of the same year, the Canongate Session received the complaint of John Mallock that John Oswald, bailie, had "strucken him with his hand upon the haffat." The bailie acknowledged his fault, but "allegit that the said Johne had provokit him in calling him ane parseoll Juge." "Wherefore," proceeds the minute, "both being fund crymnabill" they were "orderit to schaik handis both togeddir in token of reconciliation."

In 1562 "the general assemblie of the Canongate" resolved to meet every Saturday morning at seven o'clock, from March till September, and at eight from September till March, while every member was taken bound to attend under the penalty of "twelve pundis," and the minister for "doubill this soom." In April 1568, the Kirksession of Aberdeen published the following edict:—"The haill Assemblie ordainis tryall and examination of the minister, elderis, and dyaconis, and redar to be had of them, off themselvis four tymes in the yeir, concerning their liffis and conversation, according to the use off uder kirkis. And befoir the tyme off Communion that sik tryall be maid, be the haill kirk, vpone the minister, redar, elderis, and dyaconis, off their conversation." By the same Kirksession, in January 1573, was passed an ordinance in these words:—"The Assemblie ordainis the minister to charge and admonyshe on Sunday next to com, all and sundrie within this town, to compeir on the nixt assemblie day, to try and examine the lyffis of the minister, elders, and dyaconis, and to lay to their charge sik thingis as thai know to be sklanderous to the kirk."

Regular attendance at the other Courts of the
Church was rigidly insisted upon. At a meeting of
the Presbytery of Glasgow, held on the 2nd August
1597, Mr John Bell, minister of Cadder, was found
"lait of entering." He pleaded that he had "wurk-
men wirking qhairby he micht nocht cum souner,"
but the brethren "repellit" his excuse, and he was
"scharplie admonischit."

At the Reformation arose a new zeal for the suppression of sorcery by consigning to death at the
stake those believed to be guilty of the offence. And
here it is to be remarked, what has frequently escaped
observation, that Protestant Reformers did not censure the Romish Church for assailing with fire and
faggot those who practised religious error. But they
strongly condemned the Papal Church and its abettors, inasmuch that they, in professing to purge error,
burned earnest and faithful confessors. On obtaining
an ascendancy they, in token of their own fidelity,
revived the slumbering penal laws against witchcraft,
sanctioning the burning of alleged sorcerers with an
ardour not less vehement than that exercised by the
Romish clergy for the destruction of heresy. The
theme of witch-burning is reserved, for while the
Presbyterian clergy were often the accusers of persons
charged with sorcery, and witnesses of their executions, the sentences were pronounced and executed by
the secular authority. But the use of charms and

consultations with sorcerers were offences solely amenable to ecclesiastical discipline. To the Presbytery of Lanark, in July 1623, Besse Smyth, in Lesmahagow, confessed "hir charming of the heart feawers," and that "she appoyntit the wayburne leaf to be eattin at nyne morningis; the words of the charme are, 'for Godis saik, for Sanct Spirit, for Sanct Aikit, for the nyne maidens that died into the buirtrie into the Ledywell Bank, this charme to be buik and bell to me.'" Smyth's punishment is unrecorded. Before the same Presbytery, in 1630, Mrs Chancellor, wife of the laird of Shieldhill, was convicted of "medling with charmers, and burying a bairne's claithes to procure healthe." She, "in presence of the Brether, upon hir knees, confessit hir grit offence in having any medling with charmers, and promised amendement in tyme coming." In July 1645 the same Presbytery took cognisance of Janet Bailzie, a midwife, who confessed that she "repeated an oratione" when in the exercise of her calling; she was remitted for discipline to the Kirksession of Douglas. By the Kirksession of Dunfermline, Robert Shortus was, in July 1643, for "seiking charmes from his wyff," sentenced "to sit in sackcloth three Sundays upon the public place of repentance;" he was "pittied," and pardoned after two appearances.

The place of repentance was an open space in front of the pulpit, usually in the central passage. There on a stool or "pillar" the subject under discipline sat, and when called upon stood up. Brought into church at the close of the opening prayer, he was by the officer conducted to the place of penitence. When after the discourse had been sung an appropriate psalm, the penitent stood up to receive reproof and counsel. While it continued, each member of the congregation wore his hat, while the penitent stood uncovered. The Kirksession of Perth owned both a "cock-stool or cucking-stool and a repentance-stool," the former being a pillory for offenders of the worst class. In the Kirksession Records of Dalry, Wigtownshire, is named in 1693 "the low pillare," implying that a higher pillory was reserved for more flagrant offenders.

In undergoing discipline the penitent was usually clad in "sackcloth," a coarse linen garment. The vestment had many names. In southern counties it was known as the "harden gown," in Lanarkshire as "the harn gown," in the western counties as "the sack gown," and in central and eastern districts as "the linens." The ecclesiastical phrase "in sacco" at length superseded all others. In 1655 the Kirksession of Lesmahagow expended £4, 4s. 6d. in providing "a harn gown for scandalous persons." Probably one of the latest commissions for the construction of a repentance habit was the following by the Kirksession of Kirkmichael, in Ayrshire :—"September 24th, 1693. The Session appoints John Forgan to employ a Straitoun tailor to make a coat or covering of sackcloth for the said Janet Kennedy like unto that which they have in Straitoun, there having been no such thing here for these many years ; it's thought none of the tailors of this parish know how to make it." The repentance habit of Kinross is preserved in the National Museum. Offenders were latterly permitted to occupy the repentance stool "in their awn habit."

On the 30th April 1633, the Kirksession of Stirling sat in judgment on Margaret Chapman, wife of John Bennet, who by a weaver's wife was accused of " charming hir milk from out of hir breist." Chapman confessed to the use of charms, but as her object was to remedy the malady, rather than promote it, she was simply "humbled" for her offence. The Kirksession of Perth, in May 1631, reprimanded Laurence Beck and his wife for using charms in the cure of sores. The offenders acknowledged that they had expressed these lines :—

> " Thir sairs are risen through God's wark,
> And must be laid through God's help,
> The mother Mary and her dear Son
> Lay thir sores that are begun."

In December 1643 the Kirksession of Markinch extorted from Janet Brown that, in curing distempered horses, she uttered the following charm :—

> "Our Lord forth raid
> His foalie's foot staid,
> Our Lord down lighted
> His foalie's foot righted,
> Saying flesh to flesh, blood to blood
> And bone to bone,
> In our Lorde's name."

Twenty years later—that is, on the 22d January 1663, Christian Drummond was arraigned before the Kirksession of St Andrews, for attempting to cure the swollen arm of a neighbour by repeating over it a jumble of rhymes, founded upon the preceding, but which through her ignorance were wholly non-sensical.

In 1643 a parishioner of Carnbee, in Fife, on the ground that he was the seventh son of a woman, undertook "to heall the cruellis," that is, scrofulous sores, by the touch; he was subjected to discipline. To the Kirksession of Humbie, on the 23d September 1649, Agnes Gourlay acknowledged that in order to induce a cow's milk to yield cream, she had "put salt and wheat-heads into the cow's lugs," and scattered a portion of the milk into the soil, using words of incantation. The Kirksession, having consulted the Presbytery, sentenced the woman "to mak publick repentance in sackcloth." On the 9th July 1646 the Kirksession of Auchterhouse appointed a fast, "because of the scandal of witches and charmers in the district;" also for the further reason, that the neighbouring congregations had "long been starved by dry-breasted ministers"! In 1653 Bessie Chapman appeared before the Kirksession of Dunino, Fifeshire, under the charge of "consulting with witches." Her offence consisted in credulously listening to the pretensions of "twa beggar wyves," who assuring her that she was in danger from witchcraft used certain charms for its removal, afterwards depriving her of "a foure-shillin peice" in guerdon of service. On the counsel of the Presbytery, whom the Kirksession consulted, Bessie was decerned to make her repentance before the pulpit in sackcloth.

It was one of the several rules of the Kirksession of Mouswald, that persons who consulted with "familiar sprites" or witches, should for each offence be amerced in five merks, and made to stand on the church pillory in sackcloth for three successive Sundays. Catherine Fraser was, on the 12th April 1660, arraigned before the Kirksession of St Andrews for cursing Alexander Duncan and his horse, "for having raised some fulzie belanging to her, after which the horse took disease and died in short space."

Turning the riddle for the discovery of stolen goods was a common charm. On the 23d May 1667 the Presbytery of Brechin considered the case of William Boill, schoolmaster at Inschbrayock, who had

been summoned for this offence. He acknowledged
that he had rolled some stones in a chamber, for
which he was grieved. " He was sharplie rebuked,
and informed that if he used such art hereafter he
would be strictlie censured." For turning a riddle in
order to the discovery of a plunderer, Janet Hunter
was, by the Kirksession of Kilmorie in 1709, sentenced to appear in repentance three several Sabbaths
before the congregation; she was also remitted to
the civil magistrate " to be punished corporally or
pecunially."

Superstitious practices at wells, dedicated to saints,
were a fertile source of discipline. The cells of the
earlier missionaries were placed in the vicinity of
fountains, partly for convenience, but also on account
of the reverence with which were associated the ancient
basins. Adamnan relates how that a demon-possessed
spring in the territory of the Picts[1] was by the
prayers of St Columba endowed with healing qualities, a legend evidently arising from a belief that
under the Christian system water-springs formerly
associated with Baalic rites became consecrated and
purged. At the ancient wells were neophytes baptized, and other religious activities conducted.
Named in honour of the early teachers, they were
in the lapse of centuries associated with superstition.

[1] Adamnan's " Life of Saint Columba," edited by William
Reeves, D.D., Edinburgh, 1874, 8vo, p. 45.

A recent writer has enumerated about 600 wells dedicated to saints.[1]

Christ's Well, at Doune in Perthshire, was held to possess specially healing virtues on the second Sunday of May, and at this season it was largely resorted to. To stop the Christ Well pilgrimages, Kirksessions made vigorous efforts. The Kirksession of Falkirk in 1628 "ordained that if any person or persons be found superstitiously and idolatrously after this to have passed in pilgrimage to Christ's Well, on the Sundays of May, to seek their health, they shall repent *in sacco* and linen three several Sabbaths, and pay twenty pounds *toties quoties* for ilk fault; and if they cannot pay it, the baillie shall be recommended to put them in ward, there to be fed on bread and water for aught days." On the 2d May 1652, the Kirksession of Auchterhouse dealt with a woman for carrying her child to the Kirktoun Well. She informed the Court, by way of confession, that when she anointed the child's eyes with water from the well she exclaimed as a charm :—

> " Fish beare fin, and fulle [fowl] beare gall ;
> All the ill of my bairn's eyen upon ye will fall."

The Well of Strathill, in the parish of Muthil, like

[1] " Holy Wells in Scotland," by J. Russell Walker, in *Proceedings of Scottish Society of Antiquaries*, vol. v., new series, 1884, pp. 152-210.

the more reputed fountain of St Fillan, was believed
to cure lunatics.   An insane woman belonging to
Airth, in Stirlingshire, having been brought to
Strathill for cure, Mr James Forsyth, one of the
ministers. of Stirling, in a letter to Mr James
Drummond, minister of Muthil, dated 16th March
1663, supplied the information that four persons
concerned in carrying the lunatic to the well had
on citation appeared before the Presbytery of Stirling.   In answer to questions, they alleged that at
the well they had bound the patient to a stone two
several nights, but that on both occasions she was
loosed, and that though "she was very mad before,
she had ever since been sober in her wits."   The
Presbytery desired the minister of Muthil to suggest
what censure might be inflicted.[1]   In 1695 the Presbytery of Penpont consulted the Synod of Dumfries
respecting a superstition which largely prevailed
as to the virtues of the Dow Loch.   The Synod
ordered the members of Presbytery to denounce from
their several pulpits the practice of making pilgrimage
to the loch.

To the *firth-splot*, or good man's croft, we formerly
referred.[2]   At the Reformation it was discovered that
not infrequently husbandmen left untilled a portion

[1] "Geographical Collections relating to Scotland in the Advocates' Library," vol. iii. p. 97.

[2] See vol. i. p. 22.

of ground in order to avert *skaith*, or the influences of an evil power. In reference to this practice the General Assembly, on the 7th May 1594, decided, as "touching the horrible superstition used in Garioch, and diverse parts of the country, in not labouring a parcel of ground, dedicated to the devil, under the name of the *Good Man's Croft*, that application be made for an Act of Parliament to cause labour the same."

At the Reformation the observance of festival days had been prohibited. But the practice of holding the great festivals might not readily be overcome. Upon those who, on Christmas or Yule, indulged religious rites, the Reformers exercised a rigorous discipline. By the Kirksession of St Andrews in January 1573 several persons were sentenced to make "open satisfaction for observing Yule day." And in 1605 John Wyllie was summoned by the Kirksession of Dundonald on the charge of "nott yoking his plough on Yuill day;" he escaped censure by satisfying the Court that he was "at the smiddie, laying and mending the plough iernis."

The General Assembly, on the 13th February 1645, prohibited masters of schools and colleges "from granting Yule as a holiday, under the penalty of being summoned to compear before the next ensuing General Assembly, there to be censured." And on the 21st December 1649 the Kirksession of St

Andrews decreed that intimation be made from the pulpit "that no Yule be keiped, but that all be put to work as ane ordinar work day, with certification that those who use any idlenes shall be taken nottice of, and be seveirlie censured." Conformably with their menace, the Kirksession arraigned on the 29th January 1650 several persons charged with *playing jollie at the goose* on Yule day, and whom they ordained "to wait on the two next Sabbaths in the Old Colledge Kirk to be examyned and to sit altogether upon ane forme before the publict congregation, and to be rebooked there for their fault."

The Kirksession of Glasgow, on the 26th December 1683, warned the bakers of the city to discontinue the practice of baking Yule bread. Christmas mask-balls had in Catholic times been practised at Aberdeen ; they were stopped shortly after the Reformation. A Christmas game, known as "Lady Templeton," was early in the seventeenth century prohibited by the Kirksession of Ayr.[1]

The practice of extinguishing fires at Beltein, latterly at Midsummer eve, was obnoxious to the Reformed Church. In order effectually to suppress the custom, the Presbytery of St Andrews, on the 24th June 1647, asked counsel of the Provincial

---

[1] An Act of the Scottish Parliament prohibiting the observance of Christmas was, in 1712, repealed by the Parliament of Great Britain.

Synod. On the 30th September 1641 two ministers of the Presbytery of Lanark were ordained to " discharge anie solemn keeping of Michaelmas day."

While Scottish Reformers repressed those annual celebrations which derived from the usages of an elder superstition, the festivals of the Romish Church were also obnoxious to them. Of these the greater number were associated with burlesque representations, disorderly processions, impure mysteries, and profane merriment, while the frequent occurrence became socially degrading. By Knox and his reforming colleagues were put forth vigorous efforts to restrain the continuance of these unseemly demonstrations, and to confine religious celebrations chiefly to the Sabbath. Those who observed feast days in the old manner were subjected to strict discipline.

For dancing on Trinity Sunday, David Wemyss was, on the 6th June 1599, sentenced by the Kirksession of St Andrews to imprisonment in the church steeple till he obtained caution that he would " make his repentance." In his defence Wemyss pleaded that " the custom was kept in Raderny ere any of the session were born." Before the Presbytery of Lanark six persons, including a piper, were arraigned, on the 23d June 1625, " for fetching hame a may-pole, and dancing about the same upon Pasche Sunday." On the 27th December 1649, the Kirksession of St Andrews summoned before them a parishioner resid-

ing at Strathkinnes, charged with being drunk on St
Andrew's day ; he was ordered to " bring ane testi-
moniall of his carriage from the Session of Cameron,
uthyrwyse not to be suffered to remain in the
parish."

Prior to the Reformation, Sunday was held sacred
only during the hours of worship ; while the day
proper was understood to commence on Saturday
evening at six, and to terminate next evening at the
same hour. This mode of reckoning the commencement and the close of Sunday continued till some time
after the Reformation. In May 1594 the Presbytery of
Glasgow forbade a piper to play his pipes on Sunday,
" frae the sun rising till the sun going-to." By the
same Presbytery was an injunction put forth, on the
1st January 1635, that Sabbath should extend from
twelve on Saturday night till the same hour on Sunday night.

Under the sanction and countenance of the Reformers miracle-plays in which the Romish priesthood
were subjected to derision were on the Sunday evenings
acted for some time after the Reformation. On the
21st July 1574 the Kirksession of St Andrews gave
license " to play the comedy mentioned in St Luke's
evangel of the forlorn son, upon Sunday, the first day
of August next to come." This license was accompanied with the provision that the play should be
" revised by the minister, the Provost of St Salvador's

College, and the Principal of St Leonard's College,"
and further, that "the performance should not interfere with the hours of divine worship." By the same
Kirksession in 1575 plays were denounced as
"expresslie forbidden by Act of Parliament." In
1599 the Presbytery of Aberdeen decreed that "there
be nae play-Sundays hereafter, under all hiest pain."

Sunday marketing, which prior to the Reformation
was common in churchyards, cathedral alleys, and
monastic precincts, had nevertheless been forbidden
by Parliament. For a statute passed in 1503
provided that "there be na mercat nor faires haldin
upon halie daies, nor yet within kirkes, nor kirk-
yairdes, upon halie daies, nor uther daies."

On the 30th October 1560 the Town Council of
Edinburgh resolved that henceforth "the holiday
commonly called Sunday" be kept by all persons in
the burgh, and that no one make market or open
their shops, nor exercise any worldly calling on that
day, but should attend ordinary sermons forenoon and
afternoon. By an Act of the Estates passed in 1579
penalties were imposed on those who on "Sabbath-
dayes attended mercattes and faires," or used "handie-
labour," or engaged in "gamming and playing,
passing to tavernes and aile-houses," or who absented
themselves from "their Paroche Kirke." By a further
Act passed in 1593, Presbyteries and other authorities
were authorized to see that penalties were enforced.

In fulfilling their statutory duties the Presbyteries met with a keen resistance. By the inhabitants of Strathmore the right of trafficking on Sunday was strongly insisted upon, so that in 1596 the Presbytery of Meigle were necessitated to apply to the Privy Council for a vindication of their authority.

On the 15th November 1570 the Kirksession of St Andrews informed Gelis Symson, a married woman, arraigned before them on the charge of "selling candles and bread on Sundays," and of deserting worship, that if she did not desist she would be decerned " to sit in the joggis twenty-four hours." On the 30th April 1594 the Presbytery of Glasgow ordained Steven Auldsone, for working on Sunday, to pay to the church of Rutherglen twenty shillings, and to make his public repentance. By the Kirksession of St Cuthberts, on the 20th February 1622, "Johne Rid, pultriman," was convicted " for pulling of geiss upon the Lord his Sabboth in tyme of sermon." On the 16th March 1627 nine millers made confession to the Kirksession of Stow that " their milnes did gang on the Sabbath in tyme of divine service," whereupon they were ordered to make public repentance, and each to pay a penalty of "fourtie shillings."

On the 24th July 1627 the Kirksession of Stirling sentenced John Heggie, "for breaking the Sabbath be basking his netts, to mak his repentance the next Sabbath;" it was at the same time ordained that "gif he or any uther be found guiltie of the lyk offences, that is to say, ayther shutting thair cobbles, or basking their netts, from Saturday at twal hours at even to Sonday at twal hours at even they sall pay fourtie shillings, and mak thair public repentance." The Presbytery of Lanark, on the 21st August 1628, condemned "the insolencie of men and women in footracing, dancing, and playing *Barla Breks* on the Sunday," and enjoined the brethren severally to restrain the practices.

Archibald Russel, at Wester Barlymont, being on the 18th November 1641 found guilty by the Kirksession of St Andrews of "leading corn on the Sabbath evening, was ordained to crave God's mercy on his knees before the Session, and to pay 40s. penalty, which," the minute adds, "was given to ane Gordon, a distressed woman come from Ireland."

On Sunday, the 10th October 1643, the Kirksession of Saltoun, Haddingtonshire, ordered a servant woman to be summoned "for shooling muck this morning," also some youths for "playing bogill about the stacks." For "watering her kaill on the Sabbath," Margaret Brotherston was, in June 1644, sentenced by the Kirksession of Humbie "to give evidence in public of her repentance next Lord's day."

On the 31st May 1649 the Kirksession of St Andrews had before them Janet Smart, charged with "carrying water from the loch on the Sabbath day;" she escaped the sentence of making a "public repentance" by the promise "of not being found in the lyke again."

Sunday tippling was punished rigorously. The Kirksession of Stow, on the 13th May 1627, ordained William Brunton, for being drunk on Sunday, and irreverent to the Session, to "pay 40s., to stand next Sabbath in the jouges betwixt the bells, and thereafter to come after sermon in presence of the congregation and confess his fault to God, and crave mercy." On the 5th July 1636 the Kirksession of Crail ruled that those "who sall drink on the Sabbath sall be fined 20s. the first time, 30s. the second, and 10s. more every succeeding time." On the 28th January 1645 the Kirksession of Dunfermline "statute and ordainit that whosoever in this parish shall be found fra the kirk on the Sabbath day, drinking in tyme of divine service, of preaching or prayer, the drinker to pay ten shillings and the seller thereof twenty shillings. And both to mak their publick repentance before the haill congregation, whilk was intimat the next Sabbath." The Kirksession of Port of Menteith, on the 26th April 1668, sentenced three persons for "drinking a chapon of aill" on the preceding Sunday, to "sit bair headit before the pulpit, and after sermon to acknowledge their scandal on their knees." At St Andrews those who practised Sunday drinking were, as an ordinary punishment, " humbled on their knees" in presence of the Kirksession. The Presbytery of Aberdeen enjoined in 1664 that " the Lord's day be exactlie keeped, and that all attend the reading and hearing of the Word before sermon, and none depart from church before pronouncing of the blessing, and that visitors for everie part of the paroche be appointed be the ministers for visiting taverns and ail-houses ; that there be no excessive drinking, nor the people continue tippling in those places ; but that all diligent people resort to their awn houses for going about their familie duties suitable to the holiness of the day ; that there be no bargaining, feeing of servandis, or other secular exercise gone about on that day, and that notice be taken of such as travel on the Lord's day."

Attendance on divine worship was rigidly enjoined. In 1568 the Kirksession of Aberdeen decreed that every one absent from divine service should pay 6d. for each offence, a penalty of 2s. being exacted from elders and deacons. And thirty years subsequently it was decreed by the Town Council of the city that every burgess and his wife should attend church each Sunday under a penalty of 13s. 4d. for each violation of the law. In 1574 the Kirksession of St Andrews passed the following edict : " For good order to be observed in convening to hear the Word of God upon the Sabbath day, and other days in the week,

when the Word of God is preached, as well as of the
students within colleges as inhabitants of this city,
and others in the parish, the Session has ordained
captors to be chosen to visit the whole town according
to the division of the quarters, and to that effect every
Sunday there shall pass a bailie and elder, two deacons,
and two officers armed with their halberts, and the
rest of the bailies and officers to be in attendance to
assist to apprehend transgressors, to be punished
according to the acts of the kirk." On the 8th
January 1582-3 the Kirksession of Perth ordained
that " an elder of every quarter " should in turn
pass through the same each Sunday in time of
preaching before noon, and " note those found in
taverns, baxter's booths, or in the gaits, and dilate
them to the Assembly, that everyone of them that is
absent from the kirk may be poinded for twenty shillings, according to the Act of Parliament." On the
22d October 1588 the Kirksession of the united parishes
of Anstruther, Kilrenny, and Pittenweem ordained
that " the maister and mistress of every house, and
sa many as are of years and judgment (except where
need requireth otherwise) sall be present in the kirk
in due time every Sabbath to hear the sermon before
and after noon under pain of 12 pence the first fault,
two shillings the second, and for the third five shillings, and *toties quoties* thereafter."

The Kirksession of Perth, on the 29th January

1592-3, had under cognizance, for neglect of ordinances, "the Lady Innernytie," wife of Elphinstone
of Innernytie, a judge of the Court of Session. She
was allowed to escape public censure by declaring
that her non-attendance was "neither in contempt of
the word, nor of the minister, but only by reason of
her sickness," also by giving promise that she would
attend "when she shall be well in health." In 1599
the Kirksession of St Andrews decreed that whoso is
found golfing during the time of divine service, shall
for the first offence pay ten shillings ; twenty
shillings for the second ; for the third be placed on
the repentance pillar, and for the fourth be deprived
of office. In the year 1600 the Kirksession of
Glasgow enjoined the deacons of crafts to make
search among the families of freemen for "absents
from the kirk," and to impose penalties upon them.
On the 5th September 1608, Robert Orrok was
convicted by the Kirksession of Kinghorn "of being
absent fra the preaching thrie seurall Sabbathis, and
that in hie and manifest contempt of his pastour ; "
he was referred to the magistrate, to be punished
"conform to the act of his hienes' Parliament." In
1611 the Kirksession of Aberdeen enjoined "the
baillies" of the city "to caus the people to resort to
the sermons." In 1615 the Kirksession of Lasswade
enacted that "all persons attend the kirke or be
punished, gentlemen to be damnified in 6s. 8d. Scots,

men in 3s. 4d., and servants in twenty pennies." The
Kirksession of Dunino ruled in 1643 that " whosoever shall be found absent from the hearing of the
Word on the Lord's Day, shall for the first fault,
mak publict repentance and pay twa shillings, and
for the second fault pay four shillings, and *toties
quoties* thereafter." It was on the 1st July 1649
ruled by the Kirksession of Mouswald that "everie
ane absent, for everie dayes absence from the kirke
shall pay ane groat, except they can show ane reson-
able excuse, and that nane shall goe from their owne
kirk to any other upon the Lord's day."

At St Andrews, neglect of ordinances was common.
On the 21st June 1649, Mr David Lentron, portioner,
of Newton of Nydie, appeared to answer to the charge
of " not keeping of the church." His excuse as to
"the foulnes of the geat [road] in winter" was
deemed a pretence, and he was sentenced to public
censure. On the 2nd May 1654, Margaret Johnstoun
and Helen Wellwood appeared before the Kirksession
of Dunfermline, the former charged with " carrying a
pitcher of water," the latter with " carrying a burden
of cole on the Sabbath, in tyme of sermon." On
account of not having been previously charged with
any misdemeanour, both were dismissed with an
admonition.

By the Kirksession of St Andrews, Grisel Hall
was, on the 3d June 1658, sentenced to public

rebuke "for going home betwixt sermons." As "sinfull barbaratis" the Session condemned "the practice of sitting on the kirk doores [door-steps] or at the farr ends of the kirk, or gooing out to the churchyeard in tyme of publicke worship, and of sitting at doores several together chattering after sermon." By intimation from the pulpit, these practices were prohibited under high censure.

At St Andrews, children found romping on the streets on Sunday were flogged. Charles Carstairs, a child, who on Sunday, the 19th July 1649, was found "clymbing Mr Samuell Rutherfuird's yeard dyke in tyme of Divine service, was, after admonition, comitted to Alexander Cuming to see him belted [strapped] be his mother," and John Gray, Kirk Officer was directed "to help to do the samyne." In May 1649 the Kirksession of St Andrews sentenced a youth, who had profaned the Sunday, "to be scourgit in the Tolbooth by ane of the toun officers at the sight of the magistrates." The Kirksession of Dunfermline also imposed scourging. On the 25th February 1685 they sentenced two apprentices, "as twa of the perversest knaves in all the burgh, to be whipped before them for Sabbath breaking," and thereafter confined "in the bell-house."

As one of the rules of discipline, the Kirksession of Mouswald enacted, on the 1st July 1649, that a penalty be inflicted on all who on Sunday are found

"playing at nyne hollis, pennie stane, or any such lyke
idle pastymes." At St Andrews "a game played by lads
in the churchyard, called catt and dog," was prohibited, and those engaging in it warned that they
would be prosecuted as "dissorderlie walkers."

At a period when church services were unreasonably
prolonged, some persons were in the habit of seeking
respite by a brief walk in the churchyard. To Kirksessions such a practice was obnoxious. On the 24th
February 1697 the Kirksession of Ettrick appointed
two elders "every Sabbath to tak notice that nane
withdraw from the publick worship, and that no discourse be about the doors, or sitting in houses during
the time of worship, and that this be done by them
untill the elders go through once every month, that
the Sabbath be not profaned." The Kirksession of
Crathie, on the 29th June 1718, appointed their
"members to go out by turns in time of Divine service, both forenoon and afternoon, and take notice of
all people that play without in the kirk yeard in
time of sermon, discoursing about their worldly
affairs."

Proper behaviour in church was rigorously enjoined.
In 1577 the Kirksession of Anstruther Wester ordained
that William Scott "sall abyt at the dore in tym of
preachin before nun and efter, vpoun Sunday, and
see as passes furth before the blessing ; he sall cause
note them, and giv ther names to the Commissioners

appointed be the kingis majestie to be punischit as profaners of the Saboth." In July 1606, Andrew Gairnie was reprimanded by the Kirksession of Ayr, " because the minister was in the pulpit before he entered the church." On the 1st May 1608, the Kirksession of Kinghorn ordained Robert Henderson, " for the stryking his nybour upon the haffat in tyme of preaching, to stand in the gougs twa hours or els to pay twentie schillings, and also to compeir befoir the pulpit and confes his fault and craue God's mercie for the same."

Snuff-taking in church was prohibited. The Kirksession of Saltoun, on the 11th April 1641, " statute, with consent of the minister and elders, that every one that takes snuff in tyme of Divine service shall pay 6s. 8d., and give ane publick confession of his fault." And the Kirksession of St Cuthberts, on the 18th June 1640, determined that every snuff-taker in church be amerced in " twenty shillings for everie falt." In April 1643 the Kirksession of Dunfermline appointed the bellman " to tak notice of those who tak the sneising tobacco in tyme of divine service, and to inform concerning them."

During the eighteenth century Sunday desecration especially abounded in northern districts. On the 28th September 1761 the Town Council of Elgin, taking into consideration that

" the profanation of the Lord's day is become very frequent," ordained " that no person or persons shall presume to *walk in the streets, or on the fields in time of divine service;* that no person shall presume to make any disturbance on the streets, or under the forestairs after public worship is over, under the pain of three pounds Scots for each offence; that none shall presume to go into ale-houses and drink in time of divine service on the Lord's day, under the penalty of six pounds Scots—each person that shall be found drinking in such houses in time of divine service on the Lord's day, and the like sum of six pounds Scots each person who shall sell or give such ale or other liquor to them—the one half of which fines shall pertain to the informer and the other half to the Fiscal of Court; and ordain this Act to be intimated by tuck of drum."

By the Incorporated Trades of Ayr was kept a long rod for awakening apprentices, who in the Trades Gallery of the parish church slept during service.

The Church was much exercised in suppressing a practice inseparable from protracted services. So long as places of worship were without pews, women carried to church small stools as seats for their husbands and sons. Personally they leant upon woollen plaids, extended on the earthen floor. In hot weather and when the services were protracted, those exhausted by week-day toil drawing their wrappings around their heads committed themselves to sleep. Muffled sleepers were to be found in pre-Reformation times. In a sumptuary law passed by Parliament in 1457, it was ordained that "na woman come to kirk nor mercat with her face mufflalled or covered, that she may not be kend, under pains of escheit of the courchie," that is, of her head dress.

During the seventeenth century the Church Courts were constantly passing rules on the subject of plaid-wearing. In 1621 the Kirksession of Glasgow enacted that "no woman, married or unmarried, come within the kirk-doors, to preaching or prayers, with their plaids about their heads, neither lie down in the kirk on their face in tyme of prayer, with certification that their plaids shall be drawn up, and themselves raisit be the beddall."

By the Kirksession of Kinghorn, on the 4th March 1645, was denounced "the uncomlieness of women coming to church on the Sabbath to sermon with plaids about their heads . . . which provocks sleeping in the time of sermone without being espied." The Kirksession therefore ordered "that if anie woman be found in church on the Sabbath with a plaid over or about her head from this day forth she shall conforme to that act pay 6 sh. *toties quoties*, and further be liable to such censure as the sessione shall condescend upon to be inflicted for her contemptioun and disobedience." Muffled Sunday sleepers must have become intolerably numerous, when, on the 17th September 1643, the Kirksession of Monifieth provided their officer, Robert Scott, "with ane pynt of tar, to put upon the women that held plaids about their heads."

On the 24th May 1694 the Kirksession of St Andrews passed a minute in these words :

"The weamen being complained upon for their evill custome and
habit in wearing their playdes about their heades and sleiping
in the church in tyme of Divine service, quhairfoir after consideration it was ordained that hereafter none come within the kirk
dores with their plaides about their heades, especiallie on the
Sabbath, and intimation theroff to be mad on the morrow to the
whole congregation, as it was at large being Solemn Thanksgiving
for the late victorie over the malignants in the north; and for holding
hard thereto, it was appoynted that James Wood and James
Sword, balyies, attend with their officers at the kirk dores on
Sunday nixt for that effect, quhairby that they may cause every
one give obedience according as they are appoynted."

This invocation of magisterial authority had proved
ineffective, for on the 21st June the Kirksession
"ordered intimation to be made furth of the pulpit
discharging weamen's playdes from their heads in the
church, especiallie on the Lord's Day, with certification
that the Session will appoynt one of the church officers
to go throw the kirk with ane long rod and tak doune
thair playdes from their heads, quha are disobedient."
Acting on this deliverance, two persons, assuming
that what was lawful to the church officer might not
be unlawful to others, actually snatched a plaid from
a woman's head during the time of worship. Arraigned
before the Kirksession, and certain "honest women"
having testified as to their guilt, they were ordained
to be "publictlie rebookit befoir the congregation,"
and "were recommendit to the magistrats for the
ryot."

By the members of the Associate Synod in the

eighteenth century the first day of the week was associated with austerity and gloom. Every Seceder refused to shave on Sunday, while he charged with profanity all who did. Generally, the evangelical clergy abridged their toilet on the Sabbath. The writer's grandfather, a parish minister in Forfarshire, anticipated his Sunday morning toilet by shaving on Saturday evening at eleven o'clock. To these austere times succeeded a reaction. As craftsmen and others early in the present century entered upon a higher culture, they sought to appear in church with trimmed hair and well-shaved beards. Hence barbers on Sunday prosecuted an active trade. Out of this change arose a long and serious litigation. The question of Sunday observance was intimately involved. The apprentice of a barber at Dundee, who had by indenture become bound " not to absent himself from his master's business, holiday or week day, late hours or early," was requested to shave customers on Sunday mornings. To this he demurred, and the local magistrates, on his employer's complaint, resolved to enforce his attendence, remarking in a written judgment that " aid by an apprentice in shaving on the morning of Sunday before ten o'clock is not contrary to the statutes regarding the Sabbath." On advocation, Lord Jeffrey, as Ordinary, reversed the judgment, holding that a shaving shop was not of such necessity as might not admit of being closed for one day weekly. On an appeal, the Lord Justice-Clerk Boyle concurred with the Lord Ordinary, but a majority of the judges held that the work sought to be performed came within the category of necessity. The case was appealed to the House of Lords, when, on the 20th December 1837, the Lord Chancellor Cottenham, supported by all the law lords, reversed the judgment and upheld the opinion of the Lord Ordinary.[1]

By Scottish Reformers, attendance at the communion table was insisted upon. On the 9th September 1564 the Kirksession of the Canongate "ordeinit that no person get any almose [alms] except that thai haif been at the communion, saifant infantis, faderlesse, and sik persons as are into extryme seiknes and in extryme pouerte." And in the year 1603 the Kirksession of Aberdeen resolved to distrain the goods of certain persons at Footdee who from the Lord's table absented themselves "contumaciously." On the 22d June 1645 Helen Wallis, convicted by the Kirksession of Dunfermline for "not communicating at the Lord's table," was sentenced to make "hir private repentance on hir knees."

Fast-days were invested with the sacredness of Sunday. The Kirksession of Dunfermline, on the

[1] "An Outline of the Law of Scotland against Sabbath Profanation," by Hugh Barclay, LL.D. Glasgow, 1866, pp. 15-21.

21st December 1641, amerced John Smart, flesher, in eight merks for "selling a carkois of beefe and having pott on a rost at his fire the last fasting day."

Gambling was prohibited. In 1598 the Kirk-session of Stirling dealt with two persons who had played at dice till four of the morning, when they "discordit." They were remitted to the magistrates for imprisonment, "their fude to be bread and watter." In February 1654 the Kirksession of Dumfries sentenced a person found card-playing on a Saturday evening to pay 12s. to the kirk treasurer.

Rebellion against parental authority was, as a high offence, visited with severity. David Leyes, who had struck his father, was by the Kirksession of St Andrews in 1574 sentenced to appear before the congregation "bairheddit and beirfuttit, upon the highest degree of the penitent stuill, with a hammer in the ane hand and ane stane in the uther hand, as the twa instruments he mannesit his father,—with ane papir writin in great letteris about his heid, with these wordis, *Behold the onnaturall Son* punished for putting hand on his father, and dishonouring of God in him." Nor was this deemed sufficient humiliation, for the offender was afterwards at the market-cross made to stand two hours "in the jaggs," and thereafter "cartit through the haill toun." Not only so, but being again placed at the cross, proclamation in his presence was made that "if ever he offended father or mother heirefter, the member of his body quhairly he offendit salbe cuttit off from him, be it tung, hand or futt without mercy, as example to utheris to abstein fra the lyke." In 1598 the Presbytery of Glasgow seriously deliberated on the conduct of a youth, who had passed his father, "without lifting his bonnet."

A tendency to detraction long prevailed, since it was the only weapon which the feeble might urge against the strong. Writing from Edinburgh to Cardinal Wolsey in 1525, Dr Magnus, the English ambassador, remarks : "There has been right rageous winds with exceeding rain, and an open slander and a murmur raised upon me, not only in this town of Edinburgh, but through a great part of the realm, surmitting that I should be the occasion thereof, insomuch that I nor my servants could or might pass of late in the streets, neither to move from the court, but openly many women banned, cursed, swear'd, and gave me and mine the most grievous maledictions that could be to our faces."

Against a practice which had become so common and deep-seated the Reformed Church contended vigorously. The Kirksession of Canongate on the 8th December 1565 "ordainit that gif any persone or persons haif ony gruge of hatrit or malice, or any offence in his hart agane his brodir, that they and ilk ane o' thame come on Tesday in the mornying at viij houris to the Tolboth, quhan fyve of the kirk salbe present to juge the offence, and gif that it standis in thame to reconseill the same, the said fyve to be John Hart, John Short, John Mordo, John Acheson, Thomas Hunter, James Wilkie, or any fyve of them." The Kirksession of Perth in 1578 decreed that John Tod, for a slanderous speech, should stand two hours in irons. The Kirksession of Dumfries ruled that slanderers should be sentenced " to stand at the kirk-stile on the Sabbath, with branks upon their mouths," while obstinate detractors were to be pilloried in the market-place.

The brank, to which we have been introduced, was of the form of a helmet. Composed of iron bars it had a triangular piece of iron which entered the mouth. Placed on the head of the delinquent it was secured behind by a padlock. The offender wearing this degrading casque stood on the repentance stool. Soon after his elevation to the primacy, Archbishop Sharp was conducting service in the parish church of St Andrews, when a woman stood up, and in the face of the congregation, accused him of an illicit amour with her when he was a college student. The accuser was one Isobel Lindsay, a woman of humble station, resident in the city. She was arrested and brought before the Kirksession, who sentenced her to appear for a succession of Sundays on the repentance stool wearing the brank. A correspondent of the *Gentleman's Magazine* writing to that periodical in 1785 states that the father of the then church officer at St Andrews had witnessed Isobel undergoing her sentence. The brank worn by Isobel Lindsay when under discipline has been preserved.

For slandering their neighbours, Robert Shortrees and his wife were in 1646 sentenced by the Kirksession of Dunfermline to ask forgiveness "of the parties offendit before their awn doores in the street, publicklie on their knees;" the menace was added that if "Robert shall be found hereafter in the lyke fault he shall be banished out of the paroche." Janet Wely at Dunfermline was, in March 1646, sent to the pillar of repentance for calling Grissel Welwood by the name of "white bird." The Kirksession of Kinghorn, on the 28th May 1609, "be pluralitie of uoitts, thocht it meit that Patrick Key, for his misbehauiour in abusing his nybour, and in calling William Newin 'ane witchis burd' beffour the Session, suld stand twentie fowr howrs in the steipill for his penaltie."

It was one of the rules of Mouswald parish, framed in 1649, that slanderers were "to pay twentie shillings for the first fault, and to crave God and the parties sclandered mercie in the presence of the sessioun; for the second fault to pay fourtie shillings and to stand one day in the pillar with sheits; for fault the third to pay fourtie shillings and to stand thrie dayes in the pillar with sheits; and that for everie fault *toties quoties* should they confes their offence, and crave both God and the parties offended mercie, otherwayes to be put into the gorgettis."

Myse Bonar was in 1652 charged before the Kirk-session of Dunfermline with "denouncing the toune." Among other foolish utterances, she expressed a wish that "Cromwell wad come and tak all the toune upon his bak." Her sentence was a heavy one; she was condemned "to stand at the croce or tron, on ane publict mercat day, with ane paper on hir head," and on the Sunday morning thereafter "to stand in face of the congregation" and there make her further confession.

When punishments so odious were executed upon slanderers, the temptation was not inconsiderable for persons who had a dislike to any of their neighbours to charge them with this offence. So restrictive regulations became needful. It was one of the parochial laws of Mouswald "if any compleins of his neighbour for slander, and in the meintyme cannot prove the same, then the complainers themselffis shall be punished with *pæna talionis,* and underly the punishment that should be inflicted upon the person complained on, if that the fancied sclander had been proven and trew."

A similar rule was in 1691 enacted by the Kirk-session of Dalry, Kirkcudbrightshire, such being that "whosoever present before the session any bill or petition or libel anent slander, must consigne twelve shillings scots in pledge of their honest designe, to be forfeited should they faill in the probation." The sessional decree preceded by one year the commencement of proceedings in a case of scandal, which occupies by its details many pages of the register.

On the 30th October 1692, Janet Nelson, wife of John Weillis, appeared in Dalry parish church in sackcloth upon the repentance stool, and there publicly declared, as formerly she had done to the Kirksession, that she had been guilty of adultery with her husband's master, John M'Creach of M'Kistoun. As she made her public declaration, M'Creach, who was in his pew, stood up and warmly protested his innocence. Along with M'Creach was "a messenger of court," who bore a legal warrant authorizing the imprisonment of both the confessor and her husband. Adam Norval, notary, who also attended at M'Creach's instance, made an official record of the occurrence.

It now appeared that Janet Nelson or Weillis had, in the presence of several persons, subscribed a written declaration, testifying that she had presented the charge against M'Creach at the request and through the menaces of her husband, and that M'Creach was innocent. Presenting the declaration in the Commissary Court, to which he had summoned Weillis and his wife, M'Creach had, on their non-appearance, obtained judgment. Matters became complicated, for at the instance of the Kirksession, those who had attested Nelson's withdrawal expressed their regret for witnessing it, and as a statement from the pulpit was read to this effect, they verified its accuracy by severally standing up.

Janet Nelson was imprisoned in Sanquhar jail, but on her liberation a few weeks afterwards, she on the 11th December 1692, emitted a further declaration, adhering to her original confession, and alleging that her withdrawal had been procured by constraint. The Kirksession applied to the Presbytery for counsel, and on their advice it was ruled that M'Creach should have an opportunity of publicly purging himself of the charge. Accordingly on Sunday, the 4th March 1694, he in presence of the congregation at Dalry church declared his innocence in an oath which contained these words : " I, swearing by the Eternal God, the searcher of hearts, invocating Him as witness, judge and avenger, wishing in case I be guilty that He Himself may appear against me as witness."

Vituperation and scolding were cognizable offences. In 1562 the Kirksession of Aberdeen decreed that " all common skoldis, flytharis and cardis be baneist the toun, and nocht sufferit to remaine thairin for na requist ; " and on the 19th December 1592, the Kirksession of Glasgow "appointed juggs and brankis to be fixit up in some suitable place for the punischment of flyteris." By the Kirksession of Kinghorn, on the 7th August 1608, Marjorie Buit and Alison Huggan were adjudged "to be put in the gougs for their flyting and scalding in the toun." And on the 18th September of the same year, Janet Tod and Janet Ayngill were, "for missbehaviour in flytting and scalding in the audience of their neighbours and others, ordanit to stand twa hours in the gougs at the trone; Janet ane hour mair at the cros for hir dissobedience." In 1617 the Kirksession of Perth ordered "a chair of stone to be bigged in ane public part be the master of the hospital" for the "accommodation in repentance of flyteris and slanderers."

One of the code of rules passed by the Kirksession of Mouswald in 1649 provided that "notorious flytteris with their neighbouris shall stand in the gorgetis with ane paper upon thair head."

On the 3rd May 1668 the minister of Port of Menteith "did intimat unto the people, after the first sermon, and intreated them that na person should flyt nor scold on the Sabbath-day, or na ither day; or whosoever person or persons should be found scolding should be punished both in their persons and means, and [made] to stand in the jogs."

By the Church it was strongly ruled that in the conjugal union the spouses should avoid strife. On the 24th August 1623 the Kirksession of Kinghorn arraigned William Allan, who had abused his wife upon a Sunday. He was sentenced "to be layd twentie fower houris in the stockis, and thairefter to stand twa houris in the jougis upon ane mercat day, and thairefter to find caution not to do the lyk againe with notification if he sall be fund doing the same to be banischit the toun."

The abuse of husbands by their wives was a common offence. On the 2d February 1565[6] George Stene, baxter, complained to the Kirksession of the Canongate that he "culd not live with his wife Janet Mordo, be resone of wicketnes of toung and casting at him with her handis stains and dirt." The Kirksession of St Andrews, on the 15th November 1570, "warnit Gelis Symson, spouse to George Upton, that she sould be made to sit in the joggis twenty-four houris," and be heavily fined if she persevered in "miscayn her husband, flytin with her neighbouris, selling candle and bread on Sundays, and not resorting to the kirk." Margaret Short, a common offender, was by the Kirksession of Stirling, on the 23rd March 1598, handed over "to the baillies to punish her publiclie," inasmuch that she had violently abused her husband, having "mintit ane shool to him," and "cast in his face ane cap with aill." For scolding her husband the Kirksession of Ayr, in 1606, sentenced Janet Hunter "to stand in

her lynnings, at the cross on market days ; " also " to
stand at the kirk door seven days, and in the public
place of repentance." On the 29th March 1653
Margaret Markman was, for " abusing her husband
David Watertoun with most cursed, cruel, and malicious
speeches, committed to the magistrates for imprisonment in the laighest prison-house,[1] and thairaftir to be
set on the Tron on a mercat day to the example of
others, with a paper on her browe showing her
notorious scandall." For causes other than scolding
some married men had reason to be displeased with
their helpmates. On the 2d December 1564 John
Roger promised to the Kirksession of the Canongate
at the baptism of his daughter Dorothy that he would
" in na way committ the said barn to the care of his
wife, because sche afoir in druknes smorit twa former
barnis, and gif he be negligent in keeping of his said
barn that they will pursue him as ane common
mortherar of children." To the Kirksession of St
Andrews John Moris, on the 25th August 1659,
made complaint against his wife Beatrix Smith for
" wasteing and mispending their means." Beatrix
acknowledged her offence, and was warned that " if
she shall hereaftir impignorate anything," the magistrates' concurrence would be obtained " to take such
pledges from the receiver without paying debt so
contracted."

[1] Otherwise styled *the thives' hole.*

Before the Reformation, profane swearing was especially prevalent. Priests swore " by God's wounds," " by our lady," by " the wood of the holy cross," and " by all the saints." In smiting sarcastically those who indulged in imprecation, Sir David Lyndsay has adduced in his poems fifty different oaths, of which thirty-three, used by persons of quality, occur in his " Thrie Estaitis." In 1518 was passed a Parliamentary statute imposing penalties upon " swearers of abominable oaths." These penalties were levied by a scale conforming with the offender's rank or social status. Thus, " for the first fault, every prelate of kirk, earl, or lord, four shillings ; a baron or beneficed man, constituted in dignity ecclesiastical, twelve pennies ; a landed man, freeholder, vassal, feuar, burgess, and small beneficed man, six pennies ; the poor folks that have no gear to be put in the stocks, jaggs, or imprisoned for the space of four hours. And women to be weighed and considered according to their blood and estate of the parties that they are coupled with." In 1560 it was ruled by the Town Council of Edinburgh that all found guilty of blasphemy should be punished by the iron brank. On the 7th January 1585-6 the order was revived in these words : " Fynds it maist expedient that the bailyeis renew the ordour obseruet before in pvnesing of sic as blasphemys and bannis, uther be ane pecuniare sowme or be putting of thame in the jogs, according to the persoun, place, and trespas, bayth thame quhom thai sall happin to find swa doing or that sall be delaittet be the eldaris or deaconis." In 1592 the Presbytery and Town Council of Aberdeen joined in authorising employers to exact penalties from such of their servants as used oaths, and to deduct the same from their wages. With "palmers" they were empowered to punish blasphemers who were unable to pay fines, also to chastise oath-speaking children. In 1644 the Kirk-session of Glasgow appointed certain of their number to proceed on market days through the city "to take order with banners and swearers," and upon each to impose a penalty of twelve pence.

Thomas Rumkeillor was, by the Kirksession of St Andrews, on the 25th January 1649, referred to the Presbytery for "railling and cursing against the Covenant." In the same year it was ruled by the Kirksession of Mouswald that "cursers and swearers shall pay tuelf pennies *toties quoties;*" further, that "everie fighter and bloodshedder shall stand on the pillar with sheetes one day, and also to pay fourtie shillings by and atover that which the civill magistrat micht lay upon them."

In June 1651 the Kirksession of Dunfermline sentenced a woman to "stand at the croce or trone on ane publict mercat day with ane paper on her head, signifying her cursing and blasphemies." On the 5th December 1680 the Kirksession of Saltoun had at their bar one John Boyd, charged with "swearing openly at a banquet, and bragging that they [the company] might know he was a gentilman by his swearing." Boyd, who had been drinking, admitted his fault, and on his knees before the Session expressed his penitence. The Procurator-Fiscal of the Regality Court of Lesmahagow was in 1703 reproved by the Kirksession of the parish for profane swearing; it was further resolved to complain of him to the Duchess of Hamilton that " such a person may not be continued in the possession of his office."

Habitual drunkards were rigorously punished. In 1612, John Thomson, who had through excessive drinking " lost sindrie of his senses," was by the Kirksession of Stirling sentenced " to fall doun on his knees and crave God and the kirk for forgiveness, and to pay twenty shillins *ad pios usus.*" In 1645 the Kirksession of Dunino resolved to impose penalties on drunkards according to a scale. For the first offence were to be exacted six shillings, twelve shillings for a second, and so on *toties quoties.* In October 1654 the Kirksession of Dumfries " required the individual members to attend the four parts of the burgh ilka Wednesday (the day of the weekly market) from twa till six, to take note of all persons found drunk or scandalous, and to take such into custody." In May 1668 the Kirksession of Port of Menteith made the following regulation, which was publicly intimated : "No brewir within the paroch should sell aill to no person except als much as wold quenche the thirst of strangers, or to sick persons ; and not to sell aill to no ither person within the paroch, and that under the paine of ten pounds Scots, to be payed be the aill seller, and the person who drunk it to be punished as the Session shall think fit." In 1712 the Kirksession of Hawick appointed certain persons to "perlustrate the town to see who were drinking in alehouses after eight o'clock at night."

Persons guilty of manslaughter, though escaping conviction in the criminal tribunals, or subsequently pardoned, were not relieved from ecclesiastical censures. The earliest case of this sort appears in the register of the Canongate. The entry proceeds : —" The first day of Januare 1565. The whilk day the Superintendent beand present with the Assemblie [Kirksession] for the order discriwing for the repentance - making of Marjorye Brisone, quha had committed the horobill cryme of murther in slaying ane man, as at mair lenthe is confessit in hir humble supplecation to the General Kirk of Scotland at dyverse tymes be the action beand remittit to the Superintendent of Lowdiane, the said Superintendent efter the avisement ordanis the said Marjorye to be ressavit in maner following to be usit for the space of three Sondayis afoirnone and efter none, viz., that the said Marjorye sall cum to the place appointit bairfit and bair legit with ane peticot quhit out cullour, or sleffis or clayth upone hir heid, with ane knif made of tre dippit in bluide, and there beand callit upon, humblie sall require for Godis mercy and forgevines of brethern, and that thay may call upone thair God for hir to appardone hir heuie offence, and in the third Sonday to resave her again to the kirk. In taking of the quhilk ane elder of the kirk sal resave her be the hand, and tak the knyf from hir knawing hir to have gottin remission of the princes and parteis satisfiet."

In December 1599 the Kirksession of St Andrews absolved four persons for the murder of " umquhill James Smith," who had severally appeared in presence of the congregation, conformable with the regulation as to "murderous repentance." In 1619 the Kirksession of Redgorton considered the case of Colin Pitscottie, eldest son of Andrew Pitscottie of Luncarty, who was charged with the murder of Alexander Bennett. After various delays, Pitscottie appeared before the Presbytery of Perth, and acknowledged his guilt; he was ordained to make his public repentance in the kirk of Redgorton " in lyning clothes."

On the 1st August 1639, Francis Weir of Newton addressed a supplication to the Presbytery of

Lanark, entreating that he might be relieved of his long excommunication on account of the slaughter of William Carmichael, brother to Sir John Carmichael of Meadowflat, in respect that " he has now made satisfaction to the partie, and is also relaxed from the Kingis horne." The Kirksession of St Andrews, on the 14th July 1653, " appointed Laurence James Corstorphine, ' manslayer,' to begin the publicke declaration of his repentance next Lord's day." He had already " humblie confesst his terrible sinne unto the minister in private." At the instance of his Kirksession, the minister of Inverurie, on the 15th December 1661, made public intimation "that William Forbes, natural son to the Laird of Leslie, was excommunicated for murthering Kincowsay."

Owing chiefly to the lewd habits of the monks, the social degradation of the people was, in times immediately preceding the Reformation, all but complete. To remedy the prevailing licentiousness, strong measures were adopted by the authorities. In May 1562 the magistrates of Edinburgh caused a hole to be dug in the North Loch, in which persons leading impure lives might be soused. Another pool for the same purpose was known as the " corrall or quarry hole ;" it was situated on a farm lying between Edinburgh and Leith, the property of Trinity Hospital. To the punishment of ducking, persons guilty of impurity were, in the early times of the Reformed

Church, frequently sentenced by the Kirksession.
On the 16th March 1565-6, Elspeth Logan, "one of
the Quenis Gracis cukis," was, by the Kirksession of
the Canongate, adjudged "to be anis douckit in the
Corrall hollis and banischit the gait." The Kirksession of Kinghorn, on the 20th December 1607,
ordained "Johne Hagie to be put in the stepill, and
Elspet Stock in the tolbuithe till the morne, that the
ministers, elders, and magistrates sie thame punishit
aither be douking thame or els be setting thame in
the gougis, with their heads schaven for their uyle
harlatrie confessit be thame baithe." In 1602, the
Kirksession of Aberdeen, in considering the case of
Jenete Scherar, who had fallen a second time, ordered
her "to be apprehendit and put in ward, and their-
after to be doukit at the croce;" it is added,
"provyding gif sche pay ten markis of penaltie to
be fre of hir douking, and no utherways."

In the First Book of Discipline, the Reformers
demanded that adulterers should be put to death;
their desire was not fully complied with, but in 1563
Parliament enacted that "notour adulterers," meaning those of whose illicit connection a child had been
born, should be executed. The penalty was occasionally inflicted. When in 1563 Paul Methven, minister at Jedburgh, acknowledged himself guilty of
adultery, the General Assembly consulted on the
subject the lords of the Council. Methven was in

the third year subsequent to his confession, permitted to prostrate himself on the floor of the Assembly, and with weeping and howling, to entreat for pardon. Then followed the terrible sentence, that at Edinburgh as the capital, in Dundee as his native town, and in Jedburgh, the scene of his ministrations, he should stand in sackcloth at the church door, also on the repentance stool, and for two Sundays in each place.

Fornication was punished with a severity nearly equal to that which attended the infraction of the marriage vow. On the 31st September 1564, a serving girl, charged with impurity, was by the Kirksession of the Canongate (with the co-operation of the magistrates) ordered to "depart furth of the gait within forty-eight houris, under the paine of schurging and burnyng of the scheike." On the 7th October of the same year, the same Kirksession sentenced David Persoun, convicted of fornication, to be "brankit for four houris," while his associate in guilt, Isobel Moutray, was " banisit the gait," that is expelled from the parish. A week subsequently the Kirksession of Canongate issued a proclamation that all women found guilty of fornication " be brankit six houris at the croce." And on the 11th November it was decreed, with the approval of the magistrates, "that na house be let to ony persone who has committed fornication or other uncleanness, under a

penalty of xl shillings." That no female offender
might escape, "maid-wifs" were commanded to inform
the Session as to the births at which they assisted.
On the same occasion four females guilty of impurity
were condemned to "stand on the croce," two of
them to be "brankit," while all under pain of
burning on the cheek were thereafter to quit "the
commonwealth," that is the parish.

On the 2nd December 1564, the Kirksession of the
Canongate, co-operating with the bailies, ordained
certain women who were leading irregular lives, "to
sit bair-heid vpoun the croce, and there to stand three
houris—and thereafter to be banished, and if afterwards apprehendit in the lyke falt, to be schurgit,
burnt on the schiek," and sent into perpetual exile.
In 1565 Philip Walker, a fornicator from Dundee,
was, on account of "his povertie and submissiveness,"
allowed by the Kirksession of the Canongate to escape
further punishment by being warded "all nycht in
the tolbuith, with breid and water." Respecting the
punishment of adultery, the Kirksession of Aberdeen,
in 1568, decreed "that ilk persone convict in the
said cryme sall cum thre several Sundays, at the
second bell-ringing, to the kirk door, quhair the
people enteris that day, bairfutit and bairleged, cled
in sackclayth, with ane crown of paper on their heid,
with the cryme written thairabout, and remaine thair
quhile the precheour begins his sermond; and thair-

efter sall cum into the oppen place of repentans, and remain standing until the end of the preching, and then pas again to the same door, quhair thai sall remane to be ane spektakl to the haill peple, until all folkis be past hame, and departit frae the kirk." The Kirksession of Glasgow enacted in 1586 that adulterers should " satisfy six Sabbaths at the pillory, barefoot and barelegged, in sackcloth, and should thereafter be carted through the toun." Ten years later the same Kirksession had " ane pulley" attached to Glasgow bridge, whereby adulterers might be " duckit" in the Clyde.

The Kirksession of St Andrews ordained in 1576 that fornicators convicted for the first time should be imprisoned in the steeple, and that those who relapsed should be pilloried at the cross and have their heads shaved. On the 19th December 1594, the Kirksession of Glasgow enacted that the punishment of " single fornication be ane day on the cockstool, ane day at the pillar, and eight days warding in the steeple." In 1586 the Kirksession of Perth appointed James Pitlady, with a yearly salary of forty shillings " to shave the heads of fornicators and fornicatrixes." During the same year the Kirksession of Perth ordained Thomas Smith, who had for the third time confessed to the guilt of uncleanness, to be " warded, shaven, and doukit in a puddle [pool] of water, according to Act of Parliament."

By the Presbytery of Paisley, on the 16th November 1626, a man who had confessed himself guilty of adultery was ordained "to stand and abyde six Sabbaths barefooted and barelegged at the kirk door of Pasley between the second and third bell-ringing, and thereafter to goe to the place of public repentance during the said space of six Sabbaths." In 1627 the Kirksession of Stow accepted the satisfaction of Alexander Sandilands, after his having on a first conviction for fornication, "sittin eighteen dyetts" upon the stool of repentance. Margaret Brown, at Kinghorn, was, on the 25th February 1640, ordained "to sit upon the pyllar for the space of twentie-sex sabbathis, and to stand at the kirk door the haill tyme betwixt the second and third bells in sackloathe, and the hyndmost three sabbathis to be barefootit."

Among the rules of discipline framed by the Kirksession of Mouswald on the 1st July 1649, it was ordained that "everie fornicator, both man and also woman, for the first fault, should stand thrie dayes in the pillar of repentance with sheits, and to pay fourtie shillings of penaltie; for the second fault, to stand six dayes with sheits, and to pay four pundis; and for the third fault, to stand six dayes in sackclothe and to pay twentie marks." In 1643 the Kirksession of Glasgow intensified their former enactments by the decree that adulterers should stand "three hours

in the jaggs," receive "a public whipping," be imprisoned in the common jail, and be thereafter
banished from the city.   Two adulterers were in May
1642 sentenced by the Presbytery of Lanark "to go
through the whole kirkes of the Presbyterie, and at the
kirke-doore of each to stand barefoot and barelegged
from the second bell to the last."   On the 4th March
1647 the Kirksession of St Andrews determined that
fornicators should, on a first conviction, pay £10 ;
and on a relapse, £20 ; while those unable to make
payment were to be set on the cross, and to remain
fifteen days in prison, there to be fed on bread and
water.

For a century after the Reformation incestuous
crimes occupied from time to time the attention of
the higher courts.   The Synod of Fife in April
1611 ordained Laurence Ferguson, in the parish of
Kirkcaldy, who had pleaded guilty of incest, "to pas
ilk Saboth day from kirk to kirk *per circulum*
throughout the haill kirkes in the boundis of the
exerceis [Presbytery] of Kirkaldie, according as he
salbe injoyned be the brethren of the samine, and
that in sackcloth, for the space of ane yeir compleitt,
without any intermissioune of dayes, vntil the next
diocesan Assemblie to be holdin in St Androis in the
moneth of Apryl next."

The severities exercised upon social delinquents
were, if at all deterrent, very partially so.   Among

the industrial classes few were able to read, and the
songs and ballads committed to memory were usually
ribald and licentious.   Through an impure minstrelsy
the exhortations of the pulpit were more than nega-
tived.   In 1580 the Session-clerk of Perth reports
that of 211 children baptized, about 85 were born out
of wedlock.   During the seventh decade of the sixteenth century the session-clerk of Aberdeen has
entered separately the births of legitimate and illegitimate children, and from his record we learn that
the latter in 1574 numbered 27 per cent.[1]

Discipline was seldom relaxed.   There was an exception in 1585, when a pestilential distemper visited
Perth, assuming so virulent a character that infected
persons were removed from their dwellings, and being
conveyed to the burgh muir, were there lodged in
wooden huts,   To provide the means of lodgment,
penalties were exacted from those who indulged in
nuptial festivities, each one who resorted to a bridal
being called on to pay £10, while every couple who
entertained at their bridal more than four persons
were amerced in £40.   When funds derived from
this source proved unequal to the requirement, social

---

[1] It may be remarked that social irregularities still largely prevail in certain northern counties.   In the report of the Register-
General for 1883, the illegitimate births in Aberdeenshire are set
down as 12 per cent., while in the counties of Elgin and Banff the
percentage is 14.

delinquents condemned by the Kirksession were allowed to compound for not appearing on the repentance stool by what is styled " ane pecunial sum of money," which, as the parish record bears, " was applied to the support of the poor, withall that are furth in the lodges, who otherwise shall be liable to die for want, or else be compelled for hunger to stray and go abroad in the country and infect the same."

Parochial discipline was strongly exercised till the period of the Restoration, and though subsequently the jagg, the brank, and the ducking pond were rarely used, the criminal authority of the Church was not materially relaxed. But at the Revolution, it became essential that ecclesiastical authority should be restrained. By a legislative act in 1690, the civil consequences of excommunication were disallowed, while by a statute passed in 1696, the Heritors and Kirksession of every parish were empowered to appoint a parochial officer who should be charged with the maintenance of order.

In the statutory arrangement there was only a partial acquiescence, while profligacy, rampant in England since the Restoration, began in its more revolting features to extend northward. With the view of restraining the prevailing licentiousness, societies " for reformation of manners," such as already had been established in England, were formed in

Scotland. Principally concerned in their formation was Sir John Home, Lord Crossrig. In November 1699, a meeting was held in his lordship's house in Parliament Close, attended by some influential citizens, when it was determined to establish a "Society for mutual edification and reformation of manners." On the 3rd of February 1700 a schedule of rules was subscribed, but the society's progress was incidentally checked. Within a few hours after the rules had been arranged, the pile of buildings to the east of Parliament Square, which included Lord Crossrig's residence, perished in a conflagration. Therewith were destroyed the society's papers. But on the 10th September a further meeting was held, when operations were actively resumed. From the existing minute-book [1] we derive particulars as to the society's history. Those present at the meeting in September were Mr Francis Grant, afterwards Lord Cullen, Bailie John Duncan, Captain James Colt, Captain James Aikman, George Ramsay of Edington, George Fullerton of Dreghorn, Adam Freer, M.D. ; John Knox [2] and Robert Elliot, apothecaries ; William Lindsay and Adam Blackadder, merchants ; William Livingston, late deacon of the

---

[1] Minute-Book of "Society for Reformation of Manners," 131 pages folio. Laing MSS., University of Edinburgh.

[2] According to Dr Somerville (Memoirs, 175) Dr Knox was great-grandnephew of the Reformer; he had a son, an army physician, who in 1779 was residing in Scarborough.

glovers; James Pringle, ensign of the Town Guard; and Nicol Spence, writer and clerk to the Presbytery of Edinburgh. At subsequent meetings the promoters had "ministers present with them." On the 15th October, "rules" were definitely settled. These set forth that whereas the formation of societies for "the restraint of vice and immoralities" had been recommended by the Commission of the General Assembly, the society now constituted should hold weekly meetings, consecrated by prayer. From the discussions politics were to be excluded. Those only were to be chosen as members who upheld the established religion, and in their families practised Divine worship. Members were to be admitted on a unanimous vote. The meetings were to be held in the members' private dwellings. On the evening previous to each meeting, members were severally for the space of an hour to pray and meditate for the general welfare. Those at any of the meetings who came in late were to pay one shilling Scots in penalty, and those who were absent the sum of four shillings. One meeting monthly was to be occupied exclusively in devotion.

Determined to crush profligacy by a strong hand, the members instituted "a court of immoralities," with a judge, constable, and censors. As profane swearing was common, the members agreed to parade the streets a day weekly, in pairs, for the detection of blasphemers. They also resolved to visit "coffee and chocolate houses," and there to "observe such as curse, swear, or profane the name of God." Two persons detected blaspheming, Wishart of Logie and the laird of Jerviswoode, were lodged "in the guard-house."

According to the censors there was much intemperance. In entertaining their friends, opulent citizens were found "to drink with them at unseasonable hours." And tavern-drinking at late hours was common. By the society the magistrates were requested to proceed to the different taverns each evening after ten o'clock, and to call upon those who kept them to dismiss their guests. Searching personally for delinquents, the censors reported that "on Saturday, the 12th December 1701, at 12 hours at night," they had found in a tavern drinking and swearing horrible oaths, my Lord Colvill, also several colonels of the army, landowners, and others, all of whom they reported to the magistrates. An Englishman named Thomson, distinguished by the censors as "Debauchee Thomson," they in August 1702 committed to the guard-house; breaking his bail-bond he effected his escape.

"Brotherings of apprentices," or convivial initiations of members of guilds, were to the society a source of disquietude, as were the drinking practices which obtained at "lykewakes," "dergies," and "pennybrydells." Censors were sent to "bowling-greens," "kyle-alleys," and places of public gaming, to discover abuses, and to report upon them. On a strict observance of Sunday the society strongly insisted. Skating on the ice by children on Sunday was prohibited, also the "giving out on that day of postal letters."

It had been intended to plant "societies" in every district. Throughout Scotland twenty were actually established, of which six were connected with Edinburgh; that established by Lord Crossrig being described as "No. 2." Inter-communication was effected by the delegates of each society meeting together as a "Convention of Correspondents." By the Convention early in 1702 a series of queries was transmitted to the societies, to which answers were solicited. The several societies were asked whether magistrates appointed by the Heritors and Kirksessions could summarily punish delinquents for such offences as drunkenness, profane swearing, and Sabbath desecration; whether constables could personally exact fines, or whether the members of the societies could with or without a constable enter the private dwellings of suspected persons; whether parents could be fined for the profanation of the Lord's day by their children, and whether the societies could appoint constables who might legally apprehend offenders and conduct them to prison.

For two years "Society No. 2" had an average attendance of twelve members, while during the next three years the attendance averaged six. Several expedients for maintaining an interest in the proceedings were suggested without success, and "No. 2" met on the 30th December 1707 for the last time. Some of the more conspicuous members who latterly joined may be named. Not the least zealous was Mr George Drummond, afterwards a distinguished Lord Provost of Edinburgh, and one of those celebrated by the poet Allan Ramsay. Mr James Hart, latterly a member, was minister of Greyfriars Church. An intemperate opponent of the Union, he afterwards became almoner to George I., whom at the request of his brethren in the General Assembly he had congratulated on his arrival in this country. Another clerical member, Mr William Macvicar, minister of the second charge of St Cuthberts, obtained distinction by venturing in 1745, when the army of Prince Charles Edward held possession of the city, to express in public prayer his loyalty to the reigning family, and his desire that "the young man come among us seeking an earthly crown might obtain an heavenly one." Captain John Blackadder joined the society as a corresponding member; subsequently when stationed in Scotland he attended the meetings. Son of one who had suffered for maintaining his religious convictions, Blackadder was also remarkable for his Christian devotedness. As Colonel of the Cameronian Regiment, he under the Duke of Marlborough attained to military eminence.

The most notable member of "No. 2" was the celebrated Daniel Defoe. In the interests of the English government, Defoe was sent to Edinburgh in the autumn of 1706. As he had in his writings expressed a dislike to Episcopacy, he was invited to join the Society. In the minutes of a meeting held on the 25th March 1707, there is the following entry: "Baillie Duncan reports that he had some dayes been speaking to Mr Defoe about a correspondence with the Societies for reformation in England, of which he understood Mr Defoe to be a member, and Mr Defoe desiring to be admitted a member of this Societie, appeared, declaring the same, and allso his willingness to establish the foresaid correspondence with the Societies in England." On the 21st of October Defoe produced some printed papers transmitted by "the Societies in London;" these a committee were appointed to answer next day "in Mr Defoe's chamber." Defoe's signature is in the Society's minute-book, appended to the code of laws.

Subsequent to the check which, at the Revolution, was extended to the ecclesiastical courts, parochial and ecclesiastical discipline was extremely modified. Henceforth those who offended against social order were simply deprived of sacramental privileges till they were admonished and "restored." But the repentance stool and penitential vestments were permanently dispensed with. Public appearances were excused on payment of a monetary penalty. On the 29th April 1787, the Kirksession of Moffat, in consideration that "Mr Ewart had generously given four guineas for the benefit of the poor, agreed unanimously to excuse his publick appearance." In 1809 Mr Miller, younger of Glenlee, an elder of Mauchline parish, proposed to his brethren of the Kirksession that public rebukes should be discontinued, and the proposition was after some discussion agreed to. But where no penalty was forthcoming, public rebukes were in some of the rural parishes administered till thirty years later.

CHAPTER XIII.

HUNTING was the primitive occupation of every people: wild animals were destroyed, partly for their skins, but chiefly for use as food. The Scottish Celts, holding that bodily labour of all sorts was mean and disgraceful, devoted themselves mainly to the chase. They used weapons and hunting knives of flint and hard stone, while their dogs were, in Roman times, noted for their strength and ferocity. The wolf was destroyed solely for its skin ; it abounded in northern forests. According to a tradition, Malcolm II. on his return from defeating the Danes at Mortlach, in Morayshire, in 1010, was pursued by a wolf in the forest of Stochet. Just as the infuriated animal was in the act of attacking the king, a younger son of Donald of the Isles came up, who thrust his left hand, covered with his plaid, into the creature's mouth, and then by his dirk swiftly despatched it with his right. For this timely service the royal follower was rewarded with the lands of Skene in Aberdeenshire. When in later times a wolf appeared in any of the northern forests, the intruder was regarded as a common enemy, and was therefore hunted by the assembled populace. He who discovered the presence of the wolf was called upon at once to convey the tidings to the chief, who forthwith to a convenient meeting-place summoned his kinsmen and allies. When the wolf-hunt began, the country was scoured in all directions in order to arouse the intruder. An ancestor of the Clan Macgregor being successful in a wolf-hunt, led to a representation of the animal being included in the escutcheon of the sept.[1]

The wolf had his lair in the Caledonian Forest, which almost wholly covered that territory now forming the counties of Stirling and Linlithgow. In 1263 the Sheriff of Stirling was employed in repairing and extending the Royal Park at that burgh, and in connection with a payment by the Treasurer made twenty years later, it is related that a wolf-hunter had been employed by King Alexander III. The New Park at Stirling, constructed in 1263, was bounded on the north-eastern part by a ledge of rock, which retains the name of the *Wolf Crag*. In the neighbourhood of Stirling wolves were hunted in the seventeenth century. In *Wolf Crag Quarry*, in the southern shoulder of the Ochils, near Bridge of Allan, the animals long sought shelter. In the burgh seal of Stirling, the wolf forms a principal charge. The last

[1] Innes's " Scotland in the Middle Ages," p. 125

Scottish wolf was destroyed in 1680 by Sir Ewen Cameron of Lochiel.

In the "War of Inis-Thona," Ossian describes his heroes as "pursuing the boars of Runa." Latterly the boar was a denizen of eastern forests, abounding in the counties of Fife, Haddington, and Berwick. Muckross, the promontory of boars, was the original name of that spot on which the city of St Andrews now stands. A district in the vicinity, eight miles in length and averaging four in breadth, was known as the *Boar's Chase;* it was a place of royal hunting. A hamlet three miles to the south-east of St Andrews retains the name of Boarhills. By the historian, Hector Boece, is described the destruction in these parts of a boar of vast proportions which had slaughtered both men and cattle ; the tusks of the animal, sixteen inches in length, were, about the year 1528, when Boece wrote, kept in St Andrews' cathedral, and there made fast to the high altar. The family of Swinton of Swinton, in Berwickshire, derive their name from lands so called, because like Swinwood, a place in the same neighbourhood, they were in early times overrun by wild boars. Popular tradition attributes the acquisition by the Swintons of their lands in the Merse to the prowess of an ancestor in delivering the district from the ravages of swine, wild and fierce, with which it was infested. As a charge is made in 1263 by the Sheriff of Forfar, for the support of wild boars, *porci silvestres*, along with the king's horses and dogs, it is evident that at that time the boar had become extinct in the forests.

Wild cattle wandered in the southern and central forests. Of white colour, with lion-like manes and black muzzles, they were remarkable for their beauty, but withal were singularly fierce. According to Boece, they would eat nothing which the hand of man had touched. King Robert the Bruce hunted the wild ox. According to Holinshed, he in pursuing an ox, at length overtook it, and was about to thrust his spear into its loins, when it suddenly turned and made a desperate charge. Just in time to save the king's life, one of his followers ran forward, and boldly seizing the animal by the horns, overthrew it by main force. In reward King Robert bestowed on the intrepid huntsman lands and honours, with the distinguishing name of Turnbull. Among the enormities perpetrated by the Earl of Lennox and his men upon Lord Fleming in May 1570, is represented the destruction of " the white kye and bulls of his forest of Cumbernauld." [1] According to Leslie, these cattle were, in the sixteenth century, to be found in the parks of Stirling and Kincardine. Sir Robert Sibbald, who wrote about the close of the sixteenth century, remarks that in his time wild cattle roamed upon the mountains. There were formerly herds of

[1] Dalyell's " Illustrations of Scottish History," p. 521.

white cattle in the Duke of Buccleuch's park at Drumlanrig, and the race is still preserved in the forest of Cadzow.

Deer-stalking, an ancient sport, is celebrated by Ossian. "'Call,' said Fingal, 'call my dogs, the long-bounding sons of the chase. Call white-breasted Bran, and the surly strength of Luath. Fillan and Ryno, but he is not here! My son rests on the bed of death. Fillan and Fergus blow my horn, that the joy of the chase may arise; that the deer of Cromla may hear and start at the lake of roes.' The shrill sound spreads along the wood. The sons of heathy Cromla arise. A thousand dogs fly off at once, gray-bounding through the heath. A deer fell by every dog, and three by the white-breasted Bran. He brought them, in their flight, to Fingal, that the joy of the king might be great." [1]

David I. hunted the deer; he had a hunting house at Crail, in eastern Fifeshire, while localities in the vicinity, such as Kingsbarns and Kingsmuir, are evidently named in connection with the royal sportsman. Holyrood Abbey, if we are to believe a monkish legend, was founded by David to commemorate his deliverance from an infuriated stag, which, turning upon him in the chase, had almost dashed him from his horse.

In founding the Abbey of Paisley in 1160, Walter

[1] "Fingal," book vi.

the Stewart bestowed on the monks a tithe of his
hunting, with the skins of the deer slain in his forest
at Fereneze. William the Lion was an ardent sportsman. When hunting the stag at Kinghorn, Alexander
III. was, with his horse, precipitated from a cliff and
killed. In deer-hunting King Robert the Bruce had
been repeatedly balked by a white deer, which he
started among the Pentlands. At an assembly of his
nobles, he asked whether any dogs in their possession
could seize the game which had baffled his hounds,
whereupon Sir William St Clair of Roslin staked his
head that two of his dogs, Help and Hold, would kill
the deer before it crossed the March-burn. The
king accepted the offer, and in guerdon of success
pledged his forest of Pentland Muir. From an
eminence he witnessed the pursuit. Some sleuth-
hounds having startled the deer, Sir William slipped
his dogs. They gave keen pursuit, the dog *Hold*
seizing the stag in the March-burn, while *Help*, coming up, drove the creature back, and killed him on
the winning side of the stream. Embracing his
gallant baron, the king made him lord of the forest.
A similar legend, but of earlier date, is associated
with the origin of the Ducal House of Buccleuch.
Two brothers, natives of Galloway, had as disorderly
persons been exiled from that county. Familiar
with the chase, they settled at Rankleburn, in Ettrick
Forest, where their services were accepted by Brydone,

the royal keeper. Kenneth MacAlpine, who then held the sceptre, hunted in the forest soon afterwards. He pursued a buck from Ettrick cleuch to the glen now called Buckcleuch, near the junction of the Rankleburn with the Ettrick. Here the stag stood at bay, but the royal hunter and his followers were unable to proceed, owing to the steepness of the hill and a dangerous morass. One of the Galloway brothers now came up, and seizing the buck by the horns, threw the creature upon his shoulders, and bore it to the king. As his reward the sovereign granted him the name of Scott, and appointed him ranger of the forest.

In 1288 the sum of 56s. 10d. was paid by the Chamberlain to two park keepers and one fox hunter at Stirling. The practice of salting venison was familiar in the reign of David II. In 1330, the Chamberlain paid 24s. for "a chalder of large salt for salting the king's venison at Selkirk," and in the following year 16s. for salt to venison at Ettrick Forest. On the 12th March 1424 the first Parliament of James I. passed an Act for the preservation of deer-forests. The statute provides that

"The Justice Clerke sall inquire of stalkers, that slayis deare, that is to say, harte, hynde, doe and roe, and the halders and mainteiners of them; and als soone as ony stalker may be convict of slauchter of deare, he sall paie to the King, fourtie shillings: And the halders and mainteners of them sall paie ten poundes."

When James IV. was residing at Stirling Castle, and there entertaining guests, he despatched huntsmen to the hills of Kippen to procure venison. Several fine roes were brought down on the lands of Arnprior, possessed by Buchanan, a feudal chief. As the huntsmen were passing his fortalice, Buchanan seized the venison, and when the huntsmen remonstrated by claiming it for the king, Buchanan answered, "Tell your royal master that if he is king of Scotland, I am king in Kippen." With a highland laird who dared so to assert his feudal privileges, James resolved to be in amity. To Arnprior he proceeded unattended, and on reaching the gate, requested the porter to inform his master that a neighbouring king claimed an interview. Buchanan at once realized that the sovereign was at the gate, and so came forth with all humility to receive him. Explanations ensued, and Buchanan was invited to Stirling Castle to share in the royal hospitalities. This anecdote, derived from tradition, may be ascribed to the period immediately preceding the 30th April 1491, when, according to the Treasurer's Accounts, "the man of the Lard of Buchananis that brocht venyson to the king" received a payment of 9s.

For the reception of James V. and his queen, and of the Pope's ambassador, at a deer-hunt in the Forest of Athole, the Earl of Athole constructed a palace of green timber, interwoven with boughs, and provided with a moat, drawbridge, and portcullis. During the hunt, which lasted three days, 600 deer were captured. When the royal personages had departed, the palace was set on fire, since it was an honoured custom of the Highlands that a hunting lodge, graced by the presence of royalty, should afford accommodation to none of inferior station. On another occasion James V. summoned his barons to attend him to the hunting-field, with their horses and dogs, when no fewer attended than 800 persons, two-thirds of whom bore arms. In progress of the hunt 540 deer were slaughtered. During the reign of James V., messengers are by the Treasurer frequently recompensed for bearing to the Palace venison from different hunting-fields.

Queen Mary did not deem hunting an unwomanly sport. At Wemyss Castle in Fife, she first met Lord Darnley during the progress of a deer-hunt. In Mar Forest she frequently hunted. Professor William Barclay of Angers, who was in his youth attached to her court, has in his work in defence of monarchical government, described a hunt in the Forest of Athole which the Queen personally promoted. His narrative, translated from the Latin by Pennant, proceeds thus :—

"I had a sight of a very extraordinary sport. In the year 1563 the Earl of Athole, a prince of the blood-royal, had, with much trouble, and at vast expense, made a hunting match for the entertainment of our most illustrious and most gracious Queen. Our people call this a royal hunting. I was then a young man, and was present on the occasion. Two thousand Highlanders were employed to drive to the hunting ground all the deer from the woods and hills of Athole, Badenoch, Mar, Moray, and the countries about. As these Highlanders use a light dress, and are very swift of foot, they went up and down so nimbly, that in less than two months' time they brought together two thousand red deer, besides roes and fallow deer. The Queen, the great men, and a number of others were in a glen when all these deer were brought before them; believe me the whole body moved forward in something like battle order. This sight still strikes me, and will ever strike me, for they had a leader whom they followed close wherever he moved. This leader was a very fine stag, with a very high head. The sight delighted the Queen very much, but she soon had cause for fear, upon the Earl (who had been from his early days accustomed to such sights) addressing her thus :—'Do you observe that stag who is foremost of the herd? there is danger from that stag; for if either fear or rage should force him from the ridge of that hill, let every one look to himself, for none of us will be out of the way of harm, as the rest will all follow this one, and having thrown us under foot, they will open a passage to the hill behind us.' What happened a moment after confirmed this opinion; for the Queen ordered one of the best dogs to be let loose upon one of the deer. This the dog pursues; the leading stag was frightened, he flies by the same way he had come there; the rest rush after him, and break out where the thickest body of the Highlanders was. They had nothing for it now but to throw themselves flat on the heath, and to allow the deer to pass over them. It was told the Queen that several of the Highlanders had been wounded and that two or three were killed. The whole body would have escaped had not the Highlanders, by their skill in hunting, fallen upon a stratagem to cut off the roes from the main body. It was of those that had been separated that the Queen's dogs, and those of the nobility, made slaughter. There were killed that day three hundred and sixty deer, with five wolves and some roes." [1]

[1] See William Barclay's " De Regno et Regali Potestate adversus

From the "Accounts of the Thirds of the Abbey of Cupar" in 1563, we learn that the Comptroller debited himself with the sum of £124, 10s., 8d., as "the queinis maiesteis expenses in passage throucht Athoil from the huntes to Inuernes."

Alarmed at the spectacle of a naked sword, James VI. did not wince on seeing the hunter's knife. Deer-hunting was his favourite sport. From a hunt in the forest of Athole he had just returned in August 1582, when he experienced that detention at Ruthven Castle which is historically known as the Raid of Ruthven.

During his visit to Scotland in 1618, Taylor, the water poet, witnessed a great deer-hunt in the Forest of Mar, which he describes in these words:—

'The manner of the hunting is this. Five or six hundred men rise early in the morning, and disperse themselves divers ways, and seven, eight, or ten miles compass, they bring or chase in the deer, in many herds (two, three, or four hundred in a herd), to such or such a place, as the noblemen shall appoint them. Then when the day is come, the lords and gentlemen of their companies ride or go to the said places, sometimes wading up to the middle through burns and rivers; and then they, being come to the place, lie down on the ground, till those foresaid scouts, who are called the Finchel-men, bring down the deer. * * * * After we had stayed there three hours or thereabouts, we might perceive the deer appear on the hills round about us (their heads making a show like a wood), which being followed close by the Finchel, are chased down into the valley where we lay. Then

Buchananum, Brutum, Boucherium et reliquos Monarchomachos, Libri sex." Paris, 1600, 4to, pp. 279-80.

all the valley on each side being waylaid with a hundred couple of strong Irish greyhounds, they are let loose as occasion serves, upon the herd of deer. So that with dogs, guns, arrows, dirks, and daggers, in the space of two hours, fourscore fat deer were slain."

Prior to the reign of James I. deer might be stalked without any legal impediment; but as has been related, the first Parliament of James I. enacted in 1424 that "slayers of deer—namely, the hart, hind, doe, and roe," should forfeit 40s., and those who employed them the sum of £10. Further protective measures were passed in 1474, when it was ruled that those who killed deer in the time of snow should be amerced in £10. In 1551 "persons of whatsoever degree" were forbidden to kill deer under the pain of death and confiscation of movables. By a further statute passed in 1567, deer-slayers were, for the first offence, made liable to forty days' imprisonment; and for the second, to the loss of the right hand.

Of Scottish venatorial sports the further records are imperfect. During the sixteenth century and subsequently, clansmen proved their allegiance to their chiefs by accompanying them to the hunting-field. And summonses to kill venison not infrequently implied invitations to enterprises more daring. Border moss-troopers issued forth professedly to hunt deer, but in reality to drive off cattle and to plunder sheep-pens. Associated with a deer-hunt on the Cheviots is the old and popular ballad of " Chevy Chase." In August 1506, the Comptroller received 9s. from Sir Duncan Campbell of Breadalbane for four barrels, in which salted venison was sent to the King of Spain.[1]

When deer were disappearing from their lowland haunts, legislative measures were re-enacted to check their destruction. It was ruled by Parliament that from June 1682 venison be not bought or sold for seven years. Such restrictive measures proved wholly unavailing, for the expulsion of the deer became essential to husbandry even in its lower or primitive forms. For two centuries herds of deer have been found only in the uplands, or under covers artificially provided. In Mar Forest, and in the western parts of Ross and Sutherland, red deer are abundant. The roebuck is to be found in some of the western isles, also in that tract which extends from Ross-shire to Loch Lomond. But the head-quarters of deer-stalking are the Black Mount of Argyle, and the Royal Forest of Athole.

The destructive character of the fox was early recognized. By the Parliament of James II. in 1457, it was enacted that " quha ever he be that slays a fox and brings the hede to the scheref, lorde, barone or bailye, he sall have sixpence." On the 16th November 1552, David Ogilvy received from the abbot of

[1] Treasurer's Accounts.

Cupar a lease of certain lands at Glenisla, when he became bound to " nurice ane leiche of gud howndis, with ane cuppill of rachis for wolf and tod," and to be "reddy at all tymes quhene we charge thame to pas with ws or our bailzeis to the hountis." [1]   In subsequent leases of the monastery there were similar clauses.   For use in fox-hunting, a couple of greyhounds were to be kept on every considerable farm. In some districts a huntsman was salaried partly by the landowners, and partly by the tenants, the latter supplying him, in recompence, with farm produce. In addition to his salary, the huntsman received a special fee for every fox destroyed by his hounds. There was an annual fox - hunt, which continued several days.   On the occasion all the inhabitants, young and old, passed mirthfully into the fields.   In the district of Strathmore, in the county of Forfar, the yearly fox-hunt was, at the close of divine service, convened by the church beadle as the congregation retired from worship.   In reference to the practice, the Synod of Angus and Mearns, early in the eighteenth century, " charged kirk beadles against making any proclamations in the churchyard."

The marten, the otter and the wild cat abounded at an early period, and were hunted for their skins.   The marten, which latterly became rare, was a species of giant weasel, with a white or orange breast.   Pos-

[1] " Rental Book of Abbey of Cupar," ii., 107.

sessed of short limbs, it avoided its pursuers by a
succession of springs, and when hotly pressed, climbed
trees and sought refuge among the upper branches.
The marten made ravages in the poultry-yard, and
reared its young in the magpie's nest.   In summer
the otter lodges on small islets covered with rushes
or coarse grass, and by river banks, and during
winter obtains shelter in the rocks.   It was anciently
hunted for its fur, which, as an article of export, was
of considerable value.   In the reign of David II. the
custom " on ilk otyr " was by Parliament fixed at one
halfpenny ; the duty was subsequently increased.
The otter feeds chiefly on fish, and not rarely disputes
with the angler the landing of the trout secured by
his hook.   Capable of being domesticated, the creature
will bring fish to its protector, on being allowed a
liberal share of the supplies.   Otter hunting is
practised at night, and with a species of dog known
as the otter-hound.   The wild cat, like the otter,
frequents the banks of lochs and rivers ; also rocks
and corries.   In size resembling a well-sized dog, it is
of greater strength, and is remarkable for a long and
bushy tail.   The wild cat may hardly be tamed.
Quitting its lair chiefly at night, it prowls about with
cunning cautious step in quest of birds and other
prey.   The wild cat is hunted only by those keen
sportsmen who rejoice in desperate enterprises.

Hares and conies were anciently classed together

as denizens of the *cuningar* or rabbit-warren. Hares
were, from economic considerations, protected during the severities of winter. Thus in the year
1400 Parliament enacted that no one might hunt
hares in time of snow, under the penalty of 6s. 8d.
Royal warrens were protected so early as the reign of
Alexander II., trespassers being punished with death
and confiscation. In 1264 a salary of 16s. 8d. was
paid to the keeper of the warrens at Crail for a
year's service.[1] And in the reign of David II.
William Herwart obtained a charter in liferent of
the office of keeper of the king's muir in Crail and
of its "cuningare" or warren.[2] In 1358 Herwart
received as his yearly fee 40s.; he exercised his office
under the supervision of the Chamberlain.[3] In 1329
the Chamberlain made payment of 8s. to four men for
crossing to the Isle of May to catch rabbits.[4] In
the Rental Book of Cupar Abbey, a "warandar of
kunynzare," or keeper of the rabbit-warren, is named
in 1474. And in receiving from the abbey in 1475 a
life lease of two acres of the Grange of Keithock,
Gilbert Ra or Rae undertook to keep the "conyngar
fra all scaith and peryl, and promoofe and put that to
all profit at [h]is povar."[5] The tenants of the monas-

---

[1] " Exchequer Rolls," i., 4.
[2] Robertson's "Index of Charters," 57, 24.
[3] "Exchequer Rolls," i., 562.   [4] Ibid, 160.
[5] " Rental Book of Abbey of Cupar," i., 188, 203.

tery became bound to make report to the district
forester as to conies destroyed on their farms.

So early as the beginning of the fifteenth century,
the rarer feathered tribes were preserved to the sportsman, or rather to the sovereign and his court. In
1427 a law was passed that partridges, plovers, black
game, and muir-cocks be not killed from the beginning of Lent until August, under the penalty of 40s.
And in 1551 the shooting of wild-fowl was prohibited
under pain of death. It was ruled in 1555 that
partridges were not to be killed before Michaelmas,
under the penalty of £10, while barons and freeholders were empowered to severally enforce the
provision within their bounds. An Act was passed
in 1567, whereby it was provided that the shooting
of herons and "fowls of the revar" with gun or
bow be forbidden, under the penalty for the first
offence of forty days' imprisonment, with forfeiture
of movables.

In 1541 John Soutar in Millhorn was constituted
fowler of Cupar Abbey, when he became bound to
deliver to the cellarer of the monastery such fowls as
might be "slain" by himself or his assistants. In
remuneration he was to receive for a wild goose, 2s.;
for a crane or swan, 5s.; for a partridge, 8d.; and for
a plover, dottrel, curlew, wild duck, red-shank, lap-
wing, teal, and other small birds, 4d. each.[1]

[1] "Rental Book of Cupar," ii., 13.

Wild birds had materially diminished in number, when in 1621 an Act was passed forbidding all persons, save landowners, from destroying them. The Act was renewed in 1685. And in 1707 it was ruled by statute that no one should "kill, sell, or eat moorfowl from the 1st March till the 20th June, or partridges from the 1st March till the 20th August, under the penalty of twenty pounds."

Of ancient Scottish birds, one little known to fowlers and sportsmen was the capercaillie. By Lindsay of Pitscottie it is named in connection with the royal hunt, which in 1529 took place in the forest of Athole. The bird is also mentioned by James VI. in a letter to the Earl of Tullibardine, written in 1617; its existence is also denoted by Burt and Pennant. The original capercaillie became extinct before 1760, but in 1829 a pair were successfully introduced from Sweden into the forest of Braemar.

Falconry was a recognised English sport so early as the reign of Alfred in the ninth century, and it is the subject of a metrical treatise which is ascribed to Edward the Confessor. Localities in England for breeding hawks are mentioned in Domesday Book. The earliest notice of falconry in Scotland is associated with the following legend. The Danes had in one of their hostile incursions penetrated from Montrose to the vicinity of Perth, when at Luncarty they were met by Kenneth MacAlpine at the head of his army.

In the battle which ensued the centre of the Scottish army, under the king's command, was victorious, but the right and left wings were beaten and scattered. The fugitives got into a narrow lane, bounded by a bridge and a mud wall, where, with patriot intent, a farmer named Hay and his two sons, armed with spade and ploughshare, intercepted them, compelling their return to the scene of action. As in desperation they renewed the battle, the Danes, temporarily victorious, suspected a reinforcement and precipitately fled. By the king Hay was offered, in acknowledgment of timely service, as much land as a hound would course over in one heat, or across which a falcon would fly before resting. Hay, according to the legend, chose the latter, and thereby became owner of a vast territory, which accrued to his descendants.

Apart from legend, it is certain that falcons were held in high value so early as the reign of William the Lion. At this period Robert of Avenel bestowed on the abbey of Melrose his lands in Eskdale, reserving the eyries of the hawk, and when a dispute arose between his grandson Roger and the monks respecting the privileges of the monastery, it was ruled under royal authority that the monks might not lawfully destroy trees in which the hawk had an eyrie.[1]

[1] "Exchequer Rolls," i., 15, 24, 127, 511.

Alexander III. kept falcons at Forres, also at Dunipace. Shortly before his death King Robert the
Bruce had his falcon-house at Cardross repaired and
fenced. In 1342 John of the Isles, who had formerly
been in league with Edward Baliol, sent a gift of
falcons to David II. in token of respect or homage.
In the Public Accounts the goshawk and sparrow-
hawk are both named; but subsequent to the fourteenth century the peregrine was most in use. In
1489, James IV. despatched "Downy," one of his
falconers, to the English court, with a trained falcon
as a gift to Henry VII.[1] In 1496 the king's falconers
were recompensed for procuring hawks in the forest
of Athole ; also in Orkney and Shetland. Hawks had
their eyries at the Abbey Crag near Stirling,[2] also at
Craigleith, a summit of the Ochils, while the birds
there found were preserved at Craigforth, or in the
islet of Inchkeith.[3] But the more remarkable falcons
were obtained in the northern counties. Falcons
brought from the eyries of Caithness[4] James V. sent
as gifts to the King of France, to the Dauphin, and
to the Duke of Guise.

By James VI. falconry was keenly enjoyed. On
the 24th March 1626, the Treasurer - depute was

[1] " Treasurer's Accounts," i., Preface, ccxlix.
[2] Ibid., 177, 200, 275.
[3] Ibid., Preface, ccli.
[4] " Treasurer's Accounts," June to September 1539.

authorized by Charles I. to grant " the accustomed
allowances " to James Quarrier, " ane of our falconers
to have some haucks broght unto him from the
northerne parts of the kingdome." [1]   Writing in
1775, James Fea, an Orkney surgeon, remarks
that the Orcadian hawks " are the finest in the
world, insomuch that the king's falconer sends a
person annually to take them up, commonly in the
month of May, when they brood."   He adds : " From
time immemorial the king's falconer hath a perquisite
of an hen from every house in the country, originally designed for the maintenance of the king's
hawks." [2]

That hawking might, as a sport, be reserved to the
principal landowners, the Parliament of James IV.
ruled in 1594 " that no man . . . hawk . . . who
hath not a plough of land in heritage."   During the
sixteenth century, barons and knights were, when
unarmed, attended by falcons.   Hume of Godscroft
relates that when Mary of Lorraine was regent, she
urged the Earl of Angus to receive a royal garrison
into his castle of Tantallon, on which the earl looking
towards the goshawk on his wrist exclaimed, " You
greedy glede, you will never be full."   Hawks were
by the gentry borne to their places of worship, while

[1] " Earl of Stirling's Register of Royal Letters," i., 31.
[2] " The Present State of the Orkney Islands considered," by
James Fea . Holyroodhouse, 1775, 12mo, p. 21.

in making friendly visits gentlewomen carried merlins or sparrow-hawks upon their wrists.

Falcons were of high value.   For a trained bird James IV. paid £189 to the Earl of Angus, and in the reign of James VI. a pair of falcons was valued at £2000.   So long as the Dukes of Athole retained the depute sovereignty of the Isle of Man, they acknowledged fealty to the British throne by offering to the king at his coronation a pair of falcons.

In prosecuting his sport, the falconer rode on horseback, accompanied by young persons as runners, also by several dogs.   The king and nobles followed rapidly on foot.   The sport was attended with so much injury to grain that, in 1555, an Act was passed enjoining the discontinuance of the sport from spring till harvest.

The English falconers were Flemings ; those of Scotland were of Flemish descent.   The office of Grand Falconer of Scotland became hereditary in the family of Fleming of Barrochan.   From James IV. Peter Fleming received a hawk's hood, set in jewels, in acknowledgment of his having defeated the king's falcon with his tiercel ; the gift has been preserved in his family.   At the Scottish court four falconers constituted the usual staff.   A "depute-falconer" received a salary so recently as 1840, when Mr Marshall, who then held office, retired.

Archery, an early English sport, also a mode of

prosecuting vigorous warfare, was, prior to the battle
of Bannockburn, practised almost exclusively in the
chase.   But in 1318 it was ruled by the government
of King Robert the Bruce that, for the purpose of
defence, every person whose substance included possession of a cow should have a spear or a good bow
and   sheath   with   twenty-four   arrows. [1]   In 1363
David II. undertook to furnish three hundred archers
to the King of England, and in the same year Parliament consented to an arrangement whereby England,
in the case of invasion, might be helped by a company of sixty archers on the understanding that in the
event of attack, Scotland would with three hundred
bowmen be aided by her English neighbour.

In 1362 the Chamberlain paid 18s. 4d. for twelve
bows purchased by the king's order for John of
Lorn, and in 1368 a further payment was made for
twenty-one bows, to be kept at Stirling Castle for its
defence.[2]   When in 1424 James I. returned from his
long captivity he remarked that his subjects were, in
handling the bow, much inferior to the English.
Accordingly he caused to be enacted a Parliamentary
statute, which provided :

" That all men busk thame to be archars fra they be xij yeres
of eilde.   And that in ilk x lib worth of lande shal be maid bow-
merks and specialy ner paroche kirks quhar upone haly dais men
may cum, and at the lest schute thrise about and haif usage of

---

[1] "Acta Parl. Scot.," i. 474.   [2] Ibid., i. 496.

archary. And quha sa usis nocht said archary the lords of the
lande sal raise of him a wedder, and gif the lords raise not the said
payne the kingis treasurer or his ministers sall raise it to the
king." [1]

In ridicule of the prevailing awkwardness in the
use of the bow, James I., in his ballad of " Christis
Kirk," thus indulges his native humour :—

> " Ane bent a bow, sic sturt could steir him,
>   Great skayth wes'd to have scard him ;
> He chesit a flane as did affeir him ;
>   The toder said dirdum dardum ;
> Throw baith the cheikis he thocht to cheir him,
>   Or throw the erss have chard him,
> But be ane aker braid it came not neir him,
>   I can nocht tell quhat marr'd him
>   Thair,
> At Christis-Kirk on the grene that day.
>
> With that a freynd of his cryd Fy !
>   And up ane arrow drew ;
> He forgit it sa furiously,
>   The bow in flenderis flew ;
> Sa wes the will of God, trow I !
>   For, had the tre bene trew,
> Men said, that kend his archery,
>   That he had slane enow
>   That day."

Under the sanction of James II. Parliament enacted
in 1457 that—

" Wapinshawing be halden be the lords and baronys spiritual
and temporal four tymes in the yere. And that fut ball and golf
be utterly cryit doune and not usyt. And that the bowe marks

---

[1] " Acta Parl. Scot.," i. 6.

be maide at ilk paroch kirk, a pair of butts and schuting be usit ilk sunday. And that ilk man schut sex schotts at the list under the payne to be raisit upone thame that comes nocht at the list ; ijd. to be giffen to thame that cumis to the bow marks to drink. And this to be usit fra pasche till alhollomes efter, and by the next mydsomer to be reddy with all graith without failye." [1]

Subsequent to his marriage in 1503 to the Princess Margaret of England, James IV. promoted the practice of archery. His queen was an expert archer ; she shot a buck at Alnwick Park, in her northward progress. A narrative in relation to Queen Margaret's interest in the use of the bow is related by Lindsay of Pitscottie. To her son, James V., she was wont to boast of the superiority of her countrymen as archers, and at length to establish her contention she brought together representatives of the two countries, at a public competition. "There came," writes the chronicler :

" An ambassador out of England named Lord William Howard, with a bishop, and many other gentlemen, to the number of threescore horse, which were all able and waled men, for all kinds of games and pastimes, shooting, louping, running, wrestling, and casting of the stone, but they were well sayed [tried] ere they passed out of Scotland, and that by their own provocation ; but after they tint, till at last the Queen of Scotland, the King's mother, favoured the Englishmen, because she was the King of England's sister ; and therefore she took an enterprise of archery upon the Englishmen's hands, contrary her son the King and any six in Scotland that he would wale, either gentlemen or yeomen, that the Englishmen should shoot against them, either at pricks,

[1] " Acta Parl. Scot., ii. 48."

revers, or butts, as the Scots pleased. The King hearing this of his mother, was content, and quit her pawn a hundred crowns and a tun of wine, upon the English-men's hands, and he incontinent laid down as much for the Scottish-men. The field and ground was chosen in St Andrews, and three landed men and three yeomen chosen to shoot against the English-men : to wit, David Wemyss of that ilk, David Arnot of that ilk, and Mr John Wedderburn, Vicar of Dundee ; the yeomen, John Thomson in Leith, Stephen Taburner, with a piper called Alexander Bailie ; they shot very near, and warred the Englishmen of the enterprise, and won the hundred crowns and the tun of wine, which made the King very merry that his men won the victory." [1]

James V. presented silver arrows to the royal burghs, to which winners at the annual competitions were privileged to attach medals in memorial of their skill. These have disappeared, but substituted arrows belonging to Selkirk, Peebles, and Musselburgh, have been preserved. They are kept in the Archers' Hall, Edinburgh, and are in the towns to which they severally belong shot for periodically. The Mussel-burgh arrow bears medals from the year 1603. Queen Mary was an accomplished archer. In the society of Bothwell she indulged the sport of archery at Seton Palace two days after Darnley's murder. James VI. included archery among his "Sunday games." At St Andrews a portion of ground by the margin of the bay is known as *the Butts*. A locality at Peebles is so named. There is a Butts Well at the western base of Stirling Rock ; a small village which adjoins is named

[1] Lindsay's "Chronicles of Scotland," Edin., 1814, 8vo., p. 147.

Raploch, that is, the place of the bow. The old archery field at Stockbridge, Edinburgh, is now converted into recreation ground for the youth attending the higher schools.

Prior to the legislative revival of archery under James I., Robert, Duke of Albany, had despatched a body of archers to France to aid in the defence of the Dauphin against the formidable hostilities of Henry V. The Scottish archers under their captain, Alexander de Alexandry, numbered 300, and formed the principal contingent of that auxiliary force which, on the 17th May 1419, landed in France under command of Sir William Douglas, and at the battle of Beaugé restored supremacy to the House of Valois. Many members of the archers' company made settlements in France, these as a body receiving the name of the "Royal Scottish Guard." In the corps Scottish nobles sought enrolment, and in their turn drew to France many enterprising countrymen. During the regency of Mary de Medicis, widow of Henry IV., the Scottish Guard was exposed to insult. Making complaint to James VI., to whose sceptre they continued to adhere, he remonstrated successfully on their behalf. Charles I. also asserted their immunities and upheld their rights. When the Duke of Buckingham was sent in 1628 to Rochelle to aid the Huguenots against Cardinal Richelieu, a levy of two hundred Highland bowmen, under Alexander M'Naughton, proceeded to his assistance. But the duke's troops were driven back to their ships ere the bowmen had an opportunity of proving their skill.

During the fifteenth century the Scottish archers in France used a steel bow, two feet eight inches in length, two inches wide at the centre, and half an inch in thickness. They wore a close-fitting jacket of white cloth, spangled with silver gilt and embroidered with a crown in gold thread. Suspended from a white silver belt they carried a sword and a partisan, the staff of the latter being studded with golden nails. [1]

When the abbey of Kilwinning was founded in 1488, a company of archers was there established. Of this company the members practised point-blank archery, which consisted in shooting at butts twenty-six yards distant; also *papingo* archery, implying high skill. The papingo is the figure of a bird peculiar to heraldry. When used in archery it is carved in wood, and decked with party-coloured feathers; at Kilwinning it was fixed on the end of a pole, and placed in the steeple of the monastery. The archer who brought down the papingo was hailed "Captain of the Papingo;" he received a party-coloured sash, and was privileged to attach a silver medal to a silver arrow which was kept in memorial of skilful archery.

[1] "The Scots Men-at-Arms and Life Guards in France," 1418, 1830, by William Forbes-Leith, S.J., Edin., 1882, *passim*.

For the sash was substituted, in 1688, a piece of silver plate. An Archery Company, established at St Andrews in 1618, flourished till 1751, when it was discontinued. Three silver arrows, bearing seventy-nine medals, the property of the Company, are deposited in the University Museum. Among the medals are those bearing the names of the celebrated Marquis of Montrose; Archibald, the first Marquis of Argyll; and Charles, fifth Earl of Elgin, which last was appended in 1751.

The Royal Company of Archers (as successors to a community of archers who held competitions at Edinburgh early in the seventeenth century) were as a sodality constituted in 1676, and on the 6th March 1677 were sanctioned by the Privy Council. Discovered at the Revolution to be secretly disaffected, their assembling was disallowed; but having on the accession of Queen Anne appointed Sir George Mackenzie, Lord Tarbet, Secretary of State, their captain-general, they were reinstated in royal favour. From the Queen, on the 6th March 1704, they received a charter of incorporation, in which, among other privileges, they obtained the right of assembling with arms. They held no specific meeting till ten years later, but in 1714 when the state of the Queen's health suggested a further opportunity of abetting the exiled House, they met in Parliament Square, thence proceeding in a grand procession first to Holyrood Palace, afterwards to the butts at Leith. Subsequent to the Rebellion of 1715, in which not a few of the Royal Archers covertly joined, the corps did not reassemble till 1724, when in magnificent array they marched from Edinburgh to Musselburgh. On this occasion Allan Ramsay, the poet, was elected a member; with others he celebrated in verse the valour and patriotism of his associates. On the 10th June 1732 was enacted another celebration, the majority of those who took part in it being all but avowed Jacobites. Among them were the Earl of Kilmarnock and Sir Archibald Primrose of Dunipace, who, joining Prince Charles Edward in 1745, were in the following year convicted and executed as traitors. Another ardent Jacobite, connected with the corps, was James Oliphant of Gask, father of the gifted Baroness Nairne. Oliphant was an aid-de-camp to the Prince, and as such was forfeited. Subsequently pardoned and permitted to return to his estate, he was asked, on a revival of the corps, to supply a pattern for a new uniform, the old being lost. To the application he, in a letter dated " Gask, 6th November 1777," made the following answer :—

" Dr. Martin,—Few things could give me greater pleasure than to hear of the revival of the Royall Company of Archers ; it is a manly and agreeable amusement, and associats the best of the Kingdom together. I lose no time in acquainting you that my Archer's coat is still preserv'd, and shall be sent you Tuesday next by the carryer directed to your lodgings in Edinburgh. I desire you will make my compliments with it to whoever is Precess to the Company. I think myself happy to have it in my power to contribute my mite in forwarding a March, which I think is an appearance that does honour to our countrie; it is pretty odd if my coat is the only one left, especially as it was taken away in the Forty-six by the Duke of Cumberland's plunderers; and Miss Anny Graeme, Inchbrakie, thinking it would be regrated by me, went out to the court, and got it back from a soldier, insisting with him it was a lady's riding-habit, but puting her hand to the briches to take them too, he, with a thundring oath, asked if the lady wore briches ?   They had green lace, as the coat ; the knee buttons were more loose, to show the white silk puff'd as the coat sleeves. The Officers' coats had silver lace in place of green, with the silver fringe considerably deeper, fine white thread stockings, the men blue bonnets, the officers' were of velvet, with a plate japan'd of white iron, representing St Andrew, in the middle of a knot or cockade of, I think, green ribbons. An old embroidery of a former generation I have sent, in case it may be of use. The bonnet was tuck'd up and the St Andrew plac'd in the middle of the brow ; the bonnet rim watered with a green ribbon and tyed behind. The bonnets of a small size, to hold the head only, scrog'd before to the eyebrows ; the hair and wigs were worn in ringlets on the shoulders. The bow cases were linnen, with green lace like the coat, one on each side ending in silk tufts or tassels ; these were worn during the march, as sashes about the waist, and two arrows stuck in them—the bow carry'd slanting in the left hand. But I am probably mentioning circumstances that others will remember better than I ; therefore shall only add my hearty wishes for prosperity to Scotland, and the ancient Company of Archers." [1]

The effective restoration of the corps was diligently proceeded with, and on the 15th August 1776 was

[1] " The Jacobite Lairds of Gask," by T. L. Kington Oliphant, Esq. Grampian Club, 1870, 8vo, p. 386. The uniform of the laird of Gask is in a case exhibited in the Archers' Hall.

founded the Archers' Hall, near Hope Park End, in the fine dining-room of which are now represented portraits, by eminent artists, of the more distinguished members. Since Jacobite times pre-eminently loyal, the Royal Archers are the Sovereign's Body Guard for Scotland, and are allowed precedence even of the royal guards. One of the Queen's Body Guard, on her Majesty's first visit to Edinburgh in 1842, was Lawrence Oliphant of Gask, grandson of that James Oliphant who, a century before, had hazarded his life and fortune on behalf of the House of Stewart.[1]

As from the early use of the bow in securing human food arose the sport of archery, so on the primitive system of determining right by the ordeal of single combat were based the chivalrous practices of the joust and tournament. A joust was a combat between two armed knights; in the tournament the conflict was maintained between numbers on either side.

Tournaments were held by sovereign princes, who, through the instrumentality of a king-of-arms or his heralds, convened all persons of knightly rank, both native and foreign, to attend a meet for the clashing of weapons. Those summoned came forth in military array, their armorial bearings depicted on their shields and surcoats, also on the caparisons of their

[1] For further particulars see " The History of the Royal Company of Archers," by James Balfour Paul, Edinb., 1865, 4to.

horses. Each knight was preceded by an esquire, who in the right hand bore his spears, and carried with the left his helmet and crest. The tournament ground was enclosed with timber rails, defended by high-barred gates. As each knight reached the barrier he announced his arrival by sounding a trumpet, on which the heralds came forth to enter on the chivalric roll his name and arms. The knight then hung his shield upon the barrier.

As the hour of combat approached, each knight, traversing the field, chose from the different shields that of the knight with whom he preferred to combat ; he also signified his weapons by ringing with those selected on the shield of his opponent. By two pages who attended the shield, fantastically attired, the challenged knight was informed of his adversary's choice. The usual weapons were blunted lances and swords. And the combat which was commenced on horseback usually terminated on foot.

Whether at joust or tournament, each knight contended for the honour of a lady to whom he dedicated his prowess. And not infrequently the knights adopted as their heroines fair charmers whom they had not seen, and even married ladies in whom they could possess no personal interest. Tournaments were witnessed by dames and damsels of noble rank, who encouraged their favourites. The hero of the tournament received a prize from the Queen of

Beauty, a lady of high rank selected by the sovereign to preside.

So early as the reign of William the Lion tournaments were held at Edinburgh; but the authentic history of the sport does not commence till considerably later. The chamberlain's accounts for 1329 exhibit a payment of £6, 13s. 4d. to the sheriff of Edinburgh for constructing a jousting park in the vicinity. In his several tournaments David II. personally took part.[1] In his reign a tournament was attended with a sanguinary result. For in 1338, William, Lord Douglas, having expelled the English from Teviotdale, Henry of Longcastle, Earl of Derby, offered to engage him in single combat. Douglas, who accepted the challenge, was obliged to abandon it on account of a dangerous wound inflicted by the breaking of his own lance. Longcastle now summoned Alexander de Ramsay to appear at Berwick with twenty knights in armour, to be opposed by an equal number of the English chivalry. The tournament which ensued continued three days, while two combatants were slain on either side.[2]

In 1449 another tournament which issued fatally was, in the presence of James II., enacted at Stirling. On one side the combatants were two Burgundian knights, brothers, of the noble house of Lalain,

[1] "Exchequer Rolls," i., clxiii., 238, 493, 528, 531.
[2] Fordun's "Scotichronicon," ed. Goodal, xiii., c. 43.

and Sieur de Meriadet, Lord of Longueville ; on the other, three Scottish knights, two of whom were Douglases, and the third Sir John Ross of Halket. Commencing with the lance, the combatants speedily abandoned it for the battle-axe. One of the Douglases being now mortally wounded, the king threw down his gauntlet, thereby arresting the combat. The Earl of Douglas, brother of one of the combatants, had led the Scottish champions to the lists at the head of 5000 followers.

For "jousts, tournaments, and other games," James II., on the 13th August 1456, granted to the burgh of Edinburgh a portion of ground at Craigingelt Well, afterwards Greenside. Tournaments at Edinburgh were also practised near the King's Stables, under the wall of the Castle. On the 4th April 1618, Robert Scott was served heir to his brother in the King's Stables, Edinburgh, "with the office of observing the tournament, and a piece of green land at the West Port." At Stirling, tournaments were conducted in "the valley," a level hollow on the castle rock.

At Stirling James IV. frequently assembled his barons for the sport of jousting ; on each successful combatant he bestowed a lance mounted with gold. Early in 1495-6, he removed from Stirling to Edinburgh, where, in honour of the marriage of his guest, Perkin Warbeck, the alleged Duke of York, which took place on the 13th January, he held a series of tournaments. In the lists the king seems to have sustained an injury, for which a "mittane," a bandage of silk, and a sling of taffeta were provided. Warbeck's "spousing goune" of white damask was presented by the king ; also tournament dresses for himself, his six servitors, his two trumpeters, and his armourer.[1]

Among the military spectacles which, in 1503, under the direction of James IV., followed the reception of his queen, the Princess Margaret of England, were a series of tournaments held at Edinburgh. At these demonstrations attended the border chiefs, many of whom contended with each other so violently that the victor left his opponent lifeless on the field.

As a promoter of tournaments, James V. imitated his royal father. In his reign many tournaments were conducted. On these occasions knights from foreign parts challenged the skill of Scottish nobles, while the conflicts were disputed so warmly that the king had to interpose to prevent bloodshed. The death, in 1559, of Henry II. of France, consequent on his eye being pierced by the Count de Montgommeri, in a joust at Paris, gave a check to these chivalrous sports. A species of jousting was renewed at Stirling in August 1594, at the baptism of Prince Henry.

In connection with the tournament was instituted

---

[1] "Treasurer's Accounts," i. 263.

"the Round Table;" it existed in the reign of Stephen in the twelfth century, and a century later, under the rule of Henry III., was fully established. During the reign of Edward I., in 1280, Roger de Mortimer established a Round Table at Kenilworth, where, in connection with military pastimes, he entertained a hundred knights and an equal number of gentlewomen. To the Kenilworth Round Table many foreign knights were attracted by the splendour of the hospitality. In 1344, Edward III. convened a grand tilting at Windsor, which was commenced by a Round Table feast, and was continued for a week. The festivities of the Round Table were followed by the institution of the Garter, an order which, in its arrangements, symbolizes the usages of the tournament.

When, in 1424, James I. established his residence at Stirling, he there constructed a Round Table on the model of that at Windsor. The Tables at Windsor and Kenilworth embraced a circular area each two hundred feet in diameter; the diameter of the Table at Stirling is twenty-five feet. By H. M. Board of Works, in 1867, on the suggestion of the present writer, the Stirling "Round Table" was restored to its original condition; the form is octagonal.

Associated with ancient tilting was the knightly pastime of running at the ring. To a tall post, placed upright in the soil, was attached an iron rod or arm, upon which, by two springs, was suspended an iron ring, which, by the force of a stroke, might readily be borne off. Competitors mounted on horseback, and each bearing a lance of light wood, started in succession from a point about one hundred yards from the post, while all riding at full speed endeavoured to bear off the ring upon their lances. By the Stewart kings, the chapmen of Stirling, who on horseback bore their goods to the surrounding country, were privileged to practise this regal sport; hence the recreation is locally remembered as "the chapmen's sports." These sports were also conducted on the "green" at Leslie in Fife, the scene of James I.'s ballad of "Christis Kirk."

A patriotic effort to revive the ancient tournament was made by Archibald-William, thirteenth Earl of Eglinton. On Wednesday, the 28th August 1839, this enterprising nobleman assembled at Eglinton Castle a number of distinguished persons, by whom chivalrous sports and pastimes were conducted for three days, and with a splendour befitting a revival of ancient jousting. At the Eglinton Tournament were worn dresses of the reigns of Henry VIII. and Elizabeth, but several knights were attired in the old costumes of France and Spain. As Queen of Beauty, Lady Seymour wore a coronet of jewels, a jacket of ermine, and a skirt of violet velvet, with

the front of sky-blue velvet, on which in silver
was embroidered her family shield. Prince Louis
Napoleon, afterwards Emperor of the French, who
was present, wore a polished steel cuirass over a
leathern jacket, trimmed with crimson satin; a steel
vizored helmet, with a high plume of white feathers,
buckskin breeches, and russet boots. On the second
day ten knights engaged in conflict, among whom were
the Marquis of Waterford, the Earl of Eglinton, Lord
Glenlyon, afterwards sixth Duke of Athole, the Earl
of Craven, Lord Alford, and Sir Francis Hopkins.
A combat with broadswords between Prince Louis
Napoleon and Mr Lamb, an English gentleman, was
on both sides admirably sustained. On the third
day, an equestrian melée with broadswords was conducted by the Scottish and Irish knights against the
knights of England. Grand festivities closed the
pageant.

The *wapinschaw*, or weapon-show, was established
by Edward I. under " the statute of Winchester ; "
and from an extant fragment of early Scottish law, in
which the " Book of Wyntoun " or the Winchester
" lawes " is quoted, it would appear that the periodical exhibition of arms in Scotland had been derived
from the southern practice. By the Scottish statute
it is provided that every male between the ages of
sixteen and sixty shall provide himself with arms,
according to the extent of his lands or goods. The

possessor of land of the value of £15, or of goods of forty merks value, was called on to keep a horse and provide himself with a hauberk, an iron helmet, a sword, and a dagger.   A landowner with a rental not under forty nor above one hundred shillings was required to equip himself with a bow, arrows, and a dagger.   And he whose lands or goods were under the value of forty shillings was required to keep, instead of a dagger, a " gysarnis " or hand-axe.   Common persons were each to possess a bow and arrows, and all sojourning in the forest a bow and pike or bolt for a cross-bow.   By the same statute it is provided that wapinschaws be held twice a year.[1]

Assigning the adoption in Scotland of the Winchester statute to the reign of Alexander III., it would appear that for one hundred and fifty years after the first introduction, shows of arms had been discontinued.   But in 1424 Parliament enacted that "wapinschaws" be held four times a year in each shire, while in 1425 the practice was extended to burghs.[2] By the Parliament of James II., in 1456, it was ruled that " wapinschaws be made in the morning after the lawe daye after Yule,"—those who attended without being properly armed being amerced in penalties.   By the same Act it was provided that wapinschaws were to be continued monthly.[3]   In

[1] " Acta Parl. Scot.," i. 752.
[2] Ibid., ii. 10.   [3] Ibid., ii. 45.

1475 the tenants of the Cupar Abbey became bound to provide themselves with arms for the national defence, including " jakkis " [leathern coats], " hattis and splentis " [plated armour for the head and legs], " bowis and schawis " [bows and arrows], and " swurdis, bukklaris and aksys " [swords, bucklers, and axes]—all of which were to be held in readiness for display at the district wapinschaws.[1]

In prospect of an invasion by the English, it was ruled in 1481 that a wapinschaw be held every fifteen days.[2]   Two years later, sheriffs were required to make a return as to the number of fencible persons within their jurisdictions, and to inform the Court where they held wapinschaws, that the king might provide suitable inspectors.[3]   When, on the 20th November 1495, James IV. received at Stirling Perkin Warbeck, he commanded the several sheriffs to hold wapinschaws in compliment to his guest as well as in token of his being ready to afford him military support.[4]   In 1503 a statute was passed authorising the holding of wapinschaws on the 15th June and 20th October of each year.[5]   When in 1540 shows of arms had long been out of use, sheriffs and bailies were authorised to appoint captains in the

---

[1] " Rental Book of Cupar," I., xxxii. 194-6, 199, 200.
[2] " Acta Parl. Scot.," ii. 139.   [3] Ibid., ii. 164.
[4] " Treasurer's Accounts," I., cxxvi. 267.
[5] " Acta Parl. Scot.," ii. 365.

several parishes to train those bearing arms the mode of using them; this training was to be continued during the months of May, June, and July.[1] In 1574 a display of arms was decreed to be held on the 20th July and the 10th October, while on each occasion the nobility and landowners were to be horsed and harnessed, and others were to display their habergeons.

When in August 1617, James VI. made a state visit to Dumfries, he presented to the magistrates a small silver gun, mounted on a wheeled carriage, that it might be competed for as a prize at the annual wapinschaws. But periodical exhibitions of arms had now become rare, May-day sports having generally taken their place. Along with these sports, possession of the silver gun, was, at Dumfries, the subject of an animated competition, and the local poet, John Mayne, in his "Siller Gun," has graphically described the merriment with which it was associated. Proceedings commenced with a procession of the traders, which by the poet is thus described :—

> "As through the toun the banners fly,
> Frae windows low, frae windows high,
> A' that could find a neuk to spy
>   Were leaning o'er :
> The streets, stair-heads, and carts forbye
>   Were a' uproar.

[1] "Acta Parl. Scot., ii. 362-3.

Frae rank to rank, while thousands hustle
In front, like waving corn, they rustle;
Where, dangling like a baby's whistle,
The Siller Gun,
The royal cause o' a' this bustle,
Gleam'd in the sun."

May-day diversions included athletic sports and some quaint practices. "Tossing the kebar" was a favourite pastime, as were "casting the bar" and "throwing the hammer." "Climbing the greasy pole" never failed to excite hearty laughter. The performers sought to secure a leg of mutton by ascending a smooth round pole, rendered slippery by greasing. Increasing in ardour by each defeat, some one at length bore off the prize amidst noisy plaudits.

"Hurling a wheel-barrow blindfolded" was a favourite recreation, owing to the difficulty of reaching the right spot; a longer step being taken with the right than the left foot, every performer inclined to turn to the left, some actually describing a circle, and so returning to the place whence he started.

"The sack-race" excited much humour. Each competitor stepped into a corn-sack, which was made fast about his neck, his uncovered head alone escaping the ludicrous disguise. Each started at a preconcerted signal, and by vigorous effort sought to reach the goal first. But in the course of a few seconds half the competitors were *hors de combat*, while their useless struggles to resume an upright posture caused intense mirth. With those who in a rollicking fashion speeded onward, the race-course was ere long strewn at intervals. Not infrequently, all the competitors became prostrate and failed to reach the goal. By Dr William Tennant in his poem of "Anster Fair," the awkward evolutions of the sack-runners have been humorously described. Thus :—

" So leap'd the men, half sepulchred in sack,
    Up-swinging with their shapes be-monstring spy,
And cours'd in air a semicircle track
    Like to the feath'ry-footed Mercury;
Till, spent their impetus, with sounding thwack,
    Greeted their heels the green ground sturdily ;
And some, descending, kept their balance well,
Unbalanc'd some came down, and boisterously fell."

May-day sports have ceased, yet the national games, including bagpipe competitions and highland dancing, are conducted on the annual holidays and at the national gatherings. Among the more remarkable gatherings for the practice of public sports are the "Northern Meeting" at Inverness, and the great annual " Gathering " at Braemar. A yearly celebration at Innerleithen was formerly noted.

Of the Scottish game of golf the precise origin is unknown. In 1457 the Parliament of James II. passed an Act prohibiting the game, and recommending archery in its stead. The prohibition proceeded on the plea that the practice of golfing might render the people effeminate. In the reign of James VI. it was a common pastime. Along with the members of his court James practised golf at Blackheath, in Kent. During his visit to Scotland, in 1641, Charles I. played daily on the links of Leith. There, too, James VII., when Duke of York, indulged the pastime; he played so skilfully that he excelled all competitors save one Paterson, a shoemaker, by whom he was frequently overcome. When at length he could excel the leather worker, his satisfaction was intense.

Golf has a Teutonic origin ; the word is derived from the German *kolbe*, in low Dutch pronounced *kolf*, and which signifies the *game of the club*. It is played with a club and ball—the club being nearly four feet long and laden with lead ; the ball about the size of an egg, and composed of stout leather stuffed with feathers. Golf is played on *links* or tracts of sandy soil covered with short grass. Suitable golfing links exist at Prestwick, Musselburgh, North Berwick, Carnoustie, and Montrose. But the chief place of play is at St Andrews. In that city was established, in 1754, a society or club which on its roll has included the principal nobility. The St Andrews golf club meets in May and October, when competitions are conducted with a befitting ceremonial. At the close of each general competition the victors are saluted by the discharge of ordnance.

The rules of the St Andrews' club regulate other golfing societies throughout the country.

Shinty, a primitive description of golf, and not improbably its pioneer, is played with a small hard ball of wood or leather, impelled by a piece of bent timber or club. A boundary is marked on the soil, beyond which each competitor endeavours to drive his ball so as to out-distance his opponent.

The game of bowls, a product of the middle ages, has in Scotland been traced to the thirteenth century; a bowling-alley or bowling-green was attached to every manor-house. During the eighteenth century the game was practised generally, a public bowling-green being constructed in the principal hamlets. In 1769 a Society of Bowlers at Edinburgh obtained from the Governors of Heriot's Hospital a lease of ground for a public bowling-green.

Tennis, a favourite English sport, was, under the name of "catchpel," played by James IV. and his successors. The Duke of York, in 1680, constructed a Tennis Court at Holyrood Palace, near the Water Gate. John Law of Lauriston, the celebrated financier, was noted as a tennis-player.

Quoits, a game common in the south, was introduced to Scotland by James I. In an exchequer account rendered at Stirling on the 10th December 1364, the sum of £17, 12s. is allowed to Adam Thore, burgess of Edinburgh, for thirteen silver quoits and six salt cellars supplied for the king's use.[1] A native of Alva, named Rennie, was, about thirty years ago, declared champion of British quoit players.

In both kingdoms football was practised at a remote period. In order to the progress of archery, Edward III., in 1349, prohibited football to his subjects, and for the same cause it was denounced by the first Parliament of James I. A prohibitory statute of the 26th May 1424 proceeds thus—

" That na man play at the fute-ball, under the paine of fiftie schillings to be raised to the lord of the land, als oft as he be tainted, or to the Schireffe of the land or his ministers, gif the lordes will not punish sik trespassoures."

Though this provision remained unrepealed, James IV. personally indulged the sport.[2] On the 18th June 1601, the Privy Council had under consideration the subject of a quarrel which at a football match at Lochtoun in the Merse had occurred between Cockburn of that Ilk and two of his brothers on the one side, and James Davidson of Burnierig and his brother. The quarrel had been attended with pistol shooting and other violence.[3]

Football was included among the Sunday games which, in 1618, were prescribed by James VI. as

[1] " Exchequer Rolls," ii., 166.

[2] "Treasurer's Accounts," I. ccliv. 330.

[3] " Reg. of the Privy Council," vi. 262.

" lawful to be observed." During the eighteenth
century it was common in the northern and southern
provinces, also in the central counties. In Aberdeenshire the able-bodied men of every hamlet enjoyed
their usual " ba' playing," the inhabitants of one
parish challenging those of another. The game was
usually played in the village churchyard, while forty
competitors would ordinarily enter on either side.
In the " Monymusk Christmas Ba'ing," a humorous
poem, composed after the manner of James I.'s ballad
of " Christis Kirk," Mr John Skinner has effectively
depicted the coarse rough wrestling associated with
the sport. Writes the reverend bard :—

> " The hurry-burry now began,
>   Was right weel worth the seeing,
> Wi' routs and raps frae man to man,
>   Some getting and some gi'eing ;
> And a' the tricks of fut and hand
>   That ever was in being ;
> Sometimes the ba' a yirdlins ran,
>   Sometimes in air was fleeing,
>   Fu' heigh that day."

The ball might not be touched with the hand after
it had been cast upon the field. An opponent might
be tripped when near the ball, especially if he was
about to hit it with the foot, but a competitor could
not be laid hold of, or otherwise interfered with when
at a distance from the ball. The party who, out of
three rounds, hailed the ball twice, was proclaimed

victor. At Scone a game of football was played annually on Shrove Tuesday, the combatants being the married men and the single. Commenced at two o'clock, it was continued till sunset. The object of the married men was to put the ball in "the dool," a small hole in the green, while the unmarried sought to cast it into the river Tay which flows near. The party who could effect either of these objects the greater number of times was proclaimed victor.

Football sports much prevailed on the Scottish Border. Under sanction of the Duke of Buccleuch and the Earl of Home, a great match took place in the year 1815, at the junction of the Ettrick and Yarrow, between the shepherds of Ettrick and the burgesses of Selkirk; the former being led by the Ettrick Shepherd, the burgesses by their Provost. Of the three games which were determined upon, the first was gained by the burgesses, the second by the shepherds. But the third game was undecided, and terminated in confusion.

Curling, a game pre-eminently Scottish, is played upon the ice, on an open space which is called the rink. Originally played with smooth round stones taken from the strands of rivers, it was called the sport of the *channel-stane*. At Christmas 1565, Lord Darnley prosecuted the game at Peebles on a flooded meadow, which now forms part of the minister's glebe. In 1840, in the course of draining a marsh near Dunblane, the workmen dug up a curling stone, on which may be traced the date of 1551 ; it is undressed, further than in presenting two holes to which a handle had been attached. Curling stones were ⁄originally fashioned with the hammer and chisel, small niches being scooped out for inserting the fingers and thumb. Such stones were in the eighteenth century used in the more secluded districts.

Curling is noticed in the "Muses Threnodie" of Henry Adamson, published in 1638, while William Guthrie, who in 1644 was ordained minister of Fenwick, is in his memoirs. described as "fond of the innocent recreations which prevailed, among which was playing on the ice." In 1684 it is in his "Scotia Illustrata" mentioned by Sir Robert Sibbald; also in the "Description of the Orkney Isles," published in 1693 by the ingenious Mr James Wallace, minister of Kirkwall. [1] Early in the eighteenth century, the magistrates of Edinburgh, when frost had set in, yearly marshalled a procession, and, preceded by a band of music, opened the winter sports. These were conducted at the North Loch, near the present

[1] An allusion in Wallace's "Orkney" as to stones suitable for curling being found in the isle of Copinsha was, in 1695, quoted by Bishop Gibson in his translation of Camden's "Britannia," and in consequence some writers on the game have erroneously set forth that it is mentioned by the illustrious topographer in his original work.

Waverley Railway Station ; also on a sheet of water at Canonmills.

In 1795, when the Duddingston Curling Club was instituted, the Edinburgh magistrates headed a curling procession every frosty day to the Loch, returning in the evening in similar order. There are at present 300 provincial clubs, holding of the "Royal Caledonian Club," a central association which meets at Edinburgh. Under the direction of this representative body, several "Grand Matches" have been conducted. Of these, the first was, on the 15th January 1847, held at Penicuik. In 1853 a great curling pond was by the Caledonian Club constructed at Carsebreck, in Perthshire, on which have since been played five great national matches. The "roaring game," as curling is familiarly called, has been poetically celebrated by Allan Ramsay, Sir Alexander Boswell, James Hogg, Dr Henry Duncan, and Dr Norman Macleod ; it has also been mentioned by Burns. Writing in 1715, the poet-physician, Dr Alexander Pennecuik writes of the game not inappropriately :

> " It clears the brain, stirs up the native heat,
>   And gives a gallant appetite for meat."

The modern curling-stone is of a flattish, round form, weighing from thirty to forty-five pounds; it is provided with a moveable handle.[1]

[1] For a full account of the game, see " Curling : The Ancient Scottish Game," by James Taylor, D.D., Edin. 1884, 8vo.

Prior to the twelfth century, horses were used solely for riding. During the reign of William the Lion a statute was passed providing " that everyone who possessed landed or moveable property should keep at least one horse for use in the public service." Early in the thirteenth century Roger Avenel kept a stud in the valley of Eskdale. In preparing for his departure to the Holy Land, Patrick, Earl of Dunbar, sold, in 1247, to the monks of Melrose, his stud of brood mares, kept in Lauderdale. By Alexander III. a stud of horses was maintained at different stations.[1] In 1327 Randolph, Earl of Moray, made an incursion into England at the head of 20,000 cavalry.

Prior to the reign of James I. the exportation of horses was unlawful, but by that sovereign the sal of horses in England was encouraged as a matter of commerce. In 1359 a passport was obtained by Thomas Murray, *Dominus de Bothwell,* and Alan, second son of William, fifth Lord Erskine, to enable them to proceed to England with horses for sale. By James II. horses were imported from Hungary, while James IV. added to his stud by transacting with dealers in Spain and Poland. On receiving a present of valuable horses from Louis XII., James IV. sent him in return four of his best amblers. In his reign, horse-racing was instituted as a royal pastime. On the 15th April 1503 Thomas Boswell paid

[1] Innes's " Scotland in the Middle Ages," p. 131.

at Leith 18s. to the boy that " ran the Kingis hors." [1]   And on the 2d of May following, David Doule was paid by the Treasurer 28s., which " he won from the king on hors rynning." [2]

Much interested in horsemanship, James V. kept a great stud, and sent his grooms to Sweden, there to procure the best horses.   In token of affection, his uncle, Henry VIII., presented him with a valuable stud.   Upon his Master of the Horse he bestowed a landed estate, and approved horse-racing as one of the royal sports.   During the reign of Queen Mary district horse-races were instituted.   In 1552 an annual horse-race was established at Haddington, the winning prize being a silver bell.   The silver bell competed for at the Lanark races probably belongs to this period.   To this bell, which is $4\frac{1}{2}$ inches in length and $4\frac{1}{2}$ inches at greatest diameter, are attached seventeen shields inscribed with the names of the winners.   The oldest shield bears the name of " Sir Iohne Hamilton of Trabio," with the date 1628.

During the reign of James VI. horse-races were established in the principal centres.   In 1608 the Town Council of Paisley appointed an annual horse-race, voting a silver bell for the winning horse.   At Cupar-Fife a horse-race was established in 1621, at which a large silver cup of the value of £18 formed the chief prize.   In that year Parliament enacted that

[1] " Treasurer's Accounts."   [2] Ibid.

at horse-racing no person should be allowed to win more than one hundred merks, the surplus to be given to the poor.

The national frenzy which attended the Restoration culminated in a keen renewal of racing and feats of horsemanship. From the announcements in *Mercurius Caledonius* we derive that horse-racing was in 1661 actively revived. During the same year appeared at Edinburgh these two notifications :—

" The Horse Race of Lanark instituted by King William about 600 years since,[1] but obstructed these twenty-three years by the iniquity of the times, is now restored by Sir John Wilkie of Foulden, as being loath so antient a foundation should perish, and for that effect he hath given *gratis* a piece of plate of the accustomed value, with a silver bell and saddle, to the second and third horse; it is to be run the third Tuesday in May."

" The Race of Haddington is to be run on the 22d of May next; the prize is a most magnificent cup. This same antient town, famous for its hospitality, has many times sadly smarted by the armies of enemies, yet this glorious revolution hath salved up all their miseries, as very well was made appear by the noble entertainment given to the Lord Commissioner at the Lord Provost, William Seaton, his lodging, when his Grace made his entry to this kingdom." [2]

The impulse to horse-racing which obtained at the

[1] A veneration for things ancient, a leading trait of the national character, was largely utilised to their personal advantage by the Stewart kings, also by their abettors. The Lanark bell prize is apparently of the reign of Queen Mary; it certainly does not belong to a period antecedent to the reign of James IV.

[2] From " Edinburgh's Joy for his Majesties Coronation in England," a rare tract in the Advocates Library.

Restoration widely predominated. On the 15th April 1662 the Town Council of Dumfries ordered their treasurer to provide "a silver bell, four ounces in weight," as a prize to be run for, every first Tuesday of May, "by the work-horses of the burgh according to the ancient custom." Two years later the same Town Council voted "a silver cup of forty ounce weight or therby" to be run for at the ordinary course within the burgh, "by the horses of such noblemen and gentlemen as were duly entered for the race."[1] On the 23d February 1663 the Town Council of Peebles voted a silver cup to be run for annually on May-day. In the hope of propitiating the royal favour similar donations and honours to the riders of swift horses were voted by other burghs. The worst consequences followed. At these celebrations congregated idle and dissolute persons bent on mischief, while scenes of strife were so common that it became a proverb that all who had variances reserved their settlement till the race-day. Even owners and riders of horses did not forbear rude conflict. At Haddington, in connection with the races, the burgh carters prosecuted, a sport so utterly inhuman as wholly to demoralize all who might engage in it. By a local writer it is thus described :

"A cat was confined in a dryware cask containing soot, and ung at the end of a beam fixed to the top of the cross. Each

Chambers's " Domestic Annals, i., 411.

rider was armed with a wooden mell, and rode at full speed under the barrel, and gave it a blow with his mell, which operation was continued until the barrel was staved. The poor frightened cat on its release was pursued by the assembled crowd, and was very often trampled to death. The magistrates felt it their duty to put a stop to this barbarous custom; but the carters, as long as their 'play' existed, continued to ride their 'Bassies' for three times in a circle opposite the cross." [1]

Horse-racing had as a national sport become extremely degraded, when an attempt to effect its purification was made at a period when arose a strong desire to dissociate the national revels from political discontent upon the one hand, and a coarse licentiousness upon the other. On the 2d August 1777 was instituted, under the auspices of the Dukes of Hamilton, Buccleuch, Roxburgh, and Gordon, and other persons of high rank, a racing society, designated the Hunters' Club, but of which, on the 9th January of the following year, the name was changed to the Caledonian Hunt.

The membership of the hunt, restricted at the outset to forty-five, was afterwards increased to eighty, and in 1849 was fixed at seventy. The entry-money, at first a guinea, was in 1818 raised from five guineas to forty. The annual subscription, originally five, was in 1814 fixed at ten guineas. The dining hour was four o'clock until 1832, when it was altered to half-past five; in 1858 it was changed to seven. From

[1] Martine's " Reminiscences of Haddington," p. 100.

the commencement the members used their own wine, allowing " a corkage " to the innkeeper. The cost of dinner, at first half-a-crown, was in 1808 increased from 5s. to 7s. 6d. Convivial excess was discountenanced, and gambling, under a heavy penalty, was prohibited. At the first meeting, which took place at Haddington in October 1778, proceedings continued two weeks, but subsequent to 1816 the yearly races were restricted to a single week. When the first race was instituted at Kelso in 1779, the length of race was fixed at four miles; it was subsequently ruled to consist of " three four-mile heats." The weight to be carried was in July 1782 increased from ten to twelve stones. The original riding costume was a red hunting frock, and a green cape, with a horn fixed to one of the button holes; but in 1818 every member was called on to provide two coats, one being the original uniform, the other a scarlet. double-breasted coat, with flaps for pockets, and seven buttons, bearing a fox and a thistle, attached to each side. In 1822 a member was, on account of having on his coat only five buttons, amerced in a penalty.

The Hunt was eminently beneficent. On the 10th January 1787 was framed the following minute :—

" A motion being made by the Earl of Glencairn, and seconded by Sir John Whitefoord, in favour of Mr Burns of Ayrshire, who had dedicated the new edition of his poems to the Caledonian Hunt : The Meeting were of opinion that in consideration of his superior merit, as well as of the compliment paid to them, that Mr Hagart [the Secretary] should be directed to subscribe for one hundred copys in their name, for whch he should pay to Mr Burns Twenty-Five Pounds upon the Publication of his Book."

At this time the Hunt numbered not more than sixty members, so that the copies subscribed for were very considerably in excess of those required for actual use. Nor had the poet's inscription of his volume been actually carried out, for the dedication is dated the 4th April 1787, or nearly three months subsequent to the Hunt's act of subscribing.

True to patriotic traditions, the Caledonian Hunt has continued to exercise a strong benevolence. To their musician, the famous Nathaniel Gow, they, in 1798, presented ten guineas beyond his ordinary recompense, while in 1807 they resolved that for performing at their balls he should receive a stated yearly salary of twenty guineas. When, in 1827, he had become aged, and "quite unable to attend the meetings," they granted him an annuity of fifty pounds, and resolved to patronize a ball to be given for his benefit. After his death in 1833, they, in the Greyfriars' churchyard, erected a monument to his memory.

After long service, other officers were pensioned, and benefactions voted to their widows. In 1780 they granted one hundred guineas to the Charity

Workhouse of Edinburgh, and twenty guineas to the Dispensary at Kelso. When in 1793 a fire occurred during their meeting at Kelso, they gave £50 towards the relief of the sufferers. About the same time they voted fifty guineas for the army abroad. To the Patriotic Fund in 1854 they contributed £100, and they each year give a sum not exceeding £100 in charity in and around the place where their annual race meeting takes place.

In 1811, on the motion of Mr Boswell of Auchinleck, afterwards Sir Alexander Boswell, a narrative of the proceedings was prepared, and in 1865 it was resolved that the likenesses and signatures of members should be preserved. The " King's Hundred," which, in 1788, the Hunt received from George III., has since been continued from year to year, and this token of royal approval has largely tended to perpetuate the institution. Members are admitted by ballot.

As a mode of subsistence, angling in the lakes and rivers was familiar to the early Britons. By David I. fisheries were, as a source of wealth, zealously promoted ; and it was an ordinance of his reign that from Saturday evening till Monday at sunrise, angling should be foreborne. During the reign of William the Lion, the abbot of Holyrood sent his men to the herring fishery off the Isle of May, where, as a station, the fishing-boats usually assembled.

Under the government of Alexander III. considerable fisheries were established, both on the coast and upon inland waters. Estuaries yielded salmon, lamprey, and the royal sturgeon ; the lochs produced eels and trout ; and from the various inlets on the western coast were procured vast stores of excellent herring.[1]

To the abbot and monks of Cupar, King Robert the Bruce granted, in May 1327, the privilege of fishing for salmon in the river Tay, at times prohibited by statute. A payment of 57s. 1d. was made by the Chamberlain for two chalders and twelve bolls of large salt for salting six hundred salmon, with the carriage thereof.[2] By a statute passed in the year 1400, the killing of salmon from the Feast of the Assumption of the Virgin till Martinmas was prohibited under the penalty of 100s., while for a third offence the punishment was death.

While the waters of Lochfine have, from the earliest times, maintained a reputation for their abundant yield of herrings of a superior flavour, Lochleven has long been celebrated for the excellence of its trout, and Lochmaben for its interesting " vendace." By a statute passed in 1633, the trout at Lochleven were specially protected. The vendace of Lochleven, which continues to find lodgment in that solitary lake, resembles the herring in size and form, with a

---

[1] Innes's " Scotland in the Middle Ages," pp. 124, 230.
[2] " Exchequer Rolls," i. 313.

silvery skin, and the head protected by a transparent substance, representing on its upper surface the appearance of a heart. The ordinary fresh water fishes naturalized in or natives of Scotland are the salmon, char, trout, pike, and perch, while two other sorts, the bream and the roach, are peculiar to Dumfriesshire. For salmon-fishing the more remarkable waters are the Dee and Don in Aberdeenshire, the Awe and Orchy in Argyleshire, the Ness and Spey in the county of Inverness, also the Tay, Tweed, and Forth, and the rivers and lochs of Sutherland and Caithness. In southern districts a practice formerly prevailed of hunting salmon by torch-light. After the subsidence of the October floods, hunting parties were formed, provided with torches of pitch, resin, and flax. By holding torches over the water, and so casting light into its lowest depths, the hunter with a shafted trident or lister struck the salmon, which, surprised and stunned, could not possibly escape. A practice so repellent to humanity might only be excused through the unreflecting habit of those by whom it was indulged. The torch-light salmon-hunt has now all but ceased.

CHAPTER XIV.

GAMES AND PASTIMES.

COMMON to the early inhabitants of every country dancing was among the ancient Scots a favourite pastime. In evident allusion to the exercise Sir William Wallace, after arranging the position of his troops on the field of Falkirk, called out, "I have brocht ye to the ring; dance gif ye can." And in the opening lines of his poem of "Chrystis Kirk," James I. refers to dancing as a prevailing recreation. He writes :—

> " Was nevir in Scotland heard nor sene,
>   Sic dancing nor deray,
>   Nouthir at Falkland on the Grene,
>   Nor Peebles at the Play."

In the ballad of " Colkelbie Sow," written before the age of Dunbar, are named upwards of twenty native dances, while a further catalogue of dances popular in the middle of the sixteenth century is presented in the *Complaynt of Scotland*.[1]

[1] " Select Remains of Ancient Popular Poetry in Scotland," edited by David Laing, 1822, 4to, part first, ll. 296-376 ; " The Complaynt of Scotland," edited by J. A. R. Murray, 1872, p. 66.

Moorish or Morris dances were common at the court of James IV., the performers being usually Spaniards. But at Epiphany 1494, native Morris dancers, clad in a special livery, performed in the royal presence.[1] Each Morris dancer bore upon his dress a number of small bells, which played chimes during his evolutions. By the Glover Incorporation of Perth a Morris dancer's costume has been preserved. The following account of it forms the subject of a note appended by Sir Walter Scott to his "Fair Maid of Perth":—

"This curious vestment is made of fawn-coloured silk, in the form of a tunic, with trappings of green and red satin. There accompany it two hundred and fifty-two small circular bells formed into twenty-one sets of twelve bells each, upon pieces of leather, made to fasten to various parts of the body. What is most remarkable about these bells is the perfect intonation of each set, and the regular musical intervals between the tone of each. The twelve bells on each piece of leather are of various sizes, yet all combine to form one perfect intonation in concord with the leading note in the set. These concords are maintained, not only in each set, but also in the intervals between the various pieces. The performer could thus produce, if not a tune, at least a pleasing and musical chime, according as he regulated with skill the movements of his body."

Queen Mary introduced dances from France, of which, according to contemporary writers, the practice was not quite seemly. In dancing she incautiously indulged, while her people were disposed to

[1] "Treasurer's Accounts," I., ccix. 93, 179, 233.

weep ; on the day when in March 1562 tidings of the massacre of the Protestants at Vassy reached Edinburgh, she continued a ball at Holyrood. John Knox denounced her conduct on the following Sunday, and when called upon to answer for his language he was bold enough to say that her Majesty "was dancing like the Philistines for the pleasure taken in the destruction of God's people."

Mainly on account of the inopportune dances of Queen Mary's Court, and the levities with which these were accompanied, the Scottish Reformers regarded "promiscuous dancing" as a moral lesion or violation of order. They accordingly punished by fine or exposure on the pillory, those who danced at feasts or on public occasions. Even in our own times dancers at private assemblies have in isolated districts been in the ecclesiastical courts exposed to censure. For in 1863, a farmer at North Knapdale was by his pastor, a clergyman of the Free Church, refused Church membership, since by an act of dancing, he was held to have been chargeable with "scandal, flagrant inconsistency, and bitter provocation against the Lord."

Opposition to dancing by the Presbyterian clergy somewhat restrained the practice, but did not wholly subdue it. In the games declared "lawful to be observed," set forth in King James's "Book of Sports" issued in 1618, dancing is named. About a century later, that is in 1723, a weekly dancing assembly was established at Edinburgh, and was largely patronized. In 1728, the Town Council of Glasgow appointed a dancing-master, with a salary of £20, to familiarize the inhabitants with the art.

Killie-kallum, or the sword-dance, has long been practised in the Highlands. According to Olaus Magnus, it was common among the Norwegians; they derived it, he remarks, from the inhabitants of Orkney and Shetland.

Stage-playing may be traced to an early date. In the Exchequer Accounts rendered at Scone in 1264, there is a payment of £16, 2s. 9d. for "the king's charges in play." [1] On the 11th December 1366, Gilbert Armstrong, steward of the king's household, made payment of ten pounds to "the stage-players at Inchmurdoch." [2] And on the 8th May 1399, in order to the amusement of the lords auditors, the Chamberlain paid 10s. to a minstrel, and 20s. to "other players." [3]

Famous as a musician and a promoter of sports and manly exercises, James I. warmly encouraged the histrionic art. In an account to the Exchequer rendered at Linlithgow on the 5th June 1434, there is a payment of £5, 1s. 6d. to the king's stage-players in terms of his "written mandate." And in

[1] "Exchequer Rolls," i. 10. [2] Ibid. ii. 173.
[3] Ibid. iii. 484.

an Exchequer account produced at Edinburgh on the 5th September 1436, the sum of £18 is assigned as the expenses of John Turing, burgess of Edinburgh, for conducting three stage-players from Bruges to Scotland.[1] Turing received a further sum of £32 for bringing into the country four other players for the king's service, the account being under his seal vouched by Martin Vanartyne, one of the players.[2] In the same account is included a charge against the king of £33, 6s. for vestments to the stage-players with their silver decorations, also for two mantles of sable fur which had been imported.[3]

In promoting theatricals James II. was equally ardent with his royal father. For performing at his coronation Martin the player was on the 14th July 1438 paid £8, 10s.[4] Robert Mackye and Adam Rede, the royal stage-players, were, on the 13th July 1442, paid the sum of £10, 15s. 6d. in pence and penny-worths.[5] Out of the custom of Perth, on the 3d July 1447, James II. granted to Robert Mackgye, Mark Trumpats, and Adam Rede, his servitors and jesters, an allowance of £20; the payment was continued yearly.[6] By the chamberlain was paid on the 5th July 1447 the sum of £7, 13s. 8d. for white

[1] " Exchequer Rolls," iv. p. 603.

[2] Ibid., iv. p. 678.   [3] Ibid., iv. p. 680.

[4] Ibid., v. p. 35.   [5] Ibid., v. p. 114.

[6] Ibid., v. p. 263 ; Ibid., v. p. 266.

woollen cloth used in dresses to the players, who
had at the feast of Christmas performed before the
king at Stirling. On the 16th September of the
following year the account for the royal revels of the
preceding Christmas was discharged; it included
£4, 17s. for musical instruments, and £11, 17s. 1d.
for the fancy woollen dresses of the players, and
for dyeing them in various colours.[1] In the reign of
James III. Adam Rede was on the 27th July 1462
paid £3, 6s. 8d., being his half-year's fee as the king's
player.[2]

Among the sports which he vigorously promoted
James IV. included stage plays. In 1488, the year
of his succession, there occurs in the Treasurer's
accounts the following entry: "To the king himself
to play in Perth xx^{ti} lib. vij s." In the following
year Patrick Johnson and his fellows, who played to
the king at Linlithgow, also to the Spanish ambassador, were recompensed, as were certain French-
men who played before the king at Dundee.[3] In
August 1503, subsequent to his marriage, James IV.
entertained his court by the performances of certain
English comedians. To James IV. Sir David Lyndsay was in his youth a master of revels; he received
on the 12th October 1500 the sum of £3, 4s. for

[1] "Exchequer Rolls," v. p. 317.
[2] Ibid., vii. p. 144.
[3] "Treasurer's Accounts," i. pp. 91, 118, 170.

"blue and yellow taffeties," to furnish him with a coat wherein he might "play" at Holyrood for the gratification of the Court.

Prior to the reign of James V. stage-playing was simply pantomimic. And the diversions enacted in June 1538 in honour of the king's marriage to Mary of Guise were of a like character. The first perform-ance of the articulate drama took place on the 6th January 1539-60, when Sir David Lyndsay produced at Linlithgow his "Satyre of the Three Estates."[1] In representing this dramatic satire (which was repro-duced at Edinburgh and Cupar-Fife), Lyndsay pro-vided "interludes," or a pantomimic display for the common people during the intervals between the acts, when the usual audiences withdrew.

In adopting the stage as an arena on which to expose to popular contempt the corrupt manners and oppressive acts of the Romish priesthood, Sir David Lyndsay used against them a weapon fabricated by their order. The drama was originated by the Church. During the sixth century was founded in Italy the brotherhood of Gonfalone, which in silent processions represented the sufferings of the Redeemer. Miracle Plays were first performed in the fourteenth century when a company of pilgrims from Palestine were in Paris incorporated as the

[1] "The Poetical Works of Sir David Lyndsay" (edited by David Laing, LL.D.), Edinb. 1871, 12mo, I., preface xxxiii.

"Fraternity of the Passion." What prevailed in one Catholic centre was imitated in another. Holy Plays or Mysteries were in Scottish Churches performed during the hours of worship, while as performers were represented such allegorical characters as "sin," "faith," "penance," "charity," and "death." The performers were usually strolling players, who in practising religious rites wore the same habits which they displayed in their secular merry-making. Moralities were latterly performed only on the high festivals, which consequently were named play-days, while the proceedings, utterly dissociated from religion, resembled those of the ancient Saturnalia or modern Carnival. An Abbot of Unreason was annually elected by every community, who under a penalty was bound to accept office. To this functionary was latterly given the name of Robin Hood, as his acts were supposed to resemble those of the popular bandit of Sherwood. On the 24th April 1537 the Town Council of Haddington issued the following edict :—

"The quhilk day the Sys delyueris that George Rychartson sall pa to the tressaurer 20s at Whitsonday next heir aftir, and othyr 20s at zoull next thair aftir, quhilk 40s George wes awand the town becaus he would not be Abbot of Unreason."

On the 8th April 1539 the same Town Council deliberated as to whether "thai thocht expedient till haif ane Abbot of Unreason this yeir or not." A division ensued, much ardour being evinced on both sides. By a majority it was resolved to have an abbot, while any burgess chosen to the office, and who refused acceptance, was to be amerced in forty shillings. Thomas Ponton was chosen, but it is afterwards recorded that both he and another townsman who had been appointed substitute had "forsakyn the abbot-chyp," and had each paid his penalty. When on the 6th May 1555 Robert Murro was "creat burges" of Peebles, he "mad his aith as in vse is and fand his hand and his land . . . to pay his burges siluer to my lord Robine Hude."[1] At length the leaders of the popular sports became openly inimical both to the doctrines of the Church and the persons of the clergy. In 1547 Cardinal Beaton, having excommunicated for contumacy the Lord Borthwick, despatched to the curate of that parish an apparitor or macer with the injunction that forthwith in his place of worship the archiepiscopal anathema should be made public. As the apparitor entered the church he was followed by the Abbot of Unreason, who, forcibly ejecting him from the structure, dragged him to a mill-pond and there plunged him in the water. Conducted back to church the archbishop's missive was in his presence torn to pieces, and the contents cast into a bowl of wine he was compelled to swallow.[2] Through such acts of violence

[1] "Burgh Records of Peebles."   [2] Note to "The Abbot."

the existence of an Abbot of Unreason became a public scandal, and accordingly in 1555 a statute was passed in these words :—

"It is statute and ordanit that in all tymes cumming no maner of persoune be chosen Robert Hude nor Lytell Johne, Abbot of Vnressoun Quenis of Maij, nor vtherwyse, nouther in burgh nor to landwart in ony tyme to cum. And gif ony Prouest, Baillies, counsell, and communitie chesis sic ane Personage . . . . within burgh, the chesaris of sic sall tyne thair fredome for the space of fyue yeiris, and vtherwyse salbe punist at the Quenis grace will, and the acceptar of sic lyke office, salbe banist furth of the Realme. And gif ony sic persounes . . . . bin chosen outwith Burgh and vthers landwart townis, the chesaris sall pay to our Soverain Lady x pundis and thair personnes put in waird, thair to remain during the Quenis grace plesoure." [1]

Robin Hood plays, as the annual revels of the Abbot of Unreason came to be designated, were prohibited by the Reformers. On the 21st June 1567, the Lord Provost and Magistrates of Edinburgh subjected James Gillian to trial for playing Robin Hood, with the result that he was condemned to execution. Dreading a popular outbreak, the deacons of the trades entreated the magistrates, also John Knox, as minister of the parish, to stay the proceedings. As these declined to interfere, the craftsmen arose in insurrection, broke down the gibbet, shut up the magistrates in a lawyer's office, and breaking open the tolbooth, rescued Gillian and the other prisoners. Having attained their liberty, the magis-

[1] "Acta Parl. Scot." ii. 5 b. c.

trates assailed the mob, who with firearms violently
resisted.   At length the constable of the castle reconciled the belligerents, the magistrates consenting to
allow those who had engaged in the disturbance to
return to their employments.   Knox, who details the
circumstances, remarks that many persons were,
for sharing in the tumult, exposed to censure and
discipline.

The festival of *Corpus Christi,* on the second
Thursday after Whitsunday, continued to be observed
at Perth long after the Reformation.   In the Kirksession Records, under July 1577, we are informed
that—

" Mr John Row, minister, and the elders of the Church at
Perth, regretted heavily that certain inhabitants of the town had
played Corpus Christi play upon Thursday, the sixth day of
June, which was wont to be called *Corpus Christi* day ; that this
has been done contrary to the command of the civil magistrate,
and also contrary to the minister's command, which he had intimated from the pulpit ; that thereby the whole town had been
dishonoured, and great offence given to the Church of God, for
that the said play was idolatrous and superstitious."

The Kirksession further issued a declaration as to the
doctrinal errors implied in the observance.

The Play of St Obert, patron of the baxters or
bakers, was at Perth yearly celebrated on the 10th of
December in a procession attended with torches and
by a band of musicians.   One of the performers im-
personated the Devil, and all wore masquerade

dresses. A horse was led in the procession, with its hoofs enclosed in men's shoes. By imprisoning the promoters the Kirksession succeeded in checking the observance.

Uncompromising in their efforts to prevent processions and arrest pantomimic or other performances which tended to perpetuate Romish error, the reformed clergy, conscious that the popular acceptance of the Protestant faith was largely due to that formidable satire with which Sir David Lyndsay had in his plays attacked the elder system, were willing to tolerate other dramatic representations. On the 21st July 1574 the Kirksession of St Andrews granted license to Mr Patrick Auchinleck, minister at Balmerino

"to play the comedy mentioned in St Luke's Evangel of the Forlorn Son upon Sunday the first day of August next to come. But the Session desired, first, the play to be revised by my Lord Rector, Minister, Mr John Rutherford, provost of St Salvator's College, and Mr James Wilkie, principal of St Leonard's College, and if they find no fault therewith, the same to be played upon the said Sunday the 1st of August, so that playing thereof be no occasion to withdraw the people from hearing of the preaching at the hour appointed, as well after noon as before noon."

In March 1574-5 the General Assembly prohibited "clerk plays" and "comedies and tragedies made of the canonical scriptures both on Sabbath and other days," but permitted "comedies, tragedies, and other profane plays not made upon authentic parts of

scripture" on condition that these were submitted for
revision and performed on workdays only.   In terms
of this deliverance the Kirksession of Perth in June
1589 granted leave to a strolling company to repre-
sent a comedy in the city on condition that "no
swearing, banning, nor nae scurrility shall be spoken;"
and further, that "nothing shall be added to what is
in the register of the play itself." Ere the close of the
century dramas, both secular and religious, were by
the Church wholly disallowed.

By their determination to totally suppress the
drama, the clergy found themselves in strong collision with the royal authority.   In October 1599 a
body of players, known as Fletcher and Martin's
company of London, visited Edinburgh, and at once
secured the royal license to conduct their performances, also a warrant directing the magistrates to
forthwith provide them with suitable accommodation.
Informed of the contemplated procedure, the four
Kirksessions of the city parishes issued a joint
ordinance denouncing "the unruly and immodest
behaviour of the stage-players," and menacing with
censure all who should witness their performances.
On this resolution being published from the several
pulpits, the Privy Council met at Holyroodhouse, and
gave injunction " be oppin proclamation at the mer-
cate croce," that " within thrie houris," and " under
pane of rebellion," the several Kirksessions should

recall their decree.   A compromise was arranged, for
at a meeting of the Privy Council, held on the 10th
November, it was found that the "foure Sessions"
had been deceived by "some sinister and wrongous
reports," and that being "bettir advisit," they had
"cassit, annullit, and dischargit thair former act,"
and allowed "their flocks to fairly injoy the benefits
of his Majesteis libertie."[1]   It has been held, but on
insufficient authority, that Shakespeare was one of
the performers whom the Kirksessions had prohibited.

From the departure of James VI. to London in
1603 till the Restoration, Scottish theatrical entertainments were conducted only by the young and in
the public schools.   But in 1673 two Englishmen,
Edward and James Fountain, obtained a patent as
Masters of Revels, and which, they maintained, gave
them authority to legally pursue all persons who conducted public recreations apart from their sanction.
In a memorial to the Privy Council, presented on the
24th July 1679, they refer to "the playhouse,"
which they had been "at great charge in erecting."
For a time the Privy Council favoured their claims,

[1] "Privy Council Register," vi. 39-42.   For further particulars
relating to James VI.'s quarrel with the Edinburgh clergy in 1593
in reference to the Edinburgh theatre, see "Calendar of English
State Papers relating to Scotland," pp. 777-8; Spotswood's
"History," p. 456, and Calderwood's "History of the Church,"
v. 764-7.

but when they proceeded to lay impost on every
bowling-green and place of dancing, and of public
recreation throughout the kingdom, their pretensions
were disallowed.[1] In 1680 the Duke and Duchess of
York brought to Holyroodhouse a company of players
from London. They performed in the Tennis Court,
the Duke and his court giving frequent attendance.
When after an interval of thirty-five years dramatic
entertainments in the Tennis Court were renewed,
the proceeding was denounced by the Presbytery.
But the censure failed. To two plays, " The Orphan "
and " Cheats of Scapin," produced at Edinburgh in
1719, Allan Ramsay composed a prologue. Not
long afterwards Signora Violante, an Italian lady,
performed in the city with marked success. She
was in 1726 followed by Anthony Aston, a noted
comedian, who, favoured by Allan Ramsay, obtained
the patronage of the Lords of Session and of other
leading citizens. Owing to certain irregularities,
Aston was afterwards opposed by the Presbytery
and by the Society of High Constables, while the
magistrates prohibited his longer performing within
the city. Withdrawing to Glasgow in 1728, he
there encountered such formidable hostilities as to
induce his retirement.

At Edinburgh, in 1733, a body of players, called
"the Edinburgh Company," acted successfully at the

[1] Chambers's " Domestic Annals," ii. 400-1.

Tailors' Hall in the Cowgate ; they afterwards performed at Dundee, Montrose, and Aberdeen.[1]

A zealous promoter of the drama, Allan Ramsay
constructed in 1736 a theatre at Carrubber's Close,
investing in the concern the bulk of his savings.
Opened on the 8th November, Ramsay's Theatre was
by a portion of the citizens warmly patronized, but at
the close of the season was passed an Act (10 Geo.
II. chap. 28) whereby play-acting without the sanction of the Sovereign or of the Lord Chamberlain was
strictly prohibited. The good-natured but nearly
impoverished poet, in a rhyming epistle to the Lord
President Forbes, made complaint, but was nevertheless allowed without assistance to sustain his loss.

In 1746-7 was erected in St John's Street, Canongate, a new place of amusement. Intended for
dramatic performances, the statutory provision respecting a license was avoided by the announcement
that the entertainments were "concerts of musick, with
a play between the acts." Among the performers
were Digges and Mrs Bellamy, whose remarkable
dramatic talents served to arrest and sustain the
public interest. In the Canongate Theatre was,
on the 14th December 1756, produced the tragedy
of "Douglas," an event which, while advancing the
credit of the Edinburgh stage, proved in the ecclesiastical atmosphere as a thunder cloud. The author,

[1] Chambers's "Domestic Annals," iii. 397, 518, 544, 550, 583.

John Home, minister of Athelstaneford, was as one
guilty of unclerical conduct cited to appear before the
Presbytery of Haddington, and to avoid high censure
met the summons by resignation. Yet the play of
"Douglas" was elevating in tone and in sentiment
innocuous.

The Canongate Theatre was accidentally burned. On
its site a new structure with a license was on the 9th
December 1767 publicly opened, the prologue spoken
on the occasion being composed by the celebrated
James Boswell. In 1769 was founded the Theatre
Royal, on the site of the present General Post-Office.
There, on Saturday the 22d May 1784, Mrs Siddons in
the part of Belvidera first appeared before a Scottish
audience. The General Assembly was in sitting,
and many of the members gave their attendance.
The great actress played ten evenings, deriving the
sum of £967, 7s. 7d. in recompense of her art.[1]

Land Meer Processions, or Riding of the Marches,
took origin at a period when the boundaries of lands
and commons were determined by boulders and other
moveable fences, the exact position of which it was
important to mark recurrently. A proceeding, which
arose from necessity, continued in sport. At the
commencement of the present century nearly all the
minor burghs held an annual march-riding. At

[1] "History of the Scottish Stage," by John Jackson, Edin.,
1783, 8vo, p. 129.

Dumfries the riding was enacted on the 1st of October, when the Magistrates, the Town Council, and Incorporated Trades assembled at the Cross and therefrom proceeded with banners and music along the line of the burgh estate. At a particular point the cavalcade paused, when a scramble by the young for apples and sweetmeats intensified the diversion. At the close of the riding the Corporation retired to their offices to fine absentees.[1] At Haddington the Magistrates and Town Council remarked impediments and ordered their removal. They were afterwards refreshed by a dish of cockle pie.[2] In the march rides of Hawick a standard was carried by the senior bailie. In certain burghs march stones were placed, and young boys were tied to them and birched so that in after life they might better remember the landmarks. When on the last Wednesday of May the riding of the marches was practised at Lanark there was a morning procession of boys bearing tree branches. The procession stopped at the ducking hole, where those who had joined for the first time were compelled to wade in and touch a stone in the centre, when they were turned over and drenched.

At Culross on the 1st of July the memory of St Serf, the tutelary saint of the place, is commemorated by a juvenile procession. A procession of College

[1] M'Dowall's "History of Dumfries," 358.
[2] Martine's "Reminiscences of Haddington," p. 110.

students is held at St Andrews. By Bishop James Kennedy was in 1456 erected St Salvator's College, when he placed in the steeple a bell dedicated to St Catherine. On being recast in 1681 a procession attended the suspension, while the bell was named in honour of the bishop and the saint. At each celebration a personage, styled Kate Kennedy, is mounted on horseback attended by an escort. Each one concerned in the procession impersonates a character; there are Greek philosophers, Roman senators, and eminent Scottish ecclesiastics and poets. The proceedings are enhanced by music and closed by a banquet.

In allusion to the holiday processions of Ayrshire, Professor Walker, in his MS. "Life of a Manse Household in 1780," writes:

" Twice a year we (the children of Dundonald Manse) were all huddled into a crazy cart and conducted to a fair at Irvine to see a procession of tailors and weavers or an equestrian parade of coal carters, and a race run by their lumpish scarecrow horses. Long before the day of their magnificence arrived our imaginations were dwelling on its expected delights, and on the important morning we used to shift on each other, while yet in bed, the task of seeing if the sun shone through the chinks of the window shutters, none choosing to be the announcer of a heart-breaking disappointment by reporting rain, which must, as we well knew, involve our absence from the anticipated festival. On the spectacle itself we gazed with a transport as genuine as that of any Greek at the Olympic games, or of any Roman who viewed the triumph of a Scipio or an Æmilius."

The first of January, though the festival of the

circumcision in the Roman Church, was not in pre-Reformation times associated with any special rites. Hence Scottish Reformers, while subjecting to discipline those who observed Christmas, were willing that New Year's Day should be appropriated to social pleasures. Towards the closing hour of the 31st December each family prepared a *hot pint* or wassail bowl of which all the members might drink to each other's prosperity as the new year began. Hot pint usually consisted of a mixture of spiced and sweetened ale with an infusion of whisky. Along with the drinking of the hot pint was associated the practice of *first foot*, or a neighbourly greeting. After the year had commenced each one hastened to his neighbour's house bearing a small gift ; it was deemed "unlucky" to enter a dwelling " empty-handed."

Gift-bestowing on the morning of New Year's Day obtained generally. On the first of January 1489 the Treasurer presented to James IV. a personal " offerrande " ; he also handed to the king, while still in bed, ten angellis, that is £12, that he might therewith make gifts to his royal household.[1] The existence of a custom resembling first-foot is, in the Treasurer's Account, denoted by the following entry :—

" The x. of Januare [1496] giffin to Sandi Ellem, Patrick Homes man, that brocht the tithingis to the King of the first bargane in the new yere, five Scottis

[1] " Treasurer's Accounts," i. pp. 127, 171.

crovnis, ane vnicorne and half a ridare; summa
£4, 16s. 2d." [1]

With New Year's Day were, in some portions of
the Highlands, associated peculiar rites. At
Strathdown the junior anointed in bed the elder
members of the household with water, which the
evening before had been silently drawn from "the
dead and living ford." Thereafter they kindled in
each room, after closing the chimneys, bunches of
juniper. These rites, the latter attended with much
discomfort, were held to ward off pestilence and
sorcery. [2]

The direction of the wind on New Year's Day
Eve was supposed to rule the weather during the
approaching year. Hence the rhyme:—

> If New Year's Eve night-wind blow south
> It betokeneth warmth and growth;
> If west, much milk and fish in the sea;
> If north, much cold and storms there will be;
> If east, the trees will bear much fruit;
> If north-east, flee it man and brute.

The first Monday of the year, old style, known as
Handsel Monday is, in respect of a rural holiday,
the equivalent of the English Christmas. Farm
labourers, relieved from their labours, are made free
to join in the family gatherings, usual on that day,

[1] "Treasurer's Accounts," i. p. 309.
[2] "Popular Superstitions of the Highlands," by William Gran
Stewart, Lond. (1851), 12mo, pp. 174-6.

in their paternal homes. On Handsel Monday are bestowed the annual largesses to porters and parcel deliverers, and to all who have ministered to household convenience.

Candlemas, the 2d of February, held sacred by members of the Roman Church as the Purification of the Virgin, is in its ritual, derived from practices which obtained in Druidic worship. By the Church of Rome, on occasion of the festival, candles, blessed by the clergy, were carried burning in a procession. For offerings at Candlemas 1473, James III. and his queen received from the Treasurer " two crownis." [1] For the same purpose, two crowns were at Candlemas 1489, 1494 and 1495 handed to James IV.[2]

During the eighteenth century Candlemas, old style, that is, the 13th of February, was a gala-day among the young. In every parish school was held a celebration. The children proceeded to the schoolroom in their holiday attire, while the schoolmaster, seated in his desk, welcomed their approach with kindly words. Each in turn tendered a monetary offering, commonly sixpence, the children of the opulent bestowing half-crowns. The boy and girl who contributed the largest gifts became king and queen, and as such were, on a dais in the upper part of the schoolroom, ceremoniously crowned. A proces-

[1] " Treasurer's Accounts," i. p. 64.
[2] Ibid., i. pp. 129, 241, 268.

sion was enacted, when the mimic sovereigns were borne on a throne formed by crossed hands. A fire of furze and loose timber kindled in the evening was styled the *Candlemas bleeze.* In certain schools the king and queen held an evening reception, the schoolmaster, as master of ceremonies, presenting to the mimic sovereigns his more meritorious pupils. At Dumfries on occasion of the Candlemas celebration, those at the grammar-school studying Latin were expected to talk in that language only.

Associated with Candlemas is the popular rhyme :

" If Candlemas day be dry and fair,
The half o' winter's to come and mair ;
If Candlemas day be wet and foul,
The half o' winter's gane at Yule."

Shrove Tuesday is so called from being anciently associated with priestly absolution. As the day immediately precedes the commencement of Lent, it was in Scotland only known as Fastern's E'en, that is, Fasting Eve. The modes of observance varied. At Stirling young persons procured eggs, which in the morning they discoloured with various devices and in the evening boiled and ate in the fields. The inhabitants of the Border towns devoted the day to the sport of hand-ball. To games of foot-ball on Fastern's E'en the married women of East Lothian challenged the spinsters of their neighbourhood. The burgesses of Kilmarnock observed the festival by dragging their fire-engines to the cross, and after filling them with water, casting it about so as to drench the unwary.

On Shrove Tuesday was indulged the practice of cock-fighting. This most inhuman and barbarous sport was in 1681 brought into Scotland by the Duke of York. In 1683 a cockpit was erected at Leith, and there did the sport become so popular that in 1704 it was prohibited by the Town Council of Edinburgh as an impediment to business. The Leith cock-fight was at length restricted to one day yearly. From an early period of the eighteenth century till its close, cock-fighting on Fastern's E'en was an ordinary pastime. To the village schoolroom every youth bore a cock reared for his special use. At the conflict the schoolmaster presided, the craven birds or "fugies" which would not fight, also those that fell, being assigned to him as perquisites. Schoolroom dues were also payable to him. Betting was allowed, but while few profited, the spectators were rendered coarse in feeling and the young hardened to suffering. John Grub, schoolmaster of Wemyss in Fife, was the first of his order to condemn the practices of the cockpit. He composed a disputation which he caused his pupils to repeat in presence of their parents, in which the arguments for and against the sport were fairly stated. He showed in conclusion that parents unfettered by

custom would pay as generously for a lettered competition among their sons as for obtaining their distinction in the cockpit. The schoolmaster of Wemyss
flourished in 1748, but cock-fighting continued about
eighty years later.[1] Early in the century it prevailed among the gentry of eastern Fifeshire. About
the year 1810 Captain Mason of Brighton boarded
his fighting-cocks with the clergy and farmers.
About the same period Professor John Wilson, afterwards of Edinburgh, then in Oxford, entered with
ardour into the practice of a sport, which in his
maturer years he must have strongly condemned.
For birds to be used in the cockpit at Elleray he
paid five and six pounds.[2]

In the northern Highlands on Fastern's E'en was
supped a species of brose made of the skimmings of
broth, oatmeal, and eggs. And during night young
persons had placed under their pillows a cake styled
Bannich Bruader; it was discoloured by soot, and
baked with a portion of the first egg laid by a fowl.

On St Valentine's Eve the young assembled in the
several villages. The names of the blooming maidens
of the neighbourhood were inscribed on portions of
paper, and being placed in a bag were by the young

[1] " Sketches of Northern Rural Life," 1877, 12mo, pp. 172-6.
[2] " Christopher North : A Memoir of John Wilson," by his
daughter, Mrs Gordon, Edin., 1862, 2 vols. 12mo, vol. i. pp. 70,
140-3.

men eagerly drawn for. A similar proceeding was enacted with the names of the young men, which the lassies drew. The practice of despatching missives on St Valentine's Eve is comparatively modern.

On the Sunday preceding Easter or Palm Sunday the clergy of the Roman Church handed to the people tree branches to be borne in procession. Towards the cost of these processions were offerings rendered by the opulent. When James IV. was at Holyrood House in April 1489 he received from the Treasurer a demy, or fourteen shillings, for an offering on Palm Sunday; the following year his offering was eighteen shillings.[1]

On the Saturday preceding Palm Sunday the boys of Lanark paraded the streets, bearing a large willow tree decorated with daffodils, box, and other evergreens. The three last days of March were styled the *borrowing days*. When these were tempestuous a favourable summer was augured; if fine, an inclement season was anticipated. On All Fools' Day, the 1st of April, were practised those innocent impostures common on this day in nearly every European country.

Some of the rites of Beltane or May-day have been described.[2] Latterly lowland cowherds assembled in the fields, and there prepared a refection of milk and

---

[1] "Treasurer's Accounts," i., 107, 131.
[2] Vol. I., pp. 13, 14.

eggs ; their feasting concluded, they carried burning faggots from house to house. In the uplands shepherds cut in the heath a small trench, in which, kindling a fire of wood, they dressed a caudle of eggs, butter, oatmeal, and milk. As a libation a portion was spilt upon the ground. The party now individually took up a cake of oatmeal, covered with nine square knobs, which were severally taken off and cast into the fire, the names of the enemies of the flock, such as the eagle and the fox, being named in connection with each. The long subsisting practice of moistening the face with dew on the morning of May-day has all but ceased.

To the practice of frequenting wells dedicated to saints on the several Sundays of May with a view to miraculous healing has allusion been made.[1] The supposed healing qualities of Christ's Well in Menteith on May-day had attracted such crowds that in 1624 the Privy Council appointed certain commissioners to wait in its vicinity, and to forthwith imprison in the castle of Doune all who might assemble.

A day of Druidic observances in honour of the fruits, the 1st of August was, under the name of Lammas, adopted by the Roman Church as a Christian festival. The ancient origin was in their practices formerly symbolized by the herds of Haddingtonshire. About a month prior to the celebration the herds of a

[1] Vol. II., pp. 202-4.

district built in a convenient centre a tower of sods.
The tower was usually four feet in diameter at base,
tapering towards the top, which rose to a height of
about eight feet, terminating in a point containing
a hole for a flagstaff. From the time when the tower
began to assume form and prominence it was watched
nightly to prevent the attacks of neighbouring communities. The watchers were each provided with a
tooting horn wherewith in an emergency they might
summon their companions. On Lammas morning
each community chose a captain, who received a large
towel adorned with ribbons, which he bore in symbol
of office. The community then breakfasted together
on bread and cheese, drinking copiously from a spring
well, near which uniformly they encamped. Scouts
were on every side sent out to discover whether
adversaries were approaching, of whom the presence was notified by horns. When hostilities were
attempted the more powerful party commonly yielded
to the weaker without a struggle, and in token of sub-
jection laid down their colours. Occasionally fierce
struggles occurred, and at one of these four of the
combatants were killed. So many as one hundred
herds had been known to contend on each side. This
Lammas practice continued till after the middle of
the eighteenth century.[1]

[1] Paper by Dr James Anderson on "*Archæologia Scotica*," I.,
192.

The feast of the harvest-home, in early Celtic times celebrated at cairns, is popularly known as the kirn or *cairn*. A special practice called "crying the kirn" was on the last day of harvest observed on the principal farms. When the last handful of grain was secured, the reapers proceeded to the nearest eminence, and with vociferous demonstrations proclaimed that harvest was concluded. A bandster now collected the reaping-hooks, and taking them by the points, threw them upward ; the direction of the falling hook was supposed to indicate the direction in which the reaper to whom it belonged was to be employed next harvest. If a hook broke in falling, the early death of its owner was predicted. When the point of a hook sank into the soil, the owner received an augury of marriage.

The harvest-home was in Fifeshire known as *the maiden*, a derivation due not to the employment of young women in the harvest-field, but to the elevated spot or *mod-dun* where the close of reaping was announced.

The sports and drolleries of the 31st October rest upon the usages of an earlier faith. Adopted as a Christian festival, the celebration was, as preceding the Feast of All Saints, styled All-Hallow Eve—in Scottish phrase, Hallowe'en. It was the feast of ingathering ; hence in the observances are used both fruits and vegetables. With these was the unseen invoked—the future anticipated. To the young the rites were of especial interest, for the belief prevailed that with the charms of Hallow Eve were destinies associated. When two nuts placed together on the fire-grate remained in concert, those named to them were believed to possess in each other a real or a romantic interest. When nuts rested quietly, the course of affection was to prove smooth and lasting; but when one nut started up from the other, a quarrel was foreshadowed. In reference to the trial by nuts, Burns writes humorously :—

> " The auld gudewife's well-hoardit nits
>   Are round and round divided,
> And mony lads' and lassies' fates
>   Are there that night decided ;
> Some kindle couthie side by side,
>   And burn thegither trimly ;
> Some start awa wi' saucy pride
>   And jump out-oure the chimly
>   Fu' high that night.
>
> " Jean slips in twa wi' tentie e'e,
>   Wha 'twas she wadna tell ;
> But this is Jock, and this is me,
>   She says in to hersel' ;
> He bleezed owre her, and she owre him,
>   As they wad never mair part,
> Till, fuff ! he started up the lum,
>   And Jean had e'en a sair heart
>   To see 't that night."

For charming, apples were much used. From the ceiling was suspended a small stick with an apple

on the one end and a candle on the other. When
the stick was twirled, those practising the drolleries
endeavoured to seize the apple with their teeth, but
more frequently came in contact with the candle,
which scorched or greased them. Apples were set
afloat in a tub of water, into which the merry-makers
dipped their heads in order to catch one with the
teeth. But the accomplishment was difficult, and
the ardour with which it was prosecuted, usually led
to a ridiculous immersion. Eating an apple before a
mirror was a potent charm. A portion of the apple
being reserved, was on the point of a fork, extended
over the left shoulder. When the charm was thrice
repeated, the future spouse was expected to be seen
in the mirror, with extended hand.

A common Hallowe'en sport was the stepping out
hand-in-hand into the cabbage garden, and there each
with the eyes closed, pulling up the first root which
met the hand. Borne to the hearth, each stem was
examined. According as it was long or short,
thick or slender, straight or crooked, so would be
the aspect of the future helpmate. The quantity of
earth adhering to the root betokened the amount of
substance or dower. The taste of the stem further
determined whether the spouse's temper would be
sweet or acrid. The stems were now placed over the
door, one after another, when the Christian names
of those entering the house thereafter were held to

indicate those of the persons with whom the merry-makers would be wedded.

Certain rites were deemed especially solemn. When a shirt-sleeve was dipped in water, and the garment thereafter hung up to dry, the future spouse was supposed to enter the apartment and turn the sleeve. A person stole out unperceived to the peat-stack, and sowing a handful of hemp-seed, called out—

> " Hemp-seed I sow thee,
> Hemp-seed I sow thee,
> And he who is my true love
> Come after me and pu' me."

Then from behind the left shoulder, was supposed to stand forth the apparition of the future spouse in the attitude of pulling the hemp. A sieve "full of nothing" thrown up in a dark barn, was held to invoke the appearance of the future lover. When the white of an egg, or melted lead was dropped into water, the appearances were held to indicate the future dwelling. If a landscape appeared, the operator was to reside in the country ; if prominences met the eye, a town was to be his place of dwelling. There were further charms. To the nearest kiln a journey was performed solitarily and at night. The adventurer cast into the kiln-pit a clue of blue yarn. The clue was now wound up, and towards the end some one was supposed to hold the thread. To the question ،'who holds ? " an answer was expected from the kiln pit giving the name of the future spouse. The domestic drolleries of Hallowe'en have almost ceased, but in the bon-fires which at each anniversary blaze upon the northern hills the festival is perpetuated.

On the 25th December, in celebration of the upward course of the sun after the winter solstice, the Druids held a great anniversary. During the fourth century the day was associated with the event of the Nativity, and in this connection it has been observed not only by the unreformed, but by many of the reformed Churches.

At the Scottish Court in the fifteenth century Christmas was observed with much festivity and splendour. At Christmas 1489 James IV. wore a crimson satin " syd " gown, and a long robe of velvet, each lined with fur, also a short gown of velvet lined with damask, and two doublets of black satin, and one of crimson. Preceded by heralds and pursuivants he in the morning walked to high mass. Having at the altar bestowed a donation of fourteen shillings, he at noon handed largesses to his officers at arms.[1] Thereafter he had with his court recourse to games and pastimes. There were cards and dice, and " tables " or backgammon. When in 1497 James IV. observed Christmas at Aberdeen, he received from the Treasurer £156 to meet the costs of the card-tables.[2] Among

[1] " Treasurer's Accounts," preface, ccxxxvii.-ccxxxviii.
[2] Ibid., i. 310.

the out-door sports were " cach," a species of tennis, also " kiles," and langbowlis, each a form of skittles.

The diversions of the 25th December were at court continued till Epiphany, or Twelfth Day ; nor did they wholly terminate till Candlemas. At court, also in the great houses, the revels were conducted under a Lord of Misrule or Abbot of Unreason. On Hogmanay, that is the 31st December, this functionary, arrayed in a livery of green, and attended by a suite, perambulated the district, performing his escapades at the cost of private householders. In 1496 the Treasurer, on a royal precept, made to Gilbert Reade, at Stirling, a payment of ten pounds " for spilling of his hous be the Abbot of Unresoun " [1] On Hogmanay masquerading has prevailed up to our own times. While on a visit to Sir Walter Scott at Abbotsford, Captain Basil Hall makes in his journal, under the 1st January 1825, the following entry :—

" Yesterday being Hogmanay, there was a constant succession of *Guisards*—that is, boys dressed up in fantastic caps, with their shirts over their jackets, and with wooden swords in their hands. These players acted a sort of scene before us, of which the hero was one Goloshin, who gets killed in a ' battle for love,' but is presently brought to life again by a doctor of the party. As may be imagined the taste of our host is to keep up these old ceremonies. Thus, in the morning, yesterday, I observed crowds of boys and girls coming to the back door, when each one got a penny and an oaten-cake. No less than seventy pennies were thus distributed

[1] " Treasurer's Accounts," i. 270.

—and very happy the little bodies looked, with their well-stored bags."

In connection with Hogmanay, Dr Samuel Johnson, in his " Journey," describes a practice which obtained in the Hebrides. A man dressed himself in a cow's hide, upon which other men beat with sticks. As he ran round the house with his followers, the inmates, in counterfeited fright, refused him admission. Nor was he allowed to enter till he repeated on the threshold some lines of poetry.

At Deerness in Orkney, on the evening of Hogmanay, minstrel bands proceed from house to house, begging, as messengers of the Virgin, for bread and cheese and ale. Their presence is welcomed, and any householder who is overlooked regards the omission as a personal slight. Till lately, on Hogmanay the children of the peasantry, clad in white garments, entered the dwellings of the opulent, and importuned for alms in strings of verse.

In the court celebration of Twelfth Day, 1563, Queen Mary enacted at Holyrood the French pastime of King of the Bean. In her mirthfulness she arrayed Mary Fleming, one of her maids of honour, in her own robes and jewels. Randolph, the English ambassador, who was present, describes the scene in animated language.

Christmas was formerly known as Yule, from the Saxon *hiol*, or wheel, a word primarily referring to the form of the Druidic temple, latterly signifying a feast. Scottish Reformers denounced the observance of Yule as a sacred festival, and sternly refused to tolerate its festivities.[1]

There were Christmas observances peculiar to localities. On Christmas morning, in Aberdeenshire, each member of a family was, in bed, served with *Lagan le vrich*, a species of sowens, while the supper dish consisted of crappit-heads, or the heads of haddocks stuffed with oatmeal and onions. Wad, or target-shooting, also the game of football, were favourite Christmas pastimes in the northern counties.

Distaff Day, held in England on the 7th of January, had its Scottish counterpart in the *rocking*. The poet Burns names the rocking in connection with Fastern's Eve. On the day of its observance, the wives of neighbouring cottagers assembled in some central dwelling, where each worked at the distaff till the evening, when they were in the succeeding festivities joined by their husbands.

For the young there were some peculiar diversions. Hurly-hawky was practised at Stirling in the sixteenth century. One boy dragged another along the sloping side of a hill; hurly being the whirler, hawky the person whirled. On the sloping hillocks adjoining Stirling Castle the pastime was indulged

[1] *Supra*, pp. 205-6.

by the youthful James VI., when under the tutorage of Buchanan.

The Jingo Ring, a game played by girls, is derived from the practice of Romish rites. Joining hands, the players move slowly round one of their number, who with a handkerchief touches each of them in turn. In their gyrations they sing—

> " Here we go by jingo-ring,
>   By jingo-ring, by jingo-ring,
>   Here we go by jingo-ring,
>   And round about Mary matin's say."

As the players repeat the words " Mary matin's say," they each bend down, and on rising resume the song and movement without variation.

The juvenile diversion of *smuggling the geg*, founded on practices associated with the contraband trade, obtained in south - western counties. Two parties were chosen by lot ; they were of equal numbers, one being called *outs*, the other *ins*. The *outs* went out from the goal, the *ins* remained. The *outs* deposited something, such as a penknife, and then concealed themselves, calling out "Smugglers." The *ins* gave pursuit, and if the holder of the geg or deposit was captured, the parties exchanged places.

A youth who broke the rules of a game was formerly punished by *hecklebirnie*. His companions drew up in two files standing face to face, while he was made to pass between them in a stooping posture.

In his progress he, on his back, received buffets smartly applied by the bonnets of the assembly. He passed, as it were, between the fires of Baal.

During the last half century the recreations of the two countries have much assimilated, while local and quaint observances have all but ceased. Card-playing, long an all-absorbing domestic pastime, is varied by others considerably more elevating. Holidays formerly wasted in frivolity, or abused by excess, are attended by the scientific exploration of rural scenes, or by other recreations which severally tend to invigorate the understanding, inform the judgment, and refresh the heart.

CHAPTER XV.

WITH the unrestricted liberty secured at the Revolution arose a desire for social fellowship heretofore unknown. Men had hitherto assembled to concert measures against a despotic government, and provide means for the common safety. Now they met for social pastime and literary recreation. But assemblages in each other's houses were impracticable, for the domestic accommodation of even opulent citizens forbade any considerable gatherings under the family roof-tree. Clubs were instituted—that is, fellow-citizens of kindred sentiments formed themselves into associations, consenting, under the guidance of certain rules, to meet together in taverns or other public places at regular or stated intervals. From the commencement of the eighteenth century such institutions were planted in the principal towns; subsequently they obtained existence in the several provinces.

On the 12th May 1712 the Easy Club was constituted at Edinburgh. One of the prominent founders was Allan Ramsay, who, in honour of his fellow-clubmen, presented on the occasion the earliest rhymes which he is believed to have written. His inceptive ode includes these verses :—

> " Were I but a prince or king,
>   I'd advance ye, I'd advance ye ;
> Were I but a prince or king,
>   So highly I'd advance ye.

> " Great sense and wit are ever found
>   Among you always to abound,
> Much like the orbs that still move round,
>   No ways constrain'd, but *easy*.

> " Most of what's hid from vulgar eye,
>   E'en from earth's centre to the sky,
> Your brighter thoughts do clearly spy
>   Which makes you wise and easy.

> " All faction in the church or state
>   With greater wisdom still you hate,
> And leave learn'd fools these to debate,
>   Like rocks in seas, ye're easy.

> " I love ye well—O let me be
>   One of your blythe society,
> And, like yourselves, I'll strive to be
>   Aye humorous and easy."

According to the constitution, each member of the Easy Club was required to assume a dramatic name, by which he was to be addressed at the meetings and denoted in the proceedings. At first Ramsay chose the name of Isaac Bickerstaff, Steele's pseudonym in

the *Tatler ;* he was latterly known as " Gawin
Douglas." The secretary and historiographer elected
George Buchanan as his social appellative. His real
name is not entered in the papers, but he may cer-
tainly be identified as Ramsay's early associate, John
Clerk, younger of Penicuik, afterwards Sir John
Clerk, Bart., and a member of the Privy Council.
When the club started, Ramsay was twenty-six, Clerk
about twenty-eight. Among the papers is a letter
which the pseudo Buchanan had prepared for the
Spectator, in which, while discussing the merits or pecu-
liarities of social clubs, Steele had already indulged
some curious speculation. The first of the *Spectator's*
Club papers appeared on the 10th March 1711, and
the last of five others on the 8th November of the
same year. Whether Clerk's communication had
been despatched to Addison and his coadjutors and
been declined by them cannot be ascertained, but as a
graceful ebullition of social feeling, it may be printed
now. The pseudo " Buchanan " proceeds :

"Edin., August 15, 1712.—Did I think it a pardonable fault
to praise a man to his face, I could with a great deal of satisfaction
discover my judgment of your writings. However, allow me for
once to tell you that your happy talent for raising such handsome
thoughts from subjects which to men of an ordinary capacity
would seem altogether barren, makes me hope you may perhaps
find something in what I presume to trouble you with, which will
not be altogether disagreeable.

"I am a member of a civil society which goes under the name
of the Easie Club. The main reason of our assuming this name

is because none of an empty, conceited, quarreling temper can have the priviledge [*sic*] of being a member, for we allow all the little merry freedoms among ourselves, rallying one another at our meetings without the least appearance of spleen upon account of whatever we discover to be amiss or weak in any circumstance of our conversation, which produces rather love than dislike, being well persuaded of the esteem each of us hath for his fellow, and his design to see no blemish in his character.

" Our Club consists just now of eight members, all of us within some months of either side of twenty-one, unmarried, and resolved not inconsiderately to rush into a state of life even the wisest cannot foresee whether it shall be more happy or miserable, without making the tryall, and when be the luck good or bad there is no disengaging. I confess a married life has many tempting advantages, but I am affrighted when I see so many dayly instances of these being overballanced [*sic*] by a greater number of inconveniences which attend that state, and to which nothing but death alone can put a period. Therefore we are resolved as much as possible to subject every passion to the pleasure of freedom, each of us knowing how to live upon our own without the help of a well promised ill pay'd portion.

"Tho' our humours be sympathetically united, yet there are several pleasant varieties in our qualifications, or rather in what we discover ourselves to be admirers of in others. Every member at meeting is called by the name of whatever author he hath the greatest esteem for. Our Wit goes by the name of Lord Rochester; our Mathematician, Sir Isaac Newton; our Merchant, Sir Roger L'Estrange; the grave Poet, Sir Richard Blackmore; our Historian, George Buchanan; the Merchant, Robert Collinson; the Humorist, Thomas Brown, and the Censor of the Club, Isaac Bickerstaff.

" The first thing that induc'd us to join in a Society was the reading of your *Spectators*, where it is frequently recommended, and the better to make us acquainted with such fine thoughts, we have observed as one of our fundamental laws that one, two or more of the *Spectators* shall be read at every meeting. That in case any passage or sentence occur we have any scruples or doubts about, every one may give his thoughts out, and thus (as the rubing [*sic*] of two hard bodies together will smooth both) we have all been satisfied about the thing, each of us by ourselves could not be convinced of. Consider, Sir, we are but young, and have need of advice ; and seeing you are the fittest person can do it, I earnestly beg you'll lay down the best methods and rules to be observed in a Society of our constitution, and to say something in vindication of Societies in generall [*sic*] and this in particular from the implacable hatred of some here who have professed themselves irreconcilable enemies to us and all such who attempt the forsaking of vice and aiming at virtue. Hoping in some issue you'll answer the expectation of him who has a profound respect for you, and your incomparable writings, I subscribe myself your admirer.— G. BUCHANAN."

The pseudo George Buchanan was, amidst the socialities of the Easy Club, endeavouring to forget a memorable disappointment. In the year 1708 he had met at Edinburgh a celebrated beauty, Susanna, daughter of Sir Archibald Kennedy of Culzean, then in her eighteenth year. Deeply smitten he declared his love after a romantic fashion. He sent the young beauty a flute, which on receiving she proceeded to use. As no sound was emitted, she unscrewed the instrument, when a missive dropped into her lap. It bore these lines :—

" Harmonious pipe, how I envye thy bliss,
When press'd to Sylphia's lips with gentle kiss !
And when her tender fingers round thee move
In soft embrace, I listen and approve
Those melting notes, which soothe my soul to love,
Embalm'd with odours from her breath that flow

You yield your music when she's pleas'd to blow ;
And thus at once the charming lovely fair
Delights with sounds, with sweet perfumes the air.
Go happy pipe, and ever mindful be
To court the charming Sylphia for me ;
Tell all I feel—you cannot tell how much—
Respect my love at each soft melting touch ;
Since I to her my liberty resign,
Take thou the care to turn her heart to mine."

Clerk might have been a successful wooer, but that the young lady's father preferred that she should wed another suitor of higher rank, Alexander, ninth Earl of Eglinton, who consequently made her his third wife. Though disappointed in his love, Clerk was gratified to find that the object of his early affection subsequently became a patroness of his attached friend, Allan Ramsay. For in 1725 she accepted the dedication of " The Gentle Shepherd," which the author expressed in a eulogy composed in prose.

A poet of no inconsiderable elegance, Sir John Clerk is noted as author of the popular song with the alliterative opening line, " Merry may the maid be that marries the miller." Under his roof at Penicuik Ramsay spent much of his time, and when the poet died, Clerk reared in his grounds an obelisk to his memory.

James Edgar, another member of the club, whose pseudonym was latterly Michael Scot, also claims particular notice. Younger son of David Edgar of

Keithock, in the county of Forfar, he was born on the
13th July 1688, and at the time of his admission to
the club in 1713 was consequently in his twenty-
fifth year. A college student, he not long after
his admission into the club proceeded abroad,
with the professed intention of following out
his literary studies at the University of Leyden.
Within some eighteen months he was settled at Rome,
as private secretary to the Chevalier St George.[1]
Before leaving Leyden, but without notifying a
change of residence, Edgar had communicated with
the secretary of the Easy Club, and his letter after
an interval the secretary proceeded to acknowledge.
Despatched under care of a shipmaster " to the
care of Mons. Oublie, at the castle of Antwerp in
Leyden," it was in Edgar's absence brought back to
Edinburgh. The letter, which remains among the
papers of the Club, proceeds thus :—

"Last Wednesday the subject of our conversation in the Easy
Club was Friendship. We had not long discoursed of it, and
considered ourselves as engaged to one another by that nearest
relation, till we found we are justly blameable for being so much
wanting to ourselves and unfaithfull [sic] to our obligation to you
as a friend and fellow member of this Society, by so neglecting
epistolary correspondence. Upon which I was appointed to write
you as I here do without any ceremonie [sic]. That we excuse
you as not knowing whether the Club yet subsisted, and frankly
acknowledge ourselves in the wrong. But we hope that your

[1] "The Scottish House of Edgar," Grampian Club, 1873, 4to,
pp. 18-24.

good humour and agreeable easy temper will easily pardon this neglect.

" To make some amends I shall give you a short account of the state of the Club for these two last years. We had no meeting for six months after you left this place, then we had about two months' session, in which we made some improvement upon our constitution. We rejected English patrons and chose Scots authors or heroes. Rock[ingham] is now Lord Napier, Is[aac] Bick[erstaff] is Gawin Douglas, Richard Blackmore is Blind Harry, Heywood is Dr Pitcairn, Tom Brown chose Samuell Colvill (but he is ejected and extruded the Club). I continue the same. We have added Zach[ary] Boyd, Sir William Wallace, L[d.] Bellhaven,[1] Davie Lindsay, Hector Boethius, and John Barclay,[2] all of your acquaintance. We call you by the name of Michael Scot. If you are not pleased, you have the liberty of choice. During this session there was a poetick war between Gawin and Lord Napier ; we were often amused with letters and poems, and spent many evenings very aggreeably [sic]. After this we had ten months vacance [sic] till the 6th of December last, from which time we have not failed to meet once a week. The co-operating spirit gains upon us, and we grow every day more sociable, and as proof of it, by a special act have appointed the 12th of May, being the day this our Societie [sic] first met, and was constitute, an anniversary feast to be observed in all times coming by the Club, and accordingly spent the 12th of last month in countrey [sic] diversions, mirth and jollity, and ended it as true gallick juice inspired ; we remembered you frequently that day.

" Our correspondence and friendship is [sic] so sollid [sic] and

[1] The prototype was John Hamilton, second Lord Belhaven, a zealous opponent of the arbitrary measures of Charles II., and a warm supporter of the Revolution Settlement. He latterly became conspicuous by his determined opposition to the Union. He died in 1708.

[2] The prototype was the celebrated John Barclay, author of " Argenis."

secured, that we now meet in a hall or dome of our own, where we enjoy ourselves at large, free from tavern noise, and the slavish obligation of drinking contrary to our inclinations. Here we are in no fear of being overheard by such who are ready to misconstruct our innocent mirth, but have all the advantage of a private retreat.

"Our conversation is as free of party as ever. But upon all other subjects we express ourselves with a great deal of freedom. Though not in a university way, we improve so fast that in a little time we shall be able to give rules to your professors for deciding the controversies which are so disturbing to the world. There is one rule which about eighteen months ago we made a law of the Club, which may be very usefull [sic]; it has been so among us in determining many debates, and so effectually that none of the parties could ever complain of being wronged. It is this—that when any debate or argumenting arises and proves unneasie [sic] upon the complaint of any one member the Praeses shall state the controversie and call a vote for the decision, or order the disputants to remove and decide it between themselves, by FORCE or REASON. You know we are not nairrow [sic] spirited, or so churlish as to make a secret of what may be of publick use. So if you please you may communicate this to [a blank] and your other professors and wrangling *docti*. We have also attained much of the art of conversing on grave subjects, which are reckoned nauseous, dull and disaggreeable [sic] by unthinking fops and are realy [sic] so as discoursed by the PANNICK TRIBE. But in our easie and well-honoured way of treating them are the most aggreeable [sic] and edifying and afford us the greatest pleasure.

"In short (we may tell you as a friend), we look upon ourselves as the best constitute, most harmonious, aggreable [sic] and happy corporation in the three kingdoms. There is no jarring amongst us, no strife of humours, but a mutuall [sic] esteem and affection, an easie acquiessance [sic] in one another's opinions, and a frank submission of our best notions to the judgements of our fellows. Thus we live easie, and grow rich in wit and humour, by a free commerce of minds. We long for your return, to assist and bear a part with us, and hope you will make up some of our loss by frequent accounts from you; we will all rejoice in your welfare. And here I must acquaint you that our Praeses title of honour is Master Easy, disclaiming that of Lord as common among tippenny clubs.

"I shall be glad of an opportunity of giving you a fuller account of our constitution, as to how we have improved since you left us, and proud of the honour of introducing you to our green table, which, with the kindest and hearty wishes for your health and happiness, conclude this letter from your loving fellow and most humble servant,   "GEO. BUCHANNAN, *Secretary*."

"Mr Edgar.

At the Easy Dome,
Edinburgh, June 29, 1715,
And of our Club the 4th year."

While the secretary of the Easy Club was thus addressing at Leyden his quondam associate, and referring mysteriously to someone who might not be named, that associate was actually in Scotland, fomenting in the interest of his master that spirit of disaffection, which into open insurrection developed a few months later. From this course of adventure Edgar made a narrow escape; he exchanged clothes with a crofter on his father's estate of Keithock, and in this disguise escaped from those who certainly had consigned him to a traitor's death.

Two odes, or sonnets, strongly imbued with Jacobite sentiments, are included among the MSS. of the Easy Club. These may unhesitatingly be ascribed to the pseudo *Michael Scott*. One of the compositions

originally described as " Verses under the Prince's
Picture, 1710," had subsequently in a bold hand got
the following title—" Under the Pretender's Picture
with his Sword Drawn." The sonnet proceeds :—

" Born to a triple empire I submit
  To Providence in all that heaven thinks fit ;
  And if the powerful king of kings ordain
  His worthless servant in due time should reign,
  I'll sheath my sword, not claim th' avenging rod,
  Cæsar demands not what belongs to God.
  Oh ! could the sufferings of an injured heir
  Bring mercy down the guilty lands to spare,
  After the great example of my syre,
  With patience would I bear th' Almighty's ire,
  While virtuous Anna, sprung from James the just,
  Preventing greater ills, deserves the trust,
  Still let her rule, for it's her right alone,
  While I am absent, to supply my throne."

By another hand :—

" But when to do him right these lands incline,
  The pious sister will the crown resign ;
  Which to her fame will greater glory gain
  Than all the wonders of great Anna's reign."

The second Jacobite sonnet, copied on the back of
the former, is entitled, " Advice to the Duke of Marlborough, by a Penny Poet when he was at St James'
boarding and lodging there " :—

" Trust not in glittering gady height,
      Or fortune's crazy towers ;
  If justice don't prop up the weight,
      In vain's all human powers ;

> Your glorious meteor Noll's extinct,
>   Whose cursed name remains ;
> Your William's blasted trophies sink
>   In spight of all your pains ;
> But the eternal Monk shall live
>   While heaven and earth doth last ;
> To blot out { His footsteps only can retrieve
>   The loss of what is past."

In the MS., the words "blot out" precede the two concluding lines, to which they are joined by a hyphen.

If these odes were really composed by James Edgar, do we not thereby derive a clue towards discovering the authorship of those numerous Jacobite ditties heretofore anonymous? Till his death, which occurred on the 24th September 1764, Edgar possessed the means of despatching into Scotland from Rome such missives as might subserve a cause to which he had most unwisely dedicated his energies.

In the Secretary's letter to Edgar, we are informed that Tom Brown, otherwise Samuel Colvill, had been ejected from the club. The actual name of the extruded member was Andrew Brown ; and among the club's papers is a poem by Ramsay, inscribed, "On Andrew Brown hanging himself." From the opening stanza, it would seem that Brown's chief offence had been a vicious parsimony—an offence obnoxious to the sociable. The verses commence—

"Now, what could be the carle's drift,
    To which Auld Nick lent him a lift,
    Unless it were a wylie shift
        To hain his bread?
    Now he'll eat nane, and that is thrift,
        Since he is dead."

Not improbably, Andrew Brown was a near relative of that Dr Andrew Brown, commonly called "Dolphington," from his estate in Lanarkshire, who, as an Edinburgh physician, excited prejudice among the members of his profession by introducing in the treatment of fever the new system of Dr Sydenham. John Moncrieff, called "Tippermalloch," from his lands in Perthshire, had already issued his book of medical receipts, which in their absurd and disgusting details had excited loathing and contempt. Hence, as an additional disgrace to the extruded member, his successor in the club sported "Tippermalloch" as his pseudonym.[1]

The celebrated Dr Archibald Pitcairn died in October 1713, and soon afterwards Ramsay prepared for the Easy Club an elegy in his honour. Though not included among his published poems, this composition was printed by the club, and was by his friend Clerk acknowledged in the following lines :—

[1] "Analecta Scotica," ii. 176; "Locke and Sydenham, &c.," by Dr John Brown, 1858, p. 457; and R. Chambers's "Domestic Annals," iii. 52-55.

To the Ingenious Author of the Poem to the Memory of Dr Pitcairn.

So much good sense join'd with so just a thought,
And both with so much art and number wrought,
As in your poem clearly doth appear,
Can't fail to please the mind and charm the ear
Of all, but those who show their want of witt,
By crying down what they themselves can't write.
Such is your poem, and such must be its fate,
For such detraction shall enhance its rate.
Let dulness still envy and criticks rage,
Yet truth impartiall shall clear every page,
And leave them still to show their wicked spite;
For doggs who bark, yet want the power to bite,
Only, as such you are them to regard,
And let them have their barking for reward.

So may your pen continue aye to write,
And your impartiall soul [still] to indite
The praises just of those who loyal are,
And for their native soil have such a care,
As deer in midst of danger still defend
Their darling liberty for having end,
That unborn ages may the heroes know
To whom old Scotland did its freedom owe;
And then at last by whom 'twas basely sold
For the dire thirst and love of English gold,
That they may hate their execrable name
For bringing on them poverty and shame.
Thus shall you be by all good men caress'd,
Your Easy Club by loyal souls address'd,
Who with your wish'd for company are bless'd.

                                      G. B.

Included in Ramsay's published works are three
compositions written for the Easy Club—the " Elegy

on Maggy Johnstoun," the lines "On Wit," and
"The Gentleman's Qualifications Debated." In the
last the poet, in reference to a discussion in the club
on what constituted a gentleman, proceeds :—

> As in each thing we common topics shun,
> So the great prize nor birth nor riches won,
> The vote was carried thus—that easy lie
> Who should three years a social fellow be,
> And to our Easy Club give no offence
> After triennial trial, should commence
> A gentleman.

According to the rule thus poetically expressed,
the club, on the 12th May 1715, declared "that Dr
Pitcairn and *Gawin Douglas* having behaved themselves three years as good members of the Club, were
adjudged to be gentlemen." Ramsay was elected
Poet Laureate on the 2d of the preceding February.
The club had no active existence subsequent to 1715,
and it is not improbable that the sittings were suspended on account of Edgar's political disaffection,
combined with a general apprehension that the purpose of their meetings might consequently be miscon-
strued. The Club's papers, secured by the Laureate,
were attained as an inheritance by his son Allan, the
distinguished painter. Allan Ramsay, the artist, was
husband of Margaret, eldest daughter of Sir Alexander
Lindsay, Bart., of Evelick, whose sister, Mrs Murray
of Henderland, was mother of Sir John Archibald
Murray, better known by his judicial title of Lord

Murray. On the painter's death, his family papers
fell into the possession of Lord Murray, who evinced
his appreciation of the treasure by rearing in honour
of the poet a colossal marble statue in the Public
Gardens at Edinburgh. The Ramsay papers, including the proceedings of the Easy Club, and the
original MS. of the *Gentle Shepherd,* were at Lord
Murray's death exposed to sale, and being secured by
the publisher of the present work, were by him presented to Dr David Laing, the well-known antiquary.
Consequent on Dr Laing's bequest, the papers are now
in the possession of the University of Edinburgh.

Under the guidance of Allan Ramsay was formed
at Edinburgh the Select Society. This society
sought to improve the members in the art of public
speaking ; also to induce philosophical inquiry. The
first meeting, held in the Advocates' Library, was
attended by fifteen persons ; the members, who were
afterwards elected by ballot, latterly numbered an
hundred and thirty. On the roll were such social
magnates as the Duke of Hamilton, the Earls of
Aboyne, Cassilis, Errol, Lauderdale, Rosebery, Selkirk, and Sutherland, and the Lords Aberdour,
Aboyne, Belhaven, Dalmeny, and Gray, while letters
were represented by Principal Robertson, Dr Hugh
Blair, David Hume, Dr Adam Ferguson, Dr Adam
Smith, John Home, James Burnet, afterwards Lord
Monboddo, Dr Alexander Carlyle, Alexander Monro,

and William Cullen. Among the more prominent
debaters were Mr Wedderburn, afterwards Lord
Chancellor, Lord Kames, Sir Gilbert Elliot, and Principal Robertson. The club met each Friday evening
while the Court of Session was in sitting. One of the
members, Mr Robert Alexander, a wine merchant,
supplied, according to Dr Carlyle, his deficiency as a
speaker, by entertaining the members at warm
suppers. "At these convivial meetings," adds Dr
Carlyle, "the members were more improved by free
conversation than by speeches in the Society. Those
meetings in particular rubbed off all corners, as we
call it, by collision, and made the *literati* of Edinburgh less captious and pedantic than they were elsewhere."[1] The Select Society had an existence of
only six or seven years. The Duke of Hamilton,
the highest member in social rank, attended only
when under the influence of liquor, and it is not improbable that the pernicious example of one so elevated in
rank induced those more soberly inclined to withdraw
their attendance.

From the ashes of the Select Society sprung up in
1762 the Poker Club, which embraced among its
founders several leading members of the former institution. The Poker Club had a distinct practical
purpose. There was a prevailing belief, especially

[1] "Autobiography of Dr Alexander Carlyle," Edin., 1860, 8vo,
pp. 297-8.

in the capital, that in being denied the privilege of embodying a militia Scotland had by English statesmen been regarded contumeliously; and to concert measures for redress the club was organised. According to Dr Carlyle, who presents a narrative of its origin and progress,[1] the club's name of "Poker" was suggested by Dr Adam Ferguson, for reasons which the members understood, but which was to the public presented as an enigma. In reality the name was intended to imply that the society was formed to *stir up* the question at issue. Accordingly the chairman assumed a poker as his rod of office, while on the parchment diploma a poker was emblazoned as the society's symbol.

" This establishment," writes Dr Carlyle, " was frugal and moderate. . . . We met at our old landlord's . . . near the Cross, the dinner on the table soon after two o'clock at one shilling a head, the wine to be confined to sherry and claret, and the reckoning to be called at six o'clock." After the first fifteen, who were chosen by nomination, the members were to be chosen by ballot, two black balls to exclude the candidate. There was to be a new preses chosen at every meeting. William Johnston, Esq., now Sir William Pulteney, was elected secretary of the club, with a charge of all publications that might be thought

[1] "Autobiography of Dr Alexander Carlyle," Edin., 1860, 8vo, pp. 419-423.

necessary by him and two other members with whom he was to consult. The club, adds the gossiping chronicler, " continued to be in great perfection for six or seven years, because the expense was moderate, while every member was pleased with the entertainment as well as the company. During these seven years, a very close attendant told me that he never observed even an approach to inebriety in any of the members."

In 1769, owing to a quarrel with Thomas Nicholson, the landlord, the Poker Club removed its headquarters to Fortune's tavern, where the excessive charges led to a diminished attendance. Thereupon arose the Tuesday Club, which met weekly at Sommers' tavern, but ceased after two years. At the Poker Club the attendance continued steadily to fall off, till in 1784 its proceedings terminated.

The records of the Poker Club were on its discontinuance entrusted to Professor Adam Ferguson, by whose son, Sir Adam, they were in 1864 deposited in the library of the Edinburgh University. The preserved records commence in 1774 and extend till the day of winding-up. Latterly, owing to the uncertain attendance, two " attending members " were nominated as a nucleus for the next meeting, and if these did not present themselves, or make satisfactory excuse for their absence, they were mulct in the cost of two or more dinners. The imposer of penalties was Andrew Crosbie, the original of Councillor Pleydell in " Guy Mannering," who, because of the unpleasantness of his post, was humorously styled " the assassin." The assassin's " assessor " or counsel was David Hume, who was chosen in compliment to his uniform good nature and easy manners.

In 1768 the Poker Club had on its roll sixty-six members. Among these were the titled names of the Earl Marischal, the Earl of Dunmore, Lord Elibank, and Baron Grant. The literary and scientific membership included Principal Robertson, David Hume, Adam Smith, Dr Hugh Blair, John Home, John Clerk of Eldin, Islay Campbell, afterwards Lord President, George Dempster, M.P., Dr Alexander Carlyle, and Dr Joseph Black. Till September 1783 the club met weekly, when monthly meetings were substituted in the hope of reviving the general interest. But a revival did not follow, and subsequent to a meeting held on the 3d January 1784, at which five members were present, the club ceased to exist.

The Belles Lettres Society is cursorily noticed in Dr Thomas Somerville's " Life and Times." At the first meeting held in the College of Edinburgh on the 12th January 1759, it was resolved by the founders, six in number, that the society should meet each Friday evening, when " a discourse shall be pronounced," and " a question debated." Among the early subjects of debate were these sentimental themes:—"Whether mankind have been happier since the introduction of the arts, or before the invention of them; whether a good condition, with the fear of becoming ill, or a bad one, with the hope of becoming well, please or displease most; whether avarice or ambition are the predominant passions in the human mind; whether there is such a person as one disinterestedly malicious; and whether the poor sort of people are of most advantage to the rich, or the rich to the poor." These quaint topics were discussed, "whether the fool or the wise man is happier, the fool in esteeming himself, or the wise man in being esteemed by others; whether it is more useful to study men or books, and whether is popular esteem any test of merit." But the members did not reserve their dialectic skill for questions of abstract speculation. After a time they indulged debate on practical questions which involved the common welfare. They reasoned as to whether a great town or a small one is the most proper place for a university; whether the stage in its present state is of advantage to society; and whether the present prevailing game of cards tends to corrupt the morals of young people. On social and patriotic themes they debated as to whether the liberty of the press is of advantage or disadvantage to the country; whether entails are advantageous or disadvantageous; whether by the laws of nature, females are entitled to an equal share in succession with males; and whether it would not be more for the advantage of society that condemned criminals should rather be employed in public works than sent to the new or to the other world. Even questions of ecclesiastical polity were ardently contested, such as whether the settlement of ministers by presentation or by election is preferable; and whether the repenting stool should be taken away. Not without an allusion to prevailing manners strongly cynical must have been that member who proposed as a subject of discussion, whether a foundling hospital at Edinburgh to be maintained by a tax on old bachelors would be for the advantage of Scotland?

The earlier attendances on the Belles Lettres Society were limited, but in about a year after its origin, twenty and even thirty persons would be ordinarily present at the weekly meetings. These included honorary members and visitors. Among the visitors in 1760 and 1761 appear the names of Dr William Robertson, soon afterwards Principal; Dr Hugh Blair, David Hume, Dr Alexander Carlyle, Professor Adam Ferguson, George Dempster, afterwards M.P., Sir William Forbes, Bart., Dr Joseph M'Cormick, afterwards Principal of the United College, St Andrews, Professor William Cullen, and James Boswell. Of these the greater number were elected honorary members.

Ordinary members were chosen by ballot, and from those only who by respectful memorial solicited "the honour of admission." On the 7th March 1760, "Henry Dundas, Esq., student of the Civil Law," sought election, and at the second weekly meeting thereafter his name was added to the roll. As an exercise, he, on the 3d of April, "delivered a discourse on religious liberty," which, according to the record, "received the universal approbation of the society." Mr Dundas, who was then in his eighteenth year, proved so efficient as a member, that on the 29th May 1761 he was "appointed to give an occasional oration at the sitting down of the next session of the society." The eloquence wherewith this precocious youth had electrified the Belles Lettres Society was destined to move the British senate, and to obtain for the speaker, as Viscount Melville, a powerful influence in national affairs. By Dr Thomas Somerville, who joined the society in the winter of 1761, Henry Dundas is with Robert Blair named as among the "best speakers."

The minute-book of the Belles Lettres Society, containing a record of the proceedings from its commencement to the 29th May 1761, is preserved in the Advocates' Library, being there deposited by David, Earl of Buchan, one of the members.

In connection with the Belles Lettres Association, Dr Somerville names the Theological Society, which,

originating in 1759, ceased in 1764, after a dura-
tion of five years. To his attendance at these two
institutions Dr Somerville ascribes his early progress "in literature, in composition, and in solid
intellectual improvement." But the Theologians, or
many of them, adjourned to taverns after their
weekly meetings, and so, unhappily, fell into social
irregularities.[1]

A prominent literary and convivial organization
was the Club or Order of the Cape. After a less
conspicuous existence of several years, this association
acquired in 1764 a distinctive footing. Part of the
original purpose was to establish branches, whereby
provincial and colonial clubs might, with authority
derived from the parent society, "extend the benign
influence of their Order to every region under the
Grand Cape (or Cope) of Heaven."[2]

The members of the Cape Club were styled Knights
Companions, while the administration was vested in
a sovereign, a deputy-sovereign, a secretary, a trea-

[1] Dr Thomas Somerville's "Life and Times," pp. 39-42.
[2] According to Dr Robert Chambers, in his "Traditions of
Edinburgh" (ed. 1869, pp. 164-5), the Cape Club derived its
name consequent on a social incident. A burgher of the Calton
was in the habit of spending some hours each evening in the
city, often so late that the Netherbow Port was closed. He had,
therefore, to thread his way homeward towards Leith Wynd by
turning with difficulty a rectangular corner. This operation he
described as *doubling the Cape ;* and the phrase becoming familiar,
led to its being appropriated as a club name.

surer, a recorder, an assistant recorder, twelve councillors, a chaplain, and the past sovereigns. Ordinary meetings were held in "Cape-hall," which signified the private dwelling of the sovereign, while the knights resident in Midlothian observed a half-yearly festival. At these festivals the dining-hour was three o'clock, and both on these occasions and at the ordinary meetings gaming and tobacco-smoking were disallowed. Those who removed newspapers were amerced "in a green stamp," that is, one shilling and fourpence. Candidates were admitted by ballot, on the approving vote of two-thirds of the knights present. The diploma, printed on white satin, presents, in the upper part, between two cupids, an escutcheon displaying two pokers crossed, one bearing the cap of the sovereign, together with a wreath, exhibiting the motto of the Order, "Concordia Fratrum Decus." Below is a wine-flaggon, the emblem of conviviality and friendship. The printed form reads thus :—

"Be it known to all men,—That We, Sir ————, the Super-Eminent Sovereign of the Most Capital Knighthood of the CAPE, having nothing more sincerely at heart than the glory and honour of this most noble Order, and the happiness and prosperity of the Knight Companions, and being desirous of extending the benign and social influence of the Order to every region under the Cope of Heaven; being likewise well informed and fully satisfied with the abilities and qualifications of ————, Esq., with the advice and concurrence of our Council, We do create, admit, and receive him a KNIGHT COMPANION of this most social Order, by the title of Sir ———, and of C.F.D., hereby giving and granting unto him all the powers, privileges, and pre-eminences that do or may belong to this most social Order, and We give command to our Recorder to register this our patent in the Records of the Order. In testimony whereof, We have subscribed these presents at our Cape-hall, this —— day of ——— in the year of Our Lord one thousand seven hundred and ———.

——————— *Sovereign.*

——————— *Recorder."*

At the meetings of the Order, the sovereign assumed a velvet cap or crown of crimson velvet, ornamented with gold and silver lace, and in front embroidered with two hands clasped together, as a token or badge. Duly enthroned, the sovereign received each novice, by extending to him the great poker, which being taken hold of, he proceeded to raise the lesser weapon so menacingly that instant stooping became a natural impulse. As a further step in initiation, the knight-elect was required to exercise his gifts by some appropriate recital.

Among twenty-four knights created in 1764 occur the names of David Herd, the literary antiquary, who chose " Sir Scrape " as his appellative; Alexander Runciman, the painter, who became " Sir Brimstone ; " and Michael Bruce, the poet, who was styled " Sir Tomas." Thomas Lancashire, the comedian, was, as first sovereign of the Order, designated " Sir Cape." In 1766 was dubbed James Cumyng, herald painter, afterwards secretary of the

Society of Antiquaries; he was known as "Sir Nun and Abbess."

On the 10th October 1772 was admitted as "Sir Precentor" the ingenious Robert Fergusson. Elected laureate of the Order, the young bard derived from the meetings a chief source of enjoyment. The Cape Club he has in his poem of "Auld Reekie" celebrated thus :—

> " Now many a club, jocose and free,
>   Gi'e a' to merriment and glee :
>   Wi' sang and glass they fley the pow'r
>   O' care that wad harass the hour.
>   But chief, O Cape, we crave thy aid
>   To get our cares and poortith laid.
>   Sincerity and genius true
>   O' knights have ever been the due ;
>   Mirth, music, porter deepest dyed,
>   Are never here to mirth denied ;
>   And worth, o' happiness the queen,
>   Blinks bonny, wi' her smile serene."

When Thomas Lancaster died, the laureate commemorated him in these lines :—

> " Alas, poor Tom ! how oft with merry heart,
>   Have we beheld thee play the Sexton's part !
>   Each comic heart must now be griev'd to see
>   The Sexton's dreary part perform'd on thee."

On the 3d September 1774 Allan Masterton of the High School was dubbed as "Sir Pole"; on the 27th December 1774 Walter Ruddiman as "Sir Mill Dam;" on the 27th September 1782 John Rennie as "Sir

"Hatchet"; on the 8th June 1787 John Logan as "Sir Heather"; on the 14th June 1791 Alexander Nasmyth as "Sir Thumb"; and on the 26th September 1791 Henry Raeburn as "Sir Discovery."

When in September 1799 the roll closed, 650 knights were found to have been admitted. Among the more humorous pseudonyms chosen or imposed are—Sir Snore, Sir Canker, Sir Snaiknaked, Sir Sobersides, Sir Coup, Sir Truth, Sir Hayloft, Sir Beefstakes, Sir Toothache, Sir Sark, Sir Stick, Sir Fork, Sir Breeks, Sir Acid, Sir Nick, Sir Coalhole, Sir Splitbeard, Sir Spitfire, Sir Gutter, Sir Handbarrow, Sir Droddlepouch, Sir Wickstick, Sir Blackface o't, Sir Kailpat, Sir Bottle, Sir Whinbush. The sovereigns are entered after the manner of reigning princes. Thus William I., William II., William III., James I., James II., and James III., are names and designations to be found in the minute-book.

On the 11th December 1841 the Society of Antiquaries received from four surviving members of the Cape Club a cabinet containing the records, documents, and paraphernalia of the society. Along with the cabinet was handed a missive, declaring that the accompanying articles were "for depositation, it being understood that should the Club be at any time hereafter revived, either by any of the descendants of the late members or other body of respectable citizens, the documents and effects will be given up to them."

Among the MSS. so deposited are the minute-book of proceedings from 1764 to 1788,[1] and an alphabetical list of knights or members. All the insignia have been preserved.

Subsequent to the rehearsal of the tragedy of Douglas in a private lodging on the 14th December 1756, those who took part in it adjourned for festivities to the Griskin Club, which met in a tavern in the Canongate. Among those present at the rehearsal and at the Club subsequently were Principal Robertson, Dr Hugh Blair, Professor Adam Ferguson, Dr Alexander Carlyle, and John Home.[2]

During the sitting of the General Assembly of the same year was established at an inn in the West Bow the Diversorium, a gathering of the moderate clergy, members of Assembly. This institution was established by Dr Carlyle and John Home. Prior to the meeting of Assembly the founders requested Nicolson the landlord to provide for early use twelve dozen of claret, at eighteen shillings a dozen. Among the members of the Diversorium were Lord Elibank, Sir

[1] A postscript appended to the last minute bears that " the great parchment roll containing the signatures of the knights on admission, was some years ago delivered to Mr A. Sievwright (Sir Jordan), for the purpose of summoning a meeting of the existing members, with a view of reviving the Club. From enquiries recently made at his widdow [sic] there seems no doubt that the roll was ignorantly destroyed after his death along with various useless papers belonging to himself."

[2] " Life and Times of Lord Brougham," i. 541.

Gilbert Elliot, Principal Robertson, David Hume, and Professor Ferguson.[1]

On the ruins of "The Tabernacle," a literary coterie of whose proceedings there are no records, was founded the "Mirror Club," of which the leading members were Lord Abercromby, Lord Bannatyne, Lord Craig, Lord Cullen, and Henry Mackenzie. In the conversations of the "Mirror Club" originated the idea of the *Mirror*, a well-known serial, conducted after the manner of the *Spectator*. Of this pleasing and instructive periodical the first number appeared in January 1779, and the last in May 1780. From the sale the club derived a profit sufficient to purchase a hogshead of claret, also to hand a balance of £100 to the Orphan Hospital.

Chiefly memorable in connection with the poet Robert Burns, the club of the "Crochallan Fencibles" was founded in 1777 by William Smellie, printer and naturalist. With head-quarters established in the Anchor Close Tavern, kept by Donald Douglas, it was designated *Crochallan* after a song *Cro Chalein* or Colin's Cattle, which the landlord effectively sung. The word "Fencibles" was added to the title owing to the embodiment of fencible regiments to compensate for the absence in America of the regular troops, being at the time a popular topic. Burns was in January 1787 introduced to the Club by his friend Mr Smellie.

[1] "Autobiography of Dr Alexander Carlyle," pp. 308-9.

As a semi-military fraternity, the club gave its office-bearers warlike designations. William Dunbar, Writer to the Signet, a particularly mirthful associate, was *Colonel*, Lord Newton, the bibulous judge, *Muster-Master-General*, and Mr Smellie *Executioner*. In the initiatory ceremony novices were subjected to much rough handling, chiefly by Smellie. Burns, though acknowledging himself thrashed in a manner beyond his former experiences, preserved his equanimity, which was recognised as high evidence of his fraternal qualities. The *Crochallan* brotherhood he greatly enjoyed ; several of the members are celebrated by his muse. William Dunbar, whom he describes as "one of the worthiest fellows in the world," he thus poetically celebrates—

> " As I cam by Crochallan,
>   I cannilie keekit ben ;
> Rattlin, roarin' Willie,
>   Was sittin at yon boord-en',
> Sittin' at yon boord-en',
>   And amang gude companie ;
> Rattlin, roarin' Willie,
>   Your welcome hame to me."

The Bard hailed Mr Smellie in like fashion—

> " Shrewd Willie Smellie to Crochallan came ;
> The old cock'd hat, the grey surtout, the same,
> His bristling beard just rising in its might,
> 'Twas four long nights and days to shaving night,
> His uncomb'd grizzly locks, wild staring, thatch'd
> A head for thought profound and clear, unmatch'd ;

Yet tho' his caustic wit was biting rude,
His heart was warm, benevolent and good."

Two other attached friends of the poet, Alexander
Cunningham and Robert Cleghorn, were prominent
members of the Club. Inspired by their skill in
rendering the older ballads, Burns composed songs in
similar strain, to be used only at the Club. In these
compositions, he indulged his humour by scathing the
levities of a former age. Having after his death been
found in his repositories, they were, under the title of
"The Merry Muses of Caledonia," injudiciously
printed.

According to Robert Heron, there existed in Edinburgh about the close of the century a Club composed of young men of rank and fashion, known as
"The Caledonian." The Boar Club met at Hogg's
Tavern, in Shakespeare Square. Organized in 1787,
its sittings were continued every evening for about
twenty years. The officers consisted of a Poet-
Laureate, a Champion, and a Procurator-fiscal. While
dispensing with pseudonyms, the members were under
a penalty called on to address each other as "Sir,"
without using their ordinary names. As the infliction of penalties at length became oppressive, the
institution was abandoned.

The *Spendthrift* Club derived its name, not from
the extravagance of the members, but rather from
their parsimony. There were originally six, latterly

four weekly meetings, while the cost of supper, liquor, and attendance was at first restricted to four-pence-halfpenny, and latterly to sixteenpence. In 1824 the Club was wound up.

The Cormorant Club, which was noted for its fish-dinners, met at Leith. At the Soaping Club, *every member was allowed to soap his own beard,* that is, he was privileged to ventilate his own opinions. The Capilliare Club was formed in order to create a taste for certain fashionable liqueurs. About the close of the century there were social organizations known as "The Knights Nun and Abbess," "Knights of the Royal Order," "Knights of the Fleet," and "Knights of the Speech." The Marrow bone Club, composed chiefly of Lords of Session, met in the Flesh Market Close ; they recorded their proceedings in verse, and ate from plates of solid silver. "The Presbytery," an association of merchants, assembled daily in Milne's Square, High Street. "The *Pious Club*," writes Dr Robert Chambers, "met in a pie-house, so that the members might rest under the agreeable uncertainty as to whether their name arose from their piety, or from their pie-eating."[1] The members were restricted to fifteen ; and each associate was expected to consume not more than one gill of spirituous liquor. On Sunday evening, the members met for serious conversation.

[1] "Traditions of Edinburgh," Edin., 1869, p. 165.

Of the social and scientific institutions established in the eighteenth century, and which have survived to the present, the most conspicuous is the Speculative Society. Instituted on the 17th November 1764, the founders were six college students, of whom the most notable was William Creech, afterwards Lord Provost. During the University term, meetings were held weekly, when essays were read and debates conducted. Members who for several years gave regular attendance were appointed "extraordinary members," and as such exempted from active duties. From the small fee of one shilling and sixpence, the payment on admission was increased to five guineas. Several members have, in their writings, expressed the deep interest which early in life they had experienced in its discussions. From the Society Lord Cockburn derived his first notions of composition and debate. In an octavo volume are embraced sketches of distinguished members, together with interesting details of the Society's rise and progress.[1]

At the Forum, an Edinburgh literary club, young persons desirous of improving in the art of oratory conducted public discussions. In 1790 Alexander Wilson, the future ornithologist, took part in a debate as to whether Allan Ramsay or Robert Fergusson had done greater honour to Scottish poetry, by reading

[1] "Memorials of his Time," by Henry Cockburn, p. 27; "History of the Speculative Society of Edinburgh," 1845, 8vo.

his poem, *The Laurel Disputed.* He gave the palm to Fergusson.

In his autobiography Lord Brougham remarks that on the 22d December 1792 he founded at Edinburgh the Juvenile Literary Society; and among the members he names Francis Horner, Henry, afterwards Lord Mackenzie, John Forbes, afterwards Lord Medwyn, and the afterwards celebrated Dr Andrew Thomson. During the college session the society met each Saturday morning, the members presiding in rotation. Essays were read and public questions, apart from political, energetically debated. The society existed several years, and the practice of debate acquired at its meetings enabled the projector, he informs us, to enter with facility on the practice of his profession. The minute-book of the society is preserved at Brougham Hall.[1]

The Esculapian Club, consisting of physicians and surgeons, which on the 2d of April 1773 was constituted at Edinburgh, has maintained an active existence ever since. On the 14th November 1873 its centenary was celebrated by an appropriate banquet. Two volumes of the minutes of the club, preserved in the library of the Royal College of Physicians, exhibit in the roll of members many notable names. Among these the more conspicuous are Sir James Hay, Dr Andrew Duncan, Andrew and

[1] "Life and Times of Henry Lord Brougham," i. 83-6.

Alexander Wood, Benjamin Bell, and Professors Alexander Hamilton, and John and Thomas Charles Hope. The Esculapian Club has twenty-four members; it meets annually.

The Wagering Club, established on the 28th January 1775 "to promote friendly and social intercourse," continues a prosperous existence. And in practical operation the betting feature, which in some respects is calculated to excite prejudice, really serves to sustain the general interest. At one annual meeting "wagers" are chosen, for settlement at· the next, the members on a written card adhering to oné side or the other. When the cards have been fully subscribed they are sealed up, the packet being entrusted for keeping to the chairman to be publicly opened at the next anniversary. As the bets relate to events which must have been determined in the interval, those who have registered on the winning side obtain credit for their prescience, while the bets they have won, each one shilling in value, are added to the fund conducing to defray the cost of the entertainment. Some of the bets illustrate at different epochs the state of national feeling. A bet in 1798 that Buonaparte shall not be alive or known to be in existence on the 26th January 1799 was repeated in the following year. Thereafter was the bet, "that Buonaparte shall be alive at next meeting," repeated annually till the ex-emperor's death in 1821. From the beginning of the century a portion of the annual bets have related to the price of consols and of grain. Wagers in regard to the probable marriage of rich heiresses or celebrated beauties or of bachelor members of the club are frequent. In reference to an agitation now in active progress for securing a political minister for Scotland, it is interesting to remark that an antecedent movement led to the first wager of the club on the 29th January 1855, which is, " will the office of Secretary of State for Scotland be revived, or will any other public officer, to attend specially to the affairs of Scotland, be appointed betwixt and the next meeting of the Club?" Under the rule of Bain Whyt, the genial founder (whose monument adorns St Cuthbert's Churchyard), the membership was restricted to thirty, but nearly double that number have for some years taken part in the annual celebration. Among the more notable members or visitors appear the names of Sir Wilfred Lawson, Bart.; John Hunter, LL.D., Auditor of the Court of Session; Charles Mackay, comedian; Sam Bough, James D. Marwick, LL.D.; James Drummond, R.S.A.; Mr Sheriff Nicolson, and the Right Hon. Sir George Harrison, LL.D., the present Lord Provost. The surplus funds of the society were in 1862 invested in purchasing a silver medal to be worn by the chairman at the annual re-union, which is held on the last Monday of Janu-

ary. Apart from the president who is annually
chosen, are two permanent officers, the secretary and
the chaplain, of whom the latter chronicles the leading
events of the year in a humorous summary, of which
the reading forms no uninteresting part of the general
proceedings. The minute-book of the club has been
carefully preserved.

Among the clubs which have sprung up during
the progress of the century, some of the more prominent may be named. The Friday Club, so called from
the day on which it met weekly, was in 1803 originated by Sir Walter Scott. Among the early members
were Professors Playfair and Dugald Stewart, Sir
James Hall, the Rev. Archibald Alison, Henry
Brougham, Henry Mackenzie, Thomas Campbell,
Francis Horner, Malcolm Laing, Thomas Thomson,
and Francis Jeffrey. Latterly the chief promoter was
Lord Jeffrey, who, up to an advanced age, regarded
the Friday monthly meetings of the Club as "a
guide and solace."[1]

On the 27th May 1817 was established at Edinburgh the Albyn Club, one of the earliest of those
joint-stock institutions in which the members obtain
entertainment and otherwise enjoy the comforts of a
home. Among the promoters were the Marquises of
Douglas, Tweeddale and Queensberry, the Earls of

---

[1] "Life of Lord Jeffrey," by Lord Cockburn, Edin. 1852, 8vo,
i. 149-152.

Eglinton, Elgin, Fife, Glasgow and Kintore, the Hon. William Maule, afterwards Lord Panmure, and other titled and distinguished persons. Law and science had their representatives in Andrew, afterwards Lord Rutherfurd, John Hope, afterwards Lord Justice Clerk, Dr, afterwards Sir David Brewster, and Patrick Miller of Dalswinton. In 1820 the club was joined by Sir Walter Scott, and among those admitted subsequently were Archibald, afterwards Sir Archibald Alison, Bart., Robert Liston, the Right Hon. Fox Maule, the Duke of Hamilton, the Earl of Buchan, Sir John Sinclair, Bart., and Sir Henry Jardine. By one of the fundamental laws, the membership was restricted to 200, and though twelve years later the number was extended to 220, the roll did not at any time contain more than 125 names. At length, on account of embarrassments, the club was on the 11th January 1830 legally dissolved. On this event sprung up at Edinburgh the New Club, which as the city head-quarters of a large and important con-stituency, chiefly of Scottish landowners, has continued to flourish.

The Medico-Chirurgical Club was founded in 1822 with a compliment of twenty members. These assemble at dinner three times a year, in March, June, and November. At each meeting the secretary pro-duces an historical report, which embracing a vidimus of professional progress, humorously expressed, is suggestive of sparkling wit and enlivening conversation. These secretarial reports are engrossed in the minute-books, which already extend to fifteen volumes. Among the members are to be remarked the names of Dr John Abercrombie, Professor W. P. Alison, Dr James Gregory, Sir James Y. Simpson, Bart., Sir Robert Christison, Bart., and Professor James Syme.

The Heather Club was devised in 1823 for promoting a healthy recreation and social friendship, the members making an annual excursion to the Pentlands attended by a piper. The principal officers of the Heather Club are a Captain and Lieutenant.

"The Contemporary Club," which upheld Conservative principles, had among its early members Sir Walter Scott, John Hope, afterwards Lord Justice Clerk, Robert Dundas of Arniston, and about fifty others. When in 1825 John Gibson Lockhart was about to leave Edinburgh for a permanent residence in London as editor of the *Quarterly Review*, he was by the Contemporary Club, of which he was a member, invited to dinner. His reply to a letter of invitation addressed to him by the President, Mr Dundas of Arniston, now in the possession of the Publisher of the present work, proceeds thus :—

"CHIESWOOD, *November* 18, 1825.

"DEAR DUNDAS,—You may easily believe that leaving Scotland even for a season is to me no matter of pleasing contemplation. Yet having considered it as my duty to go, I cannot exert quite so much self-denial as to decline carrying with me the recollection of one meeting more with gentlemen whose society has afforded me the highest pleasure during the best years (I fear I may now begin to talk so) of my life, and whose good opinion it shall ever be my chief pride to retain and cultivate.

"This courtesy was neither merited nor expected. But I am not the less sensible to it, nor to the additional value which such a communication must ever bear from coming through hands such as yours.

"I propose being in Edinburgh on Saturday the 3d December, for the purpose of dining with the Contemporary Club, and if the Monday following should happen to suit your convenience it would mine perfectly.—Believe me, my dear sir, yours very sincerely,

"J. G. LOCKHART."

"*P.S.*—On second thoughts I take the liberty of requesting you to see Mr William Sharpe, and inform him that I request the honour of seeing the *Contemporaries* at the British Hotel, either on Saturday the 3d, or Monday the 5th of December, leaving it to *you* to determine on which of these days *your* dinner takes place, and so fixing the other, which ever it may be, for mine and the Club.

"I hope you will pardon the additional trouble. Menzies[1] will gladly relieve you of it, however, if you are busy."

Sir Walter Scott, in his "Diary," records that he was present at the dinner given to Lockhart by the Contemporaries, and which came off on Saturday the 3d December.

At the "Dilettanti Club," Professor John Wilson presided, with an abundant humour. Among the

---

[1] Afterwards the Hon. William Menzies, one of the Supreme Judges at the Cape of Good Hope.

members were J. G. Lockhart, and the early staff of *Blackwood's Edinburgh Magazine*.[1]

When, in 1835, the late Professor Edward Forbes was a college student, he, along with other young men of a kindred spirit, established a social organization, under the name of the Maga Club or Order. Each member wore across his breast a narrow silk ribbon, rose coloured and black, with the mystic letters O. E. M. worked into its texture—the initials of three Greek words signifying time, love, and learning. At the meetings of the Order, the higher class brethren wore a small silver triangle, styled " Oineromaths or Red-Ribbons." The members in 1838 sought to avoid criticism by constituting themselves into " The Universal Brotherhood of the Friends of Truth," which in the rules is described as a union of the searchers after truth, for the glory of God, the good of all, and the honour of the Order, to the end that mind may hold its rightful sway in the world." Of this latter association Forbes was Arch Magus. Its next president or leader, John, afterwards Professor John Goodsir, was, in November 1838, when in his twenty-fourth year, elected to a fellowship. The society included clergymen, physicians, artists, and other cultivators of learning.[2]

[1] " Christopher North, a Memoir of John Wilson," by his daughter, Mrs Gordon, 1862, i. 272.

[2] " Anatomical Memoirs of Professor John Goodsir," by Henry Lonsdale, M.D., Edin., 2 vols. 8vo, vol. i. pp. 59-61.

Glasgow Clubs have an appropriate chronicler in Dr John Strang.[1] Of these western fraternities some had quaint appellatives. There were the *Banditti* and *Gegg Clubs*, also those with the prefix of *Face, Pig, Duck, Crow*, and *Cowl*. Provincial Clubs resembled and imitated those in cities. Some took names from public courts and corporations. At Cupar-Fife met a " Parliament," at Falkirk a " Presbytery," at Stirling a " Session." In provincial clubs each member was designated after his farm, or his trade, or his office. In the provinces as well as in the capital, members of clubs indulged the sport of " high jinks." In this game dice were thrown by the company, those on whom the lot fell being obliged to assume and maintain a fictitious character, and repeat certain fescennine verses. When recollection failed, forfeits were imposed, compounded by a contribution to the reckoning. Written summonses to club meetings were issued quarterly. When certain Edinburgh clubs were convened, the members were invited " to hold a fast."

Among the existing Edinburgh Clubs " the Monks of St Giles " obtains a special interest. The members use a monkish costume, compose spirited verses, and under the presidentship of a Prior, hold monthly reunions. " The Monks " assemble in a hall in St

[1] " Glasgow and its Clubs," by John Strang, LL.D., London, 1856, 8vo.

Giles' Street, which is adorned with paintings executed
by the members, several of whom are artists of
reputation.

A history of those provincial clubs, of which the
records have been preserved, might prove a pleasant
exercise to the compiler, while it would amply tend
to set forth and illustrate the national manners. Of
two clubs of this rural character, of each of which
the father of the present writer was an official member,
some details may not be unacceptable. One of the earlier
of the farm clubs in this country, the Lunan and
Vinney Farming Society, was, on the 4th July
1803, established at the village of Dunnichen, near
Forfar. The founders were Mr George Dempster,
formerly M.P., who in his later years became a
zealous agriculturist; and Mr James Roger, afterwards minister of Dunino, who had acquired some
distinction as reporter to the Board of Agriculture on
the husbandry of Angus. At the initiatory meeting,
attended by thirty-four persons, of whom eleven were
landowners, Mr Roger was nominated permanent
secretary, and Mr Dempster the perpetual president.
In opening the society's business, Mr Dempster expatiated on the importance of maintaining superior
breeds of cattle and horses, on the duty of extirpating
weeds, on the necessity of a stern resistance to
smuggling, and on the desirableness of upholding the
constitution. With his approval, it was arranged

that the society should assemble at least once a year, that its proceedings should be accompanied by a modest feast at 1s. 6d., afterwards 2s. 6d. a head, and that on each occasion liquor of native manufacture should be used exclusively.

At the second meeting, held in July 1804, Mr Dempster invited attention to the rotation of crops ; suggesting various methods, and maintaining that by a proper alternation of green and grain crops, fallowing might be dispensed with. To each member he handed a slip of rules, which he termed *golden ;* they consisted of injunctions to keep the land rich and clean and dry, to use efficient manure, and to avoid two grain crops in succession. Poultry and hogs, he maintained, should be largely reared. The secretary read an essay on the rearing of horses and cattle. Prior to the reign of James I., he said, Alexander, Earl of Mar, imported horses from Hungary ; while James I. was himself a promoter of farm stock, by introducing on his lands at Falkland a superior species of milch cows. In reference to grazing, he remarked that one of the members had recently sold cattle of three years old at £18 each, while another member had reaped from about an acre a quantity of red clover which produced 154 lbs. of seed. At the meetings held in August 1805, and in July 1806, Mr Dempster recommended the cultivation of Swedish turnips, and suggested that the tops of the carrot

should be used in feeding milch cows. His former
proposal as to the disuse of fallow ground was disapproved, it being strongly held that the land required rest at least every tenth year. It was
agreed, on his recommendation, that wheat ought to
be more extensively cultivated, and that it should be
sown late in August or early in September. At the
close of the meeting an indigent person, formerly a
farmer, and then said to be in his 106th year, was
awarded a little money.

The fifth meeting, held in August 1807, was
attended with an exhibition of live stock. Various
subjects were discussed. Gypsum as a manure, recommended by the Board of Agriculture, was, on the
motion of the Rev. James Headrick,[1] disapproved.
Flax-raising was commended by several members,
and by others styled unprofitable. The question as
to whether carcases of meat might be transmitted to
distances packed in ice, was mooted and generally
affirmed.

In his address to the meeting in July 1808, Mr
Dempster recommended the cultivation of vetches, to
be sown in drills. The Chinese method of economis-

[1] This reverend gentleman was then assistant in the parish ; he
was ordained to the cure on the 11th August 1807. He recommended himself to Mr Dempster's notice by his agricultural papers
in the *Farmer's Magazine*. His " View of the Mineralogy, &c., of
the Isle of Arran," is of much value and interest. He died on the
31st March 1841, in his eighty-third year.

ing manure was explained and urged by Mr Headrick ; while the importance of draining marshes,
described as "magazines of mischief," was duly
maintained. At the meeting in 1809, the president
remarked that he had lately been making trial of
kale with a view to its more extensive use. He
regarded the sowing of spring wheat as worthy of
consideration, and exhibited a sample of naked
barley, resembling wheat, imported from Egypt, and
commended by Sir John Sinclair. By individual
members different agricultural topics were submitted
for discussion. Mr Guthrie of Craigie, an important
landowner, held that the Swedish was much inferior
to the yellow turnip, especially as the latter might be
reared on a greater variety of soils. Mr Scott of
Reswallie recommended a more general cultivation
of barley, and suggested the erection in the district
of woollen mills. He condemned the disuse of "the
Scottish" or woollen bonnet, and hoped that at next
meeting all the members would discard hats and
appear bonneted. To this proposal Mr Dempster
expressed an objection. The hat, he held, was not
cumbrous, as the bonnet was ; it protected the face
and did not retain moisture. As to woollen manufactories, these had been established in East Lothian
and elsewhere, and had failed. Manufactories of sail-
cloth and coarse linen, long common to the district,
were, he maintained, worthy of encouragement, and

no others. It was suggested that a donation should be presented to Mr Meikle, inventor of the threshing-machine, who was represented as aged and indigent.

The society's roll in September 1810 was seventy-four; it increased to eighty. At the anniversary then held, Mr Dempster remarked that sixty years ago the district was covered with furze and broom, while bogs were to be found at every turn; now the fields were clean and well drained, roads were abundant, and wheat was largely cultivated. The establishment of local farming societies he believed was most beneficial, as they brought pleasantly together landlord and tenant, and enabled them to be mutually helpful. Respecting the destruction of weeds, a member remarked that in Strathmore, a riding committee inspected farms every summer, and, as authorised in the leases, imposed fines on those who permitted weeds to grow unchecked. Of spring wheat Mr Guthrie expressed his disapproval; the grain was inferior and the straw discoloured and feeble.

There was a competition among exhibitors of live stock in 1811, Mr Dempster presenting several gold and silver medals to be used as premiums. In his presidential address, he recommended wheat-sowing in drill rather than broadcast, suggested the use of single-horse carts, and remarked that cattle might be trained for use in the threshing-mill. These proposals were generally approved, especially the drill-sowing of wheat. But naked barley was unfavourably reported upon—a third only of the seed being found to germinate, while the grain could not be threshed without difficulty. Some members discussed the respective merits of " Angus " and " Potato " oats, but the subject was left open.

In July 1812 the society held its tenth anniversary. At this meeting wheat-sowing in drill was warmly commended, a member remarking that the produce of wheat sown in this manner was one-third more than under the broadcast system. At the following meeting Mr Dempster, who had formerly congratulated the members on the general disappearance of field weeds, recommended drainage as " the most necessary of agricultural operations." He pleaded on behalf of crows that they destroyed grub, and ought to be encouraged, a view strongly supported by Mr Guthrie but objected to by Mr Headrick. Fiorin grass had at a former meeting been brought under discussion ; the subject was revived, and among those who took part in the debate was Mr John Pinkerton, the antiquary, who, being Mr Dempster's guest, was present as an honorary member. Mr Pinkerton remarked that Camden had referred to a field of fiorin grass which was so fertile as to be cut four times a year.

At the Society's twelfth anniversary, held in July

1814, Mr Dempster described the clergy as the first promoters of agriculture. " Around the monasteries," he said, "the best soil was a garden and the worst a grave." It was remarked by a member that while the Roman Catholic clergy largely cultivated and made use of wheaten-flour, it had since the Reformation been generally disused. This sentiment was confirmed by Mr Headrick, who stated that his father, who was a farmer in Ayrshire, had endeavoured to introduce wheaten-flour, but without success. A return to the use of oxen in tillage was suggested; the blight in barley, some held, might be prevented by pickling the seed; and the yellow turnip was unanimously ruled to be preferable to the Swedish.

The Society did not re-assemble. Having attained his eightieth year, Mr Dempster was unable longer to discharge the presidential duties, and as his election was for life it was deemed ungracious to choose a substitute. Mr Dempster died on the 13th February 1818, and the Society's minute-book, preserved by the secretary, became by inheritance the possession of the present writer, by whom it was deposited in the Scottish National Museum.

In the hands of the Rev. Dr J. F. S. Gordon, incumbent of St Andrew's Episcopal Church, Glasgow, are preserved the records of another provincial society, in which the writer's father held office as chaplain. The Musomanik Society had its head-quarters at

Anstruther in Fife, and was there founded in 1813 by
several resident cultivators of learning.   Of these the
more conspicuous were William Tennant, afterwards
author of the poem of "Anster Fair," latterly Professor of Oriental Languages in the University of St
Andrews, Charles Gray, afterwards Captain R.N.,
author of "Lays and Lyrics," William Macdonald
Fowler, author of "The Spirit of the Isle and other
Poems," and Matthew Forster Conolly, town-clerk of
Anstruther, latterly well known by his "Men of Fife"
and other biographical writings.

The Musomanik Society held monthly meetings;
also a grand anniversary.   In an Edinburgh news-
paper the annual meeting of 1814 is reported in the
following animated strain:—

"On the 30th of September the first anniversary of the Musomanik Club of Anstruther was celebrated there, in the hall of
Apollo, with the pomp and festivity becoming the worshippers of
that enlivening deity.   At four o'clock the brethren, whose number is precisely that of the nine Muses, being attended by many
honorary members, passed into the hall, which, from its tasteful
decorations, struck every eye with admiration.   The walls of the
chambers were hung round with pictures of ancient and modern
poets, under whose names were inscribed portions of their works,
in English, French, Italian, German, Latin, also in Greek.   Every
chair was entwined with laurels, myrtles, and *nettles;* the mixture
of the nettle leaf was appropriate, since it denoted the prickly
nature of that satire with which the rhymsters sting those who
are opposed to them.   The dinner was choice and elegant, doing
honour to the genius of the provisor.   Every dish was symbolical,
and had its innuendo denoting either the *pride* or the *vanity,*

or the *poverty* of poets. Directly before the Laureate, whose head was over-canopied by an umbrella of bays, lay the *immense roe* of a *cod-fish*, meant to be a figure not only of the multitude of modern bards, but also of that fecundity, by favour of which they are enabled to send out such voluminous productions. Much mirth was excited by a *Parnassus of paste ;* it was twin-topt, and had on each summit a sprig of laurel ; on its side appearing a *Poet of paste*, in the act of clambering ; his hand was stretched out towards the laurel sprigs, and from his mouth issued a parchment scroll, containing the motto of the Society's seal, ' Vos, O Lauri, Caspam.' The cloth removed, a sacrifice of nine copies of their *Pastimes* was offered to Apollo, every bard applying a lighted candle to the offering. The principal toasts were :—

> " May our great Patron, Dear Apollo,
> Ne'er find our brains so boss and hollow,
> If he should knock, but rhymes may follow."

" May the Shield of Good Humour throw back on our assailants the arrows of criticism."

" The Kingdom of Fife, and may she long retain her supremacy for fun, frolic, and hospitality."

At the close was sung by Mr Fowler, one of the brotherhood, the following ode, which he had composed for the occasion :—

> " Unextinguish'd spark of sky !
> Spirit that can never die !
> Hear, oh hear thy children's cry—
> Sacred Poesy !
>
> O'er this scene do thou preside,
> Joy and pleasure at thy side ;
> From thy servants, hallowed guide,
> Never, never fly !
>
> Should misfortune sullen lour
> On our short terrestrial hour ;
> Still, thy silent, secret power
> Sweeps the fiend away.

What is life without thy light ?
Cheerless gloom and sullen night !
Fancy never takes her flight !
Never dreams of day !

Then thy wand, enchantress wave !
Give, O give the boon we crave,
May we live beyond the grave,
Dear to memory ! "

The Musomanik Society possessed a seal charged with the Scottish harp, bearing an anchor on its chords, and surrounded by a chaplet. Their diploma, conferring honorary membership on Sir Walter Scott, was couched in the following terms :—

"Be it known to all men by these presents, that whereas Apollo the Sovereign Lord of Poetry, hath, by particular predilection, singled us out from the prosaic herd of men to be the special vessels of his illumination, and, in consequence of that choice, hath, in his high benignity, shed a generative ray upon the naturally barren soil of our pericraniums, thereby rendering them exceedingly rich and prolific of odes, ballads, bouts-rimés, acrostics, pastorals, epic poems, and other rhythmical effusions. And whereas, deaming it unwise and unprofitable to dissipate the richness and fecundity of our brains in the vulgar intercourse with men, we have associated ourselves into a *Musomanik Society,* in order to enjoy, by reflection of one another's fire, the coruscations of our own festive minds, by that means truly tasting, with the heightened gust of self-admiration, the pleasure of our poetical existences. Further whereas, considering that gifted as we are with sharp and penetrating wisdom, we can easily discern the seal of Apollo stamped upon the forehead of Walter Scott, Esq., whereby it is evident that the Unshorn God claims him for his own ; We the vicegerent subjects of the said Apollo in Anstruther hereby Admit, Legitimate, Enfranchise and Inaugurate, the said

Walter Scott into our Musomanik Society, freely bestowing upon him all its rights and privileges, and granting him liberty to rhyme and scribble in what shape, manner and degree he will, whether he be pleased to soar in the Epopee, to sink in the Song, to puzzle in the Riddle, to astonish in the Ode, or to amuse and make merry with the Bouts-rimés.--Given at the Hall of Apollo at Anstruther, &c.   WM. TENNANT, *Recorder*."

By the author of "The Lady of the Lake" the complement of the Anstruther rhymsters was acknowledged in the following letter :—

"GENTLEMEN,—I am, upon my return from the country, honoured with your letter and diploma, couched in very flattering terms, creating me a member of the Musomanik Society of Anstruther.   I beg you will assure the Society of my grateful sense of the favour they have conferred upon me, and my sincere wishes that they may long enjoy the various pleasures attendant upon the hours of relaxation which they may dedicate in their corporate or individual capacity to ' weel timed daffing.'—I remain, Gentlemen, your much obliged humble servant.   WALTER SCOTT."

At the monthly meetings strings of rhymes were supplied by the president, to which lines were forthwith added by the members. Specimens of their poetical competitions were printed in a volume entitled "Bouts-Rimés, or Poetical Pastimes round the base of Parnassus." Of these two examples will suffice to show that the "musomaniks" considerably shared a poetic inspiration.

MORNING ON ARTHUR'S SEAT.

On Arthur's lofty top   sublime,
Seared by the iron hand of   time,

I sit and view the coming   day,
Smiling from Portobello   bay !
On Abercorn the ruddy   dawn
Tinges each tower, and tree, and   lawn ;
On high the waning pale-faced   moon
Is lost ere she attains her   noon.
But see with radiant orb   entire,
Beaming appears the god of   fire !
O'er Duddingstone's enchanting   lake,
While scarce a leaf the breeze doth   shake,
The wild duck skirrs on rattling   wing,
Condolence to its mate to   bring.
Few are thy charms, Edina ! oh, how   few !
With scenes like these, content, I'd bid thee long   adieu !

THE POET.

With eye of fire, and haughty brow   sublime,
The Poet fears thee not, destructive   Time.
He toils, unmindful of the passing   day,
To gain at last the never-fading   bay ;
He courts the beauties of the golden   dawn,
He dwells delighted on the dewy   lawn.
But chief at night when the resplendent   moon
Climbs the blue heaven to gain her silent   noon,
Entranced he stands, wild fancy reigns   entire,
And his high numbers burn with more than mortal fire !
Heedful he views the calm unruffled   lake ;
Careless he feels the earth with thunders   shake ;
He soars aloft on fancy's eagle   wing,
From her high halls her airy forms to   bring ;
Or, snugly seated with a chosen   few,
Bids the vain world, and all its pomp,   adieu !

The Musomanik Society ceased after an active existence of about four years.

Reactionary to the rigid austerity prescribed by the

societies for the reformation of manners, which arose
at the time of the Union, prevailed a movement of
which the promoters fostered levity and abhorred
restraint.   Writing under May 1726, Wodrow remarks :—

" We have sad accounts of some secret Atheisticall Clubs in or
about Edinburgh. . . . I am told they had their rise from the
Hell-fire Club about two or three years ago at London, the secretary of which, I am well informed, was a Scotsman, and came
down not long since to Edinburgh ; and I doubt not propagat
their vile wickedness. He fell into melancholy, . . . and physitians
prescribed bathing for him, and he dyed mad at the first
bathing." [1]

These clubs, each possessing an unhallowed name,
and associated with demoralising orgies, had their
real origin in the more degrading rites of a rude and
pre-Christian superstition.   The fires with which
their observances were associated symbolized not
the spiritual Gehenna, but the sacrificial fires of
Druidic worship.   There were Baalic or " hell-fire "
clubs in the capital and on the coast.   Of a " Hell-fire "
club at Edinburgh, the president was named " the
Devil " ; it assembled in secret haunts, and, according
to Dr Robert Chambers, practised rites not more fit
for seeing the light than the Eleusinian mysteries." [2]
The Sweating Club, partaking of the same character,
flourished at Edinburgh about the middle of the

[1] Wodrow's " Analecta," iii. 309.
[2] Chambers's " Traditions of Edinburgh," 1869, p. 170.

century. In a state of intoxication, the members
sallied forth at midnight, when they attacked or
jostled any inoffensive citizen whom they chanced to
meet.

On the west coast, at every point where prevailed
a contraband trade, a Hell-fire Club obtained scope
and footing. Those who constituted the membership
were the smugglers and their abetters, who had
banded against the excise, and who kindling fires on
the coast to guide the skippers in making for the
shore, leapt through the burning embers, as did the
boys through the Beltane fires.

The contrabandist clubs of eastern Fifeshire culminated in a society which met at Anstruther under
the designation of the Beggar's Benison.

Of this fraternity the existence may be traced to
1732, when it was instituted as a knightly order. At
its origin and long afterwards, the members assembled
annually in the ruin of Castle Dreel, at Anstruther,
where in a small chamber designated "the temple"
they enacted their mysteries. At the annual meeting,
on the 30th November or "collar day," they severally
bore upon their breasts a silver medal, while the chief
or sovereign wore a medal pendant from a green sash. [1]

[1] In his "Memoirs of the Hon. Henry Erskine" (pp. 147-155),
Colonel Alexander Fergusson, who supplies some notices of the
"Beggar's Benison," remarks that each knight wore a sash, and
that the medals were of gold. In reality the sovereign only possessed a sash, and all the medals were of silver. By Colonel

The "temple" derived a dim light from an upper window. Towards the centre was placed a small table designated "an altar," on which were placed symbols such as those used by John Wilkes in his Order of St Francis, and which were irreverently consecrated by the monks of Isernia. At the sound of a small trumpet or breath-horn were novices severally admitted to the initiatory rite. The ceremonial was derived from the Druidic rites of Ashtoreth and those of the Roman Lupercalia. When proceedings in "the temple" had closed, festivities were conducted in the inn. There the knights were entertained with verses in the style of William Dunbar and with prose dissertations in the strain of Rabelais.

The Beggar's Benison having some years fallen into abeyance, was revived about 1764 by John M'Nachtan, who, at Anstruther held office as Collector of Customs. The Order was then described as being founded by James V., in commemoration of an incident which· happened to him while travelling in disguise. In the dress of a piper he had proceeded on foot to the annual fair at Anstruther, when, finding

Fergusson has been presented as an illustration a seal displaying three fishes in a triangle, and which he holds had some mysterious connection with the Order. In point of fact, the seal so represented is that of the Burgh of Anstruther-wester, which the Town-Clerk, being also Secretary of the Benison, had accidentally placed in the "Pandora Box," which contained the symbols of the Order.

that the Dreel burn which he required to cross was in flood, he accepted the service of a sturdy beggar-woman, who bore him through the stream upon her shoulders, and from whom, on rewarding her with gold, he received a *benison* or blessing. The story is fictitious.

In *Ruddiman's Magazine* for 1768, it is set forth "that on Wednesday the 30th November 1768, being Collar-day of the most puissant and honourable Order of the Beggar's Benison, the Knights Companions re-elected as Sovereign, Sir John M'Nachtane, being the fourth year of his guardianship." In his *Humphrey Clinker*, composed in 1770, Dr Tobias Smollett has, in Mr Melford's letter to Sir Watkin Phillips, described a dinner given by the chairmen of Edinburgh to their patrons after the Leith races, and " the Beggar's Benison " is named as one of the toasts.

The Knight Companions of the Order, thirty-two in number, included Thomas Alexander Erskine, the eminent musician, afterwards sixth Earl of Kellie ; Lord Newark, whose progenitor was the celebrated General David Leslie ; Sir Charles Erskine, Bart., a brave officer who fell at the battle of Laffeldt in 1747 ; James Lumsdaine of that ilk, James Lumsdaine of Stravithie, William Ayton of Kippo, and David Anstruther of the old family of that name. But the most ingenious of the early members was Colonel Alexander Monypenny of Pitmilly, who was constituted laureate. To his pen has been ascribed a humorous composition, of which is preserved the following fragment :—

> " Oh, were you e'er in Crail toun ?
>   Igo and ago ;
>   An' saw you there Clerk Dischington ?
>   Iram coram dago.

> " His wig was like a droukit hen,
>   Igo and ago ;
>   The tail o't like a grey goose pen,
>   Iram coram dago.

> " Ken ye ought o' Sir John Malcolm ?
>   Igo and ago ;
>   If he's a wise man I mistak him,
>   Iram coram dago.

> " Ken ye ought o' Sandy Don ?
>   Igo and ago ;
>   He's ten times dafter than Sir John,
>   Iram coram dago.

> " To hear them o' their travels talk,
>   Igo and ago ;
>   To go to London 's but a walk,
>   Iram coram dago.

> " To see the wonders o' the deep,
>   Igo and ago ;
>   Wad mak a man baith wail and weep
>   Iram coram dago.

> " To see the leviathen skip,
>   Igo and ago ;
>   An' wi' his tail ding oure a ship,
>   Iram coram dago."

Colonel of the 56th Regiment, Colonel Monypenny

was representative of a family which had possessed
the lands of Pitmilly from the thirteenth century ; at
a very advanced age he died in December 1801, surviving, after the lapse of half a century, to remark
that his popular *Benison* ode was parodied by Burns
in an Epistle to Captain Grose. The families of
Dischington, Malcolm, and Don, of which the representatives are depicted in the Colonel's verses,
deserve a passing notice.

Prior to 1330, William of Dischington married
Elizabeth, younger sister of King Robert the Bruce.
His eldest son John, a skilful architect, reared the
Gothic fabric of St Monan's Church, which was com-
pleted at the cost of David II., his near relation. His
descendant, Sir William Dischington, obtained in
1429 the lands of Airdrie. Three members of the
house, Thomas, George, and Andrew Dischington,
were charged with being privy to Rizzio's murder.[1]
In 1626 Sir Thomas Dischington was one of the
keepers of the royal park at Farnham.[2] The Town-
Clerkship of Crail became in the family an hereditary
office. George Dischington succeeded his father as
" Clerk of Crail " in 1642, and was in turn succeeded
in 1708 by his son George, who was doubtless the
" Clerk " of the ode.

---

[1] " Register of Collegiate Church of Crail," Grampian Club,
1877, pp. 13-15.

[2] Earl of Stirling's " Register of Royal Letters," i. 101.

Sir John Malcolm of the Beggar's Benison was originally a writer in Kirkcaldy; he succeeded to the baronetcy of Lochore, and possessed the estates of Balbedie and Grange, the latter not distant from Anstruther. Originally distinguished by wealth and culture, the Malcolm family were latterly to be remarked for their peculiar manners. Ignorant and boastful, Sir John's eccentricities subjected him to ridicule. He died prior to 1747, and in the baronetcy was succeeded by Sir Michael Malcolm, who when he came to the family honours was a working joiner, first at Kinross, afterwards in London. Sir Michael was also celebrated in rhyme, probably by the laureate of the Benison. Thus:—

> " Balbedie has a second son,
>   They ca' him Michael Malcolm;
> He gangs about Balgonie dykes
>   Huntin' and hawkin';
> He's stown away the bonny lass,
>   And kept the widow waukin'."

Alexander, described as "Sandy" Don, Colonel Monypenny's third hero, was parish schoolmaster of Crail. He was a relative of Sir James Don of Newton, and the scion of an old family which owned an estate at Doune in Perthshire. The schoolmaster of Crail was famous for his jocundity.

Among other officers, the "Beggar's Benison" engaged the services of a chaplain, who was *bona fide* a clergyman in orders. The diploma by which the

Reverend John Nairne, minister of Anstruther, was on the 27th May 1767 constituted a knight brother and chaplain of the order, has been preserved. Representing on its engraved surface certain Isernian symbols, the diploma proceeds :—

"By the supereminently beneficent and superlatively benevolent Sovereign of the most ancient and most puissant Order of the Beggar's Benison and Merry Land [1] in the fourth year of his guardianship, and in that of the Order 5771. Having nothing more sincerely at heart than the happiness of our well-beloved subjects in our celebrated territories of Merry Land, and the promoting of Trade Manufactures and Agriculture in that delightful colony, and whereas we are well-informed that the Rev. John Nairne has all manner of inclination, as well as sufficient ability and other qualifications for these laudable purposes, and willing that such well-qualified and bold adventurers should have all suitable encouragement, we do therefore elect, admit and receive him, &c."

In respect of his chaplaincy, Mr Nairne was styled "Dean of the Order for the shire of Argyle and of the Western Isles." He held office till his death in 1795, when as his successor was appointed the Right Reverend David Low, D.D., Bishop of Ross, who ministered to a small congregation at Pittenweem, the adjacent burgh. Bishop Low died in 1865 at the age of eighty-seven. Several years previously

[1] The term Merry Land was suggested by Colonel Monypenny, the laureate, in allusion to the ballad of "The Jew's Daughter," of which there was a special version published in Fife. See Percy's "Reliques," Lond. 1869, 12mo, p. 20; and Johnson's "Scots Musical Museum," iv. 499.

he requested that in the records of the Benison his name might be expunged from the proceedings of each of the forty anniversaries in which he had taken part. This request suggested the propriety of destroying the register. Already the order had ceased, for on the 30th November 1836 the knights met for the last time. The dissolution was agreed upon, Lord Arbuthnot only expressing his dissent. After a considerable interval, and when he had become the sole surviving member, the secretary, Mr Conolly, handed the balance of funds, amounting to £70, to certain local administrators, in order to provide prizes in reward of merit at the Anstruther schools.[1]

[1] To our friend Dr J. F. S. Gordon, incumbent of St Andrew's Church, Glasgow, son-in-law of the latest secretary and last surviving member, Mr M. F. Conolly, we are indebted for many of these particulars.

END OF VOL. II.